52 SHABBATS

52 SHABBATS

Friday Night Dinners Inspired by a Global Jewish Kitchen

FAITH KRAMER

Photographs by Clara Rice

Some of the recipes in this cookbook previously appeared in
a modified form in j, *The Jewish News of Northern California*

ISBN: 978-1-951412-18-0
Ebook ISBN: 978-1-951412-26-5
LCCN: 2020915638

Manufactured in Hong Kong, China.

Design by Andrea Kelly
Food styling by Bebe Black Carminito

10 9 8 7 6 5 4 3 2 1

The Collective Book Studio®
Oakland, California
www.thecollectivebook.studio

To my mother, mother-in-law,
grandmothers, and the generations of
Jewish cooks before me who created
and preserved the taste of Judaism.

CONTENTS

INTRODUCTION

It's Friday night. We've gathered good food and good people together to share and celebrate. It's time to focus on what is within us and the joy we have in life and others. Welcome to the Shabbat table.

Around the world, at sunset on Friday night, Jews, their families, and their friends come together to celebrate with food, wine, bread, community, and ruach (spirit). It's the start of Shabbat, the Jewish Sabbath, the holiday that comes once a week. For some, this dinner is just a festive meal. For others, it is part of their religious observance. For most, Shabbat is a space to celebrate, recharge, and share with those you care for—a time to look at our relationships with ourselves, with others, and with the world at large.

The arc of Jewish beliefs and observances is large, but sitting down and eating a meal together for Shabbat is one of the most basic and connects us back to ancient rituals and customs. Today, our Friday night dinners may or may not be traditional or observe all the Jewish religious laws, but they add meaning and sustenance to our lives. We may add new twists, and make them more individualized, inclusive, and multicultural. (That's why the book's title uses the English "Shabbats" rather than the Hebrew "Shabbatot.")

No matter what your Friday night custom is (or even if you don't really have one), embracing this weekly Shabbat ritual brings an element of understanding as the activities and food can connect us, through history, geography, and tradition, to Jewish communities and ways other than our own.

The recipes in this book are drawn from ingredients and techniques from around the Jewish world, ranging from ancient cultures to modern Chabad outposts in Southeast Asia and from thriving communities to ones that no longer exist in their homelands. I didn't try to replicate regional recipes. Instead, I started with the traditional foods and preparations and found new ways to add flavor and meaning to my table and now to yours. Much like our ancestors adapted the food of their homelands, I adapted their food ways and ingredients into recipes that reflect those values and traditions while creating dishes full of life, flavor, and heritage that work for our tables today.

The 52 primary recipes are organized by season, starting with fall. The introductions to the seasonal chapters address the major Jewish holidays that fall within each one, such as Rosh Hashanah in fall, Hanukkah in winter, and Passover in spring, and offer recipe suggestions for each. In the recipe introductions and short essays within the chapters, I discuss special ingredients and detail some stories, customs, history, and current facts from and about different international Jewish communities. And after each seasonal recipe, I offer a "Make It Shabbat" menu, with suggestions for how build the dish into a full Shabbat dinner. Whenever appropriate, tips for making dishes ahead are offered to help you manage the time-consuming part of holiday and Shabbat cooking.

This book shares flavors from around the Jewish world: seasonings from Libya and Ethiopia; sauces from Morocco, Lebanon, and Yemen; and herbs, spices, and more from the Middle and Near East. Standbys are transformed: Pomegranate molasses brings a sweet-tart taste to brisket; falafel makes a crispy crust for a pizza; baked potatoes are stuffed with ground turkey, cumin, cinnamon, cloves, and other spices; roasted chicken is enhanced by fresh herbs or shawarma seasoning; and a spicy beef stew with dried fruit becomes the filling for tamales, to name just a few.

The state of Kerala inspired the South Indian–Inspired Fish Cakes with Coconut-Cilantro Chutney (page 120), North Africa the Fish in Spicy H'raimi-Style Tomato Sauce (page 48), Latin America the Matzo Ball and Pozole Chicken Soup (page 60), and Greece the Oregano Roast Chicken with Leek-and-Mint Fritters (page 62).

There are vegetarian and plant-based choices, too, from Almost Homemade Hummus (page 96) to Peppers Stuffed with White Beans, Bulgur, Chard, and Tomatoes (page 54) to Spinach and Dill Phyllo Pies (page 126).

There are also more than forty other recipes for sauces, side dishes, accompaniments, and desserts, as well as some American and Eastern European Jewish food fundamentals, including some of the classics I have been asked for most often

such as Chicken Soup with Matzo Balls (page 196), Real Deal Chopped Chicken Liver (page 202), and Friday Night Challah (page 204).

Follow the suggested menus, mix and match the recipes, or add favorite dishes to create your own Friday night dinner. How you enjoy Friday night is up to you. Try adding in different traditions and observances. Add discussions or learning sessions. Play games. Sing songs. Make it a party. Make it all about family. Invite new friends and old. Celebrate the joy of Friday night whenever you can. It is your Friday night dinner.

From my table to yours, Shabbat Shalom.

JEWS, JEWISH FOOD & THE GLOBAL JEWISH KITCHEN

There is a reason that there is a global Jewish kitchen. The worldwide Jewish community is not a monolith. It is made up of Jews of many backgrounds, heritages, beliefs, and customs. Here is an overview of some of the major divisions.

ASHKENAZI JEWS

Often called Eastern European Jews, Ashkenazi Jews have migrated far beyond those borders. In many Western countries, they form the largest groups of Jews. The Ashkenazi originally settled near the border of what is now Germany ("Ashkenazi" comes from the ancient Hebrew name for that area) and France and moved eastward through Central Europe to Lithuania, Latvia, Poland, the Ukraine, and Russia. Many of these Jews migrated to America, Canada, England, and Australia during the last decades of the nineteenth century and first decades of the twentieth century.

MAGHREBI JEWS

These are North African Jews from the Maghreb region of western North Africa under Arab, Moorish, and Ottoman rule. They include Jews from Morocco, Libya, Algeria, and Tunisia. (Some include Egyptian Jews in this grouping.) While Maghrebi communities go back 2,000 years, they were heavily influenced by Sephardic Jewish migration.

MIZRAHI JEWS

Those that remained settled in the Middle and Near East, with ancient roots in the Fertile Crescent (part of which is now Israel) as well as Syria, Yemen, Iraq, Iran, and Central Asia are considered Mizrahi. Many Mizrahi (from the Hebrew word for "Eastern") communities existed alongside Sephardic ones after the Spanish and Portuguese expulsion of the Jews. Some Jews from Iraq settled in India (particularly around Kolkata and Mumbai), forming what became known as the Baghdadi Jews. Business opportunities eventually lured some of the Baghdadi Jews to Shanghai, where they remained until the Communist takeover of China.

SEPHARDIC JEWS

These are the descendants of Jews who originally settled in the Iberian Peninsula. (The term "Sephardic" is taken from an ancient Hebrew word thought to refer to what is now Spain and Portugal.) After fifteenth-century persecution and inquisitions, many fled to other countries, with a majority migrating to lands controlled by the Ottomans, including Turkey, Syria, Greece, and the Balkans. Others made their way to the Netherlands, India, and other countries. Some eventually landed in the New World.

OTHER COMMUNITIES

In addition to these main groups, there are many other distinct Jewish groups with their own customs, such as the Beta Israel of Ethiopia; the Bene Israel, Cochin Jews, and Bene Menashe of India; the Romaniote Jews (who trace their ancestry to ancient Jewish populations in the Byzantine and Greece); the Italkim, or Roman, Jews of Italy whose community dates back more than 2,200 years ago; and others throughout the world. Some of these communities became homes to Jews from other areas over the centuries. Many members of these communities were forced to leave or chose to migrate and have settled primarily in the United States and Israel.

Besides where they come from, Jews are also distinguished by their denomination. In America, for example, depending on family customs, beliefs, and level of ritual observance, Jews might be Orthodox (the most traditional and, until relatively recently in history, the only branch of Judaism), Conservative, Reform, Renewal, or Reconstructionist (among others). Within each branch there is a wide range of beliefs and practices. In addition, many Jews regard themselves as unaffiliated and/or cultural or secular Jews and do not follow any organized form of Judaism.

The basis for all the denominations and religious traditions of these diverse Jewish communities is the same: the Torah, the Hebrew Bible. The Torah is interpreted by the Talmud, which was written 1,500 to 2,000 years ago, shifting Jewish worship from Temple offerings to prayer.

HOW JEWISH FOOD EVOLVED

Wherever Jews settled they adapted, incorporating local foods to meet religious, dietary, and symbolic needs. The resulting dishes are tied to where the community came from and where they migrated to by economics, politics, and geography. So the foods of Venice were influenced by those of Sicily, as Jews migrated to the northern city and brought with them imports from the Moors such as eggplants and a taste for sweet-and-sour foods. Waves of Jewish migration also brought fish and chips to England and bagels to America.

My grandmother's parents emigrated from Russia, so the food I ate in her kitchen would have been recognized by Ashkenazi Jews from Central and Eastern Europe—although her stuffed cabbage might not be sweet enough for the Poles, where beet sugar was a big business, or too bland for Hungarians, where years of Ottoman rule left a taste for spices.

Central and Eastern European food traditions began when Jews settled in the Rhine Valley, and spread as persecution and opportunity drove them ever farther eastward. It is in many ways a cold-weather cuisine. Cabbage and cucumbers were fermented into sauerkraut and pickles. Freshwater fish and meats were smoked and salted. Meat was scarce and often used as a component of other dishes to make it go further. Beans and grains were plentiful. Once potatoes were introduced, they were widely eaten. Warm-weather produce was relished in season and preserved for when it was not.

Those who first settled in the Iberian Peninsula had very different food influences. The Jews who lived near northern Spain had diets that reflected the legacy of the Roman Empire, such as grapes, wheat, and olives. Those in the southern end of the peninsula were influenced by the occupation of the Moors, and incorporated spices such as cumin, cinnamon, nutmeg, and black pepper in their cooking as well as rice, almonds, citrus, eggplants, spinach, and artichokes.

The spread of the Sephardic Jews after their fifteenth-century expulsion from the Iberian Peninsula affected Jewish food cultures in their new homes, from Turkey to the Netherlands to India. The immigrant Sephardic Jews changed their cooking in turn, as they began to learn new regional specialties from the population at large and the local Jews.

Many of the Mizrahi Jews of the Middle and Near East did not migrate, or generally at least not as far, and their food traditions grew up side by side with their Arab neighbors, affected by the same geographic and economic factors but always shaped by the Jewish dietary laws. Others traveled the spice routes and silk roads and settled in Central Asia, China, and India, adapting local cuisines as they went.

Jewish communities in India, Italy, Greece, Ethiopia, and Egypt also developed distinct food ways. As Jews from around the world migrated to Europe, Israel, and the Americas, their traditional foods began to morph to accommodate new tastes and available ingredients.

My grandmother seasoned her food with onion, salt, pepper, and maybe a pinch of paprika. I use those, but I also reach for sumac, cumin, allspice, and a wealth of other spices. Tahini (ground sesame seeds) and berbere (a key Ethiopian spice mixture) are staples. I flavor my food with pomegranate molasses, tamarind, and harissa (North African hot sauce). From the stews of Ethiopia to the curries of India, what I stir in my pot is inspired by Jewish kitchens around the world.

The recipes in this book honor the wide variety of customs from diverse Jewish communities and the cultures they found themselves in throughout history, but often in a way that carries on the desire to adapt, adjust, or transform tradition.

FOOD AS A SYMBOL

Food in Judaism is often treated as a symbol of blessings, wishes, or thankfulness. Probably the most famous is the custom of eating fried foods at Hanukkah to commemorate when one day's worth of oil for the menorah lasted for eight. From potato pancakes called latkes (which means "little oily thing") to jelly donuts (sufganyiot), this tradition continues to evolve.

Symbolism at the table for Shabbat includes having two loaves of bread for the blessing, as a connection to the offerings at the Temple and a remembrance of the double portion of manna that was provided during the long Exodus. Wine (or grape juice) is also an important symbolic element of the meal. In some traditions, including fish in the meal represents a wish for the Jews to increase in the world, since fish are seen as multiplying rapidly.

Food becomes almost a form of prayer, when we imbue it with our words and wishes and then consume it. You'll see more about holiday food symbolism throughout the book.

BUT IS IT KOSHER? JUST A LITTLE ABOUT JEWISH DIETARY LAWS

Jews come with a handbook. Among the tenets for how to live our lives—given to us by the Torah and interpreted by the Talmud as well as ancient and contemporary rabbis—are dietary rules called kashrut. In the simplest terms, when ingredients and preparation follow the laws of kashrut, the resulting food is known as kosher, or "fitting" and "proper." Food that does not meet those criteria is known as treif (from the word for "torn").

Kosher food has several properties. Meat must come from animals with cloven hooves that chew a cud, which is why pork is not eaten. Permitted animals must be slaughtered according to religious standards, and meat taken only from certain parts. Meat must not be eaten with milk, cheese, or other dairy products. Fish must have fins and scales, so shellfish are not eaten. Commercial food production must be monitored and certified kosher (the certification seal is known as a hechsher). There is much more to it than this, but that's a quick overview.

Do most Jews follow these rules? No. But observance of these dietary laws is a huge part of what has created the Jewish cuisine.

All the recipes in this book use ingredients that are available kosher. (If that is not a concern, you can source these same ingredients without a hechsher.) Some recipes also include non-dairy options. The menus do not mix meat and milk to make sure that the dishes are accessible to those who observe kashrut.

HOW TO SHABBAT

There are many published and online resources for how and why to celebrate Shabbat, for expanded prayers and blessings, and for the blessings written in Hebrew or in English transliteration. Do what works for you and your guests.

The breadth of beliefs, customs, and practices are broad. Some are traditional, others more personalized.

Shabbat is often referred to as a queen, or a bride. So, it's fitting to make a bit of a fuss over the Shabbat table if you can. Adding flowers, using a special tablecloth, or making a special meal all mark the day.

Celebrating Shabbat by yourself, with a partner, or with family are all special, but it is considered a mitzvah (which can be translated as both a command or a good or correct action) to invite others to join you and share in what is a joyous celebration.

Shabbat starts eighteen minutes before sundown on Friday nights, so the timing will vary each week, and ends Saturday nights after the first three stars are spotted.

FRIDAY NIGHT LIGHTS

While some will only light the candles as proscribed just before sundown, others wait until all the guests have arrived even if it is after the start of Shabbat.

Most Jews light two candles, although others light a candle for every member of the household, or have family members and/or guests light their own. Sephardic Jews traditionally light seven candles (or wicks in oil), one for each day of the week, as well as ones for family members and loved ones who have died.

Any candlesticks can be used; many households have special ones just for Shabbat. Candles should burn through dinner. Shabbat candles are available but tea lights and regular candles work. Traditionally, women light the Shabbat candles and lead the prayer, but in many families, others take on that role or everyone joins in.

To begin, light the candles then cover your eyes while saying the blessing. A common custom is to bring hands up to the candle flames and wave or circle them back toward you three times and then cover your eyes and recite the blessing. Sephardic tradition is to say the blessings before lighting the candles.

Blessed are you Adonai, our God, Ruler of the Universe, who has sanctified us by commanding us to light Shabbat candles.

Now is the time to offer personal prayers or share thoughts. Finally, wish all present *Shabbat Shalom* (or a Shabbat of peace).

This is also a good time to bless one's children, a custom evolving from Jacob blessing his grandsons. There are separate blessings for boys and girls, but some now combine them into a more gender-neutral blessing. An adult places a hand on top of the child's head and says:

May God Make you like Ephraim and Menashe and Sarah, Rivka, Rachel, and Leah. May Adonai bless you and guard you. May Adonai lift the divine face towards you and be gracious unto you. May Adonai's face smile at you and grant you peace.

BLESS THE BREAD AND WINE

The next step is to say the blessings over wine (Kiddush) and bread (Hamotzi).

Have ready two uncut loaves (even two rolls work) but one loaf is fine if that's what is available. Wrap or cover the bread with a napkin or special challah cloth. While challah is traditional for many American and European Jews, the type of bread does not matter as long as the loaf is made of at least 20 percent rye, barley, wheat, spelt, or oat flour.

Fill either one big wine cup to share or individual cups with wine or grape juice. Some families have special silver Kiddush cups.

Raise the wine glass (and guests raise their individual cups) and recite the blessing. (The one below is abbreviated; check the internet and other resources for the full Shabbat blessing.) Drink the wine.

Blessed are you Adonai, Our God, Ruler of the Universe, Creator of the fruit of the vine.

Guests can say the prayer with the host, or simply add an "Amen" at the end.

Next comes the Hamotzi.

To bless the bread, uncover both loaves, hold them up, say the blessing, and tear off a piece of bread and eat it, passing pieces or slices of bread to others.

One custom is to dip the piece of bread in or sprinkle on salt. Dipping the bread in salt has several symbolic meanings, including recalling the salt used on Temple offerings and the Jews' convenant with God, since salt does not spoil or turn rancid. Participants can say the blessing along with the host or add "Amen" at the end.

Blessed are you, Adonai, our God, Ruler of the Universe, who brings out bread from the earth.

TIME TO EAT, DISCUSS, AND MAYBE SING

In my family, when everyone sits down to eat, we all hold hands, and we say the Shehechiyanu, a blessing said to celebrate the moment, as a way of being thankful for being with friends and family and being able to enjoy Shabbat together.

Blessed are you, Adonai, our God, Ruler of the Universe, who has granted us life, sustained us, and enabled us to reach this occasion.

Dinner is served, and it's a time to catch up and talk, and perhaps share readings, discuss Shabbat, Torah, social justice, or other topics. After dinner, some of us sing Shabbat songs or play games.

In more observant homes, special blessings would be said before and after the meal.

OTHER SHABBAT CUSTOMS

Some Jews attend services Friday night and/or Saturday at local synagogues. They may refrain from using electronics, handling money, working, or driving during Shabbat, and wrap up the holiday on Saturday night with Havdalah, a special ceremony to prepare for the end of a holy day of rest and peace and reentry into the rest of the week.

ABOUT THE INGREDIENTS

These are my preferences for the common ingredients that are used throughout 52 Shabbats. Look throughout the book for essays on specialty ingredients I use frequently, such as tahini and pomegranate molasses.

BUTTER

Use a good quality unsalted butter. If substituting vegan margarine, reduce the amount of salt in the recipe.

CARROTS

All carrots should be well scrubbed before using and, unless specified in a recipe, they don't need to be peeled.

CAYENNE PEPPER

This fiery powder is ground dried red chiles and is often called ground red pepper. Just a pinch adds a good amount of heat to a dish. If unavailable, use hot (sharp) paprika or crushed red pepper to taste.

CRUSHED RED PEPPER

Also known as crushed chile flakes. These are dried chiles that have been crushed and cut into small particles, usually including the seeds. It's used for heat and spice. Hotness and flavor depend on the type of chiles used. Taste as you add to avoid over spicing. Recipes are written for the most commonly available flakes. If using crushed red pepper without seeds or chile flakes such as Aleppo or Urfa (common in the Middle East and Turkey and available in spice and specialty stores), you may need to use more flakes than if using the standard variety. Aleppo and Urfa chile flakes also add a nice complexity to dishes and are worth seeking out.

EGGS

All recipes are written for large American eggs. To substitute medium eggs or extra-large eggs when mixing in as an ingredient or for baking, for up to 3 eggs use the same number of eggs. For 4 large eggs, use 5 medium eggs or 3 extra-large. Recipe results may vary, especially when baking. All eggs should be at room temperature.

FLOUR

Unless otherwise noted, all flour is unbleached, all-purpose flour without additives and with a protein content of 10 to 11.7 percent. To determine the protein percentage, check the nutrition label. If the label shows 10 grams of protein per 100 grams of flour, it is 10 percent. If the serving size is less than 100 grams, multiply accordingly.

FLOUR, BREAD

I use brands that are between 12 and 12.7 percent protein. This higher protein content results in better gluten structure and a higher rise. Look for unbleached flour without additives.

GARLIC

I only call for fresh garlic in this book. Frozen or jarred may be substituted if necessary.

HERBS

Use fresh parsley or cilantro--never dried. I prefer flat-leaf parsley (also known as Italian parsley) but the curly leaf variety may be substituted if necessary. For other fresh herbs such as mint or dill, do not substitute dried as a garnish. If using a dried substitute for fresh mint or dill as a recipe ingredient, use one-third as much as the recipe calls for to prevent over seasoning. If replacing dried herbs in a recipe with fresh, triple the amount called for. Dried whole-leaf herbs such as oregano or mint should be crumbled by hand before measuring.

KOSHER SALT

Kosher salt (see right) refers to a particular kind of coarse salt, one that has a shape designed to maximize contact with food as an aid in kashering (removing the blood from) meat to obey traditional Jewish dietary laws. ("Kosher" means "fit or proper to eat.") Kosher salt is used in a

About kosher salt

In my grandmother's day, she had to salt her meats and drain them on a slanted wooden board before cooking. Today most kosher meats come ready to use, but that hasn't diminished the market for this special salt. Its popularity has expanded beyond its traditional use because of how it interacts with, and is absorbed by, food.

Technically, all brands and types of salt without additives are considered kosher, but if a recipe specifies kosher salt, the author is referring to the larger grain used for salting kosher meat. It also works well for bagel or challah toppings, rubs for meat and poultry, in brines for pickles and other fermented foods, and as a finishing salt.

There are two main brands of kosher salt in the United States and they are very different in structure, which affects how salty they taste by volume.

Morton Salt's kosher salt is flatter and finer (so there are more grains of salt in a teaspoon). Diamond Crystal's version has larger, pyramid-shaped crystals (so there are fewer grains in a teaspoon). By weight, all salt is the same (table, sea, and kosher). It is by volume that over-or under-salting becomes an issue. One teaspoon of finely ground table salt or sea salt is as salty as 1¼ to 1½ teaspoons of the Morton or 1¾ to 2 teaspoons of Diamond Crystal. (To further confuse matters, a finely ground kosher salt is now available for use in salt shakers. When a recipe specifies kosher salt in this book, it is referring to the coarse salt, not the finely ground one. Use finely ground kosher salt as you would table salt.)

If you are unsure what type of kosher salt you have, a recipe doesn't specify which type to use, or you need to substitute table salt or fine sea salt, start with half of the amount specified, taste, and add more. Coarse sea salt is closer to kosher salt in volume and salinity, but it too varies between producers. Start with less, taste, and add more as needed.

few recipes in *52 Shabbats,* including in a spice rub and when broiling chicken livers, but unless otherwise specified, "salt" in an ingredients list refers to table or finely ground sea salt. *See* Salt.

LEMON JUICE

For the best flavor, use freshly squeezed lemon juice.

NON-DAIRY PRODUCTS

Choose non-dairy milk or yogurt that is unsweetened and unflavored.

OIL, VEGETABLE

I like neutral-tasting vegetable oils for general cooking and frying. My preference is for grape seed, sunflower, or safflower oil, but canola or corn oil is also fine.

OIL, OLIVE

When olive oil is specified in a recipe for cooking, use any good-tasting pure olive oil. Extra-virgin olive oil is specified and preferred for use in salad dressings and uncooked sauces or as a garnish.

PAPRIKA

Dried ground paprika comes in sweet, hot (also called sharp), and smoked versions. A paprika that is not marked hot or smoked is sweet. Use regular, sweet paprika unless directed otherwise.

SALT

Unless otherwise specified, for the salt in the recipes in this book, use fine sea salt or table salt without iodine or other additives. Iodized table salt may taste and react differently in some dishes. (see Kosher Salt, page 17)

SUGAR

All sugar is granulated white sugar unless otherwise noted.

About instant-read thermometers

An instant-read thermometer gives cooks a more precise idea of what's going on inside cooked food. It's helpful for chicken, meats, and other solid foods such as challah. Insert the thermometer's thin metal spike into the middle of the thickest part of meat, chicken or other food (without touching bone) for the most accurate measure. Depending on which style of thermometer you choose, a digital readout or analog dial shows the temperature. The spike is only inserted while testing; it does not stay inside the food while it cooks. Meat, candy, or deep-fry thermometers cannot be substituted.

HOW TO USE THIS BOOK

In the seasonal chapters, every recipe has a suggested menu, giving you a total of a year's worth of Friday night dinners. But the recipes can be mixed and matched so you can create your own individualized menu.

Main courses often work well in smaller portions as appetizers or starters. The menus focus on recipes from the book but also include recommendations for other items such as a green salad, steamed green beans, pasta, and fruit salad for you to prepare as you like.

Serve the recipes as part of the suggested menu or however you see fit, substituting personal or family favorites or purchased food wherever desired. Feel free to make Shabbat dinner simpler. Focus on one big flavor item and keep the rest simple.

Purchased hummus is a great shortcut, as are premade and ready-to-reheat foods such as rice or other grains; canned beans and lentils; frozen falafel; ready-to-eat pickled vegetables; and cut, cleaned, and chopped produce. Purchased salad dressing can reduce preparation time. Ready-to-use chicken broth or vegetable broth is a time saver when making sauces or stews. Dessert is easy to outsource with commercially baked goods or sorbet, or make it even simpler by serving fresh fruit.

Check out local and online specialty stores for the sauces and spice mixes listed in the recipes and fundamentals chapter so they are ready to go (or make extra to have for other recipes.) Buy (or make) a simple green salad mix or steam some vegetables as a side dish. Purchased challah or other bread is just as appropriate as homemade. Even substituting take-out items for some or all of the menu works.

Most recipes will double well. Often there are suggestions on how to prepare all or part of a dish in advance, helpful for those who might not be able to make a full meal right before Shabbat.

The main ingredient of a Friday night dinner menu is intention—purposefully setting aside and honoring the specialness of the day. As long as you have that, you have Shabbat.

fall

52 *SHABBATS* STARTS IN WITH ROSH HASHANAH,

the ritual beginning of the Jewish year. Since I live in North America, this coincides with fall, and my Shabbat dinners tend toward roasted, braised, and simmered foods as the weather begins to chill, days shorten, and summer fruit and vegetables fade from the marketplace, replaced by sturdier alternatives.

It's a time to appreciate the blessings of family, friends, and home, as these next months are full of major Jewish holidays, with their communal observances, remembrances, and introspection.

Foods that offer a bit of comfort are welcome additions to the Shabbat table this season, such as Central Asian–inspired Layered Chicken and Rice Plov (page 34), an all-in-one meal with vegetables and herbs, or Spice-Rubbed Chicken on Root Vegetables (page 28). Add some brightness to the plate with Fish in Spicy H'raimi-Style Tomato Sauce (page 48) or to the palate with Pickle-Brined Roast or Oven-Fried Chicken (pages 32 and 33).

HOLIDAYS & SPECIAL DAYS

The Jewish year is divided into twelve lunar months, adjusted with occasional leap months to align it to the solar year. Jewish holidays are always on the same dates on the Hebrew calendar, but the dates change on the secular, solar-based (Gregorian) calendar.

Fall brings us the Hebrew months of Tishri, Heshvan, and the first part of Kislev.

Holidays during this time include Rosh Hashanah, Yom Kippur, Sukkot, and—though not specifically Jewish—Thanksgiving.

Rosh Hashanah is the start of Tishri, the seventh month of the Hebrew calendar, but it's considered the beginning of creation and the start of the ritual New Year. Home observance centers around shared meals, often including symbolic foods that add an extra level of meaning or intention. Dipping challah in honey and eating foods with honey such as Roast Salmon with Citrus-Honey Sauce (page 46) or Sweet-and-Tart Silan-Roasted Carrots with Lentils (page 24) communicates our wish for a sweet year. Carrots also represent a wish for prosperity and multiplying good deeds.

For some Jews, no meal can be considered festive without meat, and for many Eastern European Jews that meat is brisket. Here Pomegranate Molasses Brisket (page 38) delivers rich, tender, slow-cooked beef in a sweet-and-sour sauce with a Middle Eastern accent and a connection to pomegranates, a biblical fruit. The number of its many seeds is associated with the number of mitzvot (commandments or good deeds) mentioned in the Torah. And

leftover meat can be used in a personal favorite of mine, Brisket Fried Rice (page 41).

Yom Kippur is a day of fasting, atonement, and prayer. The custom is to have a full meal the night before the holiday without spicy, salty, or heavy flavors and then break the fast with a light meal after sunset the next day when Yom Kippur concludes. For a pre-fast dinner, try Whole Roast Chicken with Herbs (page 30). Break the fast with Mostly Make-It-Ahead Shakshouka (page 100) or Spinach and Dill Phyllo Pies (page 126).

Sukkot is a harvest festival that also commemorates the forty years of the Exodus. It lasts eight days (seven in Israel), so it overlaps with Shabbat. Meals are eaten in a small hut (a sukkah; "sukkot" is the plural) built in yards and balconies or in community sukkot at synagogues and other Jewish institutions. It is a celebration of bounty, heritage, and shared experiences, where the custom is to invite others to dine and drink.

One Sukkot tradition is to eat filled or stuffed foods, to symbolize the abundance of the season. For meals in a sukkah or for the Shabbat during the holiday, try homey, grandma-inspired Stuffed Cabbage Meatloaf (page 42), Eggplant Overflowing with Lamb (page 44), or Peppers Stuffed with White Beans, Bulgur, Chard, and Tomatoes (page 54) drizzled with Garlic Sauce (page 210).

Heshvan, also known as Marcheshvan, is when the Beta Israel (see page 75) celebrate Sigd (also called Mehlella or Amata Saww), fifty days after Yom Kippur. The community fasts and, dressed in white, joins together to celebrate the acceptance of the Torah. They then break the fast with a feast. It is a national holiday in Israel, where most Beta Israel now live. To celebrate, try Berbere Lentils and Cauliflower (page 26) or Ethiopian Spiced Pot Roast (page 73).

Thanksgiving falls during Kislev, and although it's a national and not a Jewish holiday, it is celebrated by American Jews. The Pilgrims were said to have modeled their observance after Sukkot. The Za'atar Roast Turkey (page 108) is a great choice for a smaller gathering. Turn any Thanksgiving turkey leftovers into a Middle Eastern–inspired Shabbat by making Turkey with Tahini Sauce in a Sweet Potato Crust (page 36).

SWEET-AND-TART SILAN-ROASTED CARROTS WITH LENTILS

Serves 4 as a main course, or 8 as a side dish

Carrots are symbolic in Judaism of asking for prosperity and for our blessings to multiply. Combined with the sweetness of silan (see What Is Silan, opposite) or honey, they make an edible wish for a Happy New Year at Rosh Hashanah.

This dish is bursting with color and flavor, honoring the joy of Shabbat, and is a satisfying plant-based main course. The colorful carrots are roasted in a sweet but slightly tart sauce that brings out their richness, and are complemented with lots of robustly spiced lentils. This protein-packed recipe makes a hearty main but is also a lovely side dish, either served together or separately.

MAKE IT SHABBAT:

STARTER/APPETIZER: *Whole Roasted Garlic (page 218) with cheese and Matzo Crackers (page 208) or other crackers*

MAIN COURSE: *Sweet-and-Tart Silan-Roasted Carrots with Lentils*

SIDE DISH: *Green salad with Lemon, Za'atar, and Garlic Dressing (page 219)*

BREAD: *Friday Night Challah (page 204)*

DESSERT: *Mango and Cardamom Mini Cheesecakes (page 184)*

FOR THE LENTILS

1 cup green or brown lentils
3 cups Vegetable Broth (page 197) or purchased
¼ teaspoon ground black pepper
¼ teaspoon ground cumin
¼ teaspoon paprika
½ cup chopped fennel or celery
½ cup chopped onion
1 teaspoon minced garlic
1 teaspoon minced jalapeño, optional
¼ teaspoon salt, plus more if desired

FOR THE CARROTS

2 tablespoons olive oil, plus
    more for the baking sheet
1 cup silan, honey, or agave syrup
¼ cup water
2 tablespoons fresh lemon juice
¼ teaspoon ground cumin
¼ teaspoon ground cardamom
¼ teaspoon cayenne pepper or paprika
⅛ teaspoon ground cloves
1 pound multicolored carrots, peeled, large
    carrots cut into thirds
1 teaspoon coarse sea salt
2 tablespoons tahini
2 tablespoons chopped fresh mint or flat-
    leaf parsley

TO MAKE THE LENTILS

In a large saucepan, stir together the lentils, vegetable broth, black pepper, cumin, and paprika and bring to a simmer over medium heat. Stir in the fennel, onion, garlic, and jalapeño (if using), and return to a simmer. Cover and cook, lowering the heat as needed to maintain a gentle simmer, until the lentils are tender and the liquid is absorbed, 15 to 20 minutes. Add the salt and stir well. Taste and adjust the seasoning, if desired. Remove from the heat, drain any excess liquid, and set aside while you make the carrots.

TO MAKE THE CARROTS

Preheat the oven to 450°F. Line a rimmed baking sheet with parchment paper or aluminum foil. Grease the parchment paper with olive oil.

In a wide, flat dish, whisk together the silan, water, olive oil, lemon juice, cumin, cardamom, cayenne, and cloves. Add the carrots and toss until evenly coated.

Place the carrots in a single layer on the prepared baking sheet. Set aside any left-over silan mixture.

Lower the oven temperature to 400°F. Roast the carrots for 40 to 50 minutes, or until tender and browned, tossing in the pan juices every 10 to 15 minutes.

Reheat the lentils, if desired, or keep them at room temperature. Add any leftover silan mixture to the lentils and stir to combine. Transfer the lentils to a large serving dish and top with the roasted carrots. Sprinkle with the coarse salt, drizzle with the tahini, and garnish with the fresh mint.

MAKE IT IN ADVANCE: *The lentils and carrots can be cooked up to 3 days ahead. Store the lentils, carrots, and leftover silan mixture separately in airtight containers and refrigerate.*

What is silan?

Silan is a thick syrup made from dates. It's also known as date honey, date syrup, or date molasses. When honey is mentioned in the Torah, they are talking about silan. It's made by boiling or steaming dried dates, mashing or pressing them, and then cooking the resulting liquid down into a syrup with a complex, sweet, and slightly tart flavor. It is sweeter and less sour than similar fruit-based syrups such as pomegranate molasses. It's a great drizzle for both savory and sweet dishes.

Silan plays a role in many Mizrahi, Maghrebi, and Middle Eastern dishes and is a component of a traditional Iraqi charoset (a symbolic nut-and-fruit mixture eaten at Passover Seders). You can find it in kosher, Middle Eastern, and specialty markets as well as online. Look for a brand without added sugars, preservatives, or thickeners. Honey or agave syrup are good substitutes.

BERBERE LENTILS AND CAULIFLOWER

Serves 6

Berbere, a heady blend of hot, sharp, and earthy spices from Ethiopia, does double duty here, flavoring both roasted cauliflower and simmered lentils bathed in tomato sauce. Berbere can be found online, in spice stores, and at specialty and African markets. It varies in heat, so if this is the first time you've used a particular mixture, you may want to start with a smaller amount and add more as you go. If purchased berbere is not available, try my Basically Berbere (page 215).

This recipe is a hearty and satisfying main dish, but you can also make just the roasted cauliflower or just the lentils and serve either as side dish for recipes like the Shawarma Roast Chicken (page 110) or Grilled Lamb Chops with Bitter Herbs Salad (page 116).

Adding the onions to the hot, dry pan, is a common Ethiopian cooking technique and helps give the dish its distinct flavor and character.

MAKE IT SHABBAT:

STARTER/APPETIZER: *Chile, Ginger, and Spice Charred Eggplant Dip (page 132) with vegetable sticks*

MAIN COURSE: *Berbere Lentils and Cauliflower*

SIDE DISH: *Green salad with Tahini Dressing (page 220)*

BREAD: *Challah Pull-Apart Rolls (page 206)*

DESSERT: *Raisin and Almond Twirls (page 187)*

FOR THE CAULIFLOWER

¼ cup olive oil, plus more for the baking sheet
1 teaspoon berbere or Basically Berbere (page 215)
¼ teaspoon salt
¼ teaspoon ground black pepper
¼ teaspoon ground ginger
¼ teaspoon ground cardamom,
2 tablespoons fresh lemon juice
1 (2- to 2½-pound) cauliflower, cut into 1½-inch florets
2 cups chopped red onion
2 cups 1-inch chopped green bean pieces
½ cup peeled garlic cloves, halved if large

FOR THE LENTILS

1 cup minced red onion
2 tablespoons extra-virgin olive oil
2 teaspoons minced garlic
2 teaspoons berbere or Basically Berbere (page 215)
½ teaspoon salt, plus more if desired
¼ teaspoon ground black pepper
¼ teaspoon ground ginger
¼ teaspoon ground cardamom
1½ cups chopped fresh tomatoes
1 (15-ounce) can tomato sauce
3 cups cooked brown or green lentils, homemade or canned (see Note)

FOR SERVING

¼ cup chopped tomatoes
3 tablespoons chopped fresh flat-leaf parsley or cilantro
¼ cup dairy or non-dairy sour cream or plain Greek yogurt, optional

TO MAKE THE CAULIFLOWER

Preheat the oven to 450°F. Line 2 large rimmed baking sheets with parchment paper or aluminum foil. Grease the paper with olive oil.

Pour the olive oil into a large bowl. Add the berbere, salt, pepper, ginger, cardamom, and lemon juice and stir until combined. Add the cauliflower, red onion, green beans, and garlic and toss until evenly distributed and well coated. Transfer the cauliflower mixture along with any seasoned oil remaining in the bowl to the prepared baking sheets and spread them into a single layer.

Roast for 45 to 55 minutes, or until the cauliflower is tender and the green beans are charred, using a spatula to turn them every 15 minutes. Transfer the vegetables and any browned bits to a bowl and set aside.

TO MAKE THE LENTILS

In a saucepan over low heat, cook the onion, stirring often and adding water 1 teaspoon at a time, if needed, to prevent sticking, until it begins to soften, 5 to 7 minutes. (If you added water, cook until the onions are soft and the pan is dry.)

Add the olive oil, raise the heat to medium, and cook, stirring, until the onions begin to sizzle, 3 to 5 minutes. Add the garlic and sauté until golden, 1 to 2 minutes. Add the berbere, salt, pepper, ginger, and cardamom and sauté until fragrant, about 30 seconds. Add the chopped tomatoes and sauté until they begin to soften, about 3 minutes.

Add the tomato sauce and bring to a simmer, stirring often. Add the cooked lentils, stir to combine, and return to a simmer. Lower the heat to medium-low, cover, and continue to simmer, stirring occasionally, for 10 minutes. Remove the lid and cook, stirring often, until the sauce is thickened but not dry, about 5 minutes longer (add water, 1 tablespoon at a time, as needed, if the sauce gets dry). Taste and add salt, if desired.

TO SERVE

Transfer the lentils to a large serving dish and top with the roasted cauliflower and vegetables. Garnish with the chopped tomatoes and the parsley. Top with dollops of sour cream (if using) and serve hot, warm, or at room temperature.

NOTE: *You'll need 2 (15-ounce) cans of lentils, rinsed and drained, or 1¼ cups dried. To cook dried lentils, rinse and drain the lentils, picking out any debris. Place in a large saucepan with 3¼ cups of vegetable broth or water and ¼ teaspoon salt. Bring to a simmer over medium heat. Lower the heat and simmer until the lentils are tender but not mushy, 20 to 25 minutes. Drain, rinse under cold running water, and drain again.*

MAKE IT IN ADVANCE: *The lentils in sauce can be made up to 3 days ahead and refrigerated in an airtight container. The vegetables can be roasted up to 2 days ahead and refrigerated in an airtight container.*

SPICE-RUBBED CHICKEN ON ROOT VEGETABLES

Serves 6 to 8

For more than twenty-five years, Dawn Margolin knew exactly what she would be serving, and so did her guests around her oversized dining table: this recipe for chicken served with vegetables roasted in the tantalizing pan juices. The flavors are influenced by Morocco, where she was born during her family's stint at the U.S. Naval Base there. Dawn keeps the rest of the meal simple, serving just challah and a green salad on the side. Dessert is always her One-Pan Banana Bread (page 183).

"Knowing what I was going to make each week made me more comfortable to invite guests without stressing about it. I always asked the guests to bring the salad, because making salad causes me stress," she said with a laugh. My adaptation is here. Dawn uses a whole chicken. I use chicken parts, which I think is simpler.

5 tablespoons olive oil, divided
3½ to 4 pounds bone-in, skin-on chicken parts
2 teaspoons salt, divided
2 teaspoons ground black pepper, divided
3 teaspoons ground cumin
1½ teaspoons ground turmeric
¼ teaspoon cayenne pepper
2 tablespoons fresh lemon juice
2 cups (½-inch slices) carrots
2 cups (½-inch chunks) peeled potatoes
2 cups (½-inch chunks) peeled sweet potatoes
2 cups (½-inch chunks) peeled and seeded butternut squash, or additional potatoes or sweet potatoes
2 cups (½-inch chunks) diced onion
10 large garlic cloves, peeled
1 cup Chicken Broth (page 194) or Vegetable Broth (page 197) or purchased, plus more if needed
3 tablespoons chopped fresh cilantro or flat-leaf parsley
2 large heads Whole Roasted Garlic (page 218), optional

MAKE IT SHABBAT:

STARTER/APPETIZER: *Almost Homemade Hummus (page 96) with Matzo Crackers (page 208)*

MAIN COURSE: *Spice-Rubbed Chicken on Root Vegetables*

SIDE DISH: *Green salad with Whole Lemon Dressing (page 218)*

BREAD: *Friday Night Challah (page 204)*

DESSERT: *One-Pan Banana Bread (page 183)*

Preheat the oven to 400°F. Grease a 9-by-13-inch or larger baking pan or roasting pan with 1 tablespoon of olive oil.

If you're using chicken breasts, cut any larger pieces in half. In a small bowl, stir together 1½ teaspoons of salt, 1½ teaspoons of black pepper, the cumin, turmeric, cayenne, lemon juice, and remaining 4 tablespoons of olive oil. Transfer 2 tablespoons of the spice paste to a medium bowl and set aside. Brush or rub the remaining spice paste on all sides of the chicken pieces and set aside on a plate.

Place the carrots, potatoes, sweet potatoes, squash, onions, and garlic cloves in the baking pan. Set aside.

In a bowl, add the chicken broth, remaining ½ teaspoon of salt, and ½ teaspoon of black pepper to the reserved 2 tablespoons of spice paste and stir until combined. Pour the mixture over the vegetables and toss until combined. Spread out the vegetables into a single layer in the baking pan.

Loosely cover the baking pan with aluminum foil and roast for 30 minutes. Remove the baking pan from the oven and brush or spoon the pan juices over the vegetables, adding more broth, 1 tablespoon at a time, if the pan seems dry.

Place the chicken pieces, skin side up, on top of the vegetables in a single layer. Brush or spoon some of the pan juices over the chicken. Roast, uncovered, for about 50 minutes, basting the chicken and vegetables every 15 to 20 minutes with the pan juices. (Add more broth, 1 tablespoon at a time, if needed.)

Cut into a piece of chicken; it is done when the juices run clear when you cut into the thickest piece. An instant-read thermometer inserted into the thickest part but away from the bone of a chicken piece should read 160°F for white meat and 175°F for dark meat, when checked a few times over 3 minutes.

Tent the chicken loosely with foil and let rest for at least 10 minutes. Sprinkle with the cilantro, garnish with the roasted garlic (if using), and serve.

MAKE IT IN ADVANCE: *The vegetables, pan juices, and chicken can be stored in separate airtight containers and refrigerated for up to 3 days.*

WHOLE ROAST CHICKEN WITH HERBS

Serves 4 to 6

Turning the chicken over partway through roasting helps make sure the thighs and breasts cook evenly and the chicken achieves a crispy texture all over. If you can't find some of the fresh herbs, it's fine to compensate with larger quantities of the others.

MAKE IT SHABBAT:

STARTER/APPETIZER: *Real Deal Chopped Liver (page 202) with Matzo Crackers (page 208)*

MAIN COURSE: *Whole Roast Chicken with Herbs*

SIDE DISH: *Tamarind Okra or Zucchini (page 168) and/or green salad with North African Dressing (page 219)*

BREAD: *Friday Night Challah (page 204)*

DESSERT: *Twice-Baked Lemon Cookies (page 185) with fresh berries*

FOR THE HERB STUFFING

½ cup chopped green onions
¼ cup chopped fresh flat-leaf parsley
¼ cup chopped fresh cilantro
¼ cup chopped fresh mint
¼ cup chopped fresh dill
1 tablespoon minced lemon zest

FOR THE SPICE MIX

1½ teaspoons salt
1 teaspoon ground black pepper
½ teaspoon ground cumin
½ teaspoon paprika
¼ teaspoon ground sumac or ½ teaspoon minced lemon zest
¼ teaspoon dried mint

FOR THE CHICKEN

1 whole chicken (3½ to 4½ pounds)
½ cup olive oil, divided
2 cups white wine or Chicken Broth (page 194) or purchased, plus more if needed
2 tablespoons fresh lemon juice

The popularity of poultry

Today, probably no food is seen as quintessentially Jewish as chicken (except for maybe matzo). But it wasn't always that way. The Jews probably didn't start eating chicken until they were conquered by the Romans. The Talmud eventually declared chickens the choicest of birds and made the chicken egg a standard of measurement and a symbol of fertility. But despite their favored status, once Rome fell, chicken production was limited in many parts of the world.

Geese were the predominant poultry among early Ashkenazi Jews. But as the Dark Ages ended and the Ashkenazi moved east in the fifteenth century, chicken once again become important, with many families raising small flocks for the eggs. The wealthy could afford to serve chicken on Shabbat. The poor might eat chicken only when a hen was too old to lay eggs.

For Sephardic and Mizrahi Jews, eating chicken remained popular, but expensive, since it cost much more than beef or lamb.

It wasn't until innovations in chicken production in the nineteenth and twentieth centuries that chicken became widely available and synonymous with Shabbat dinner for much of the Jewish world.

TO MAKE THE HERB STUFFING

In a medium bowl, mix together the green onions, parsley, cilantro, mint, dill, and lemon zest. Reserve ¼ cup of the mixture in a separate bowl and set both bowls aside.

TO MAKE THE SPICE MIX

In a small bowl mix together the salt, black pepper, cumin, paprika, sumac, and dried mint. Reserve ½ teaspoon of the spice mix and set both aside.

Preheat the oven to 400°F.

TO MAKE THE CHICKEN

Remove the giblets and neck (if any) from the chicken cavity and discard or save them for another use. Cut away any excess fat at the neck and rear of the chicken. Wipe the chicken cavity clean of any debris with paper towels.

Rub the chicken inside and out with ¼ cup of olive oil. Rub the larger portion of spice mix over the inside and outside of the chicken. Pack the larger portion of the herb stuffing into the chicken's cavity. Do not truss the chicken (it roasts more evenly this way).

Pour the wine into a roasting pan and place a rack inside. Place the chicken on the rack, breast side down.

Lower the oven temperature to 350°F. Roast the chicken for 30 minutes. Brush or spoon the pan juices over the chicken. Using a large fork and tongs, carefully turn over the chicken so it is breast side up. Brush or spoon the pan juices over the chicken and continue to roast for another 40 minutes (for a 3½ pound chicken) to 60 minutes (for 4½ pound chicken). Baste every 20 minutes and add a little more wine if needed. The chicken is ready when the juices run clear when you cut into the thickest piece and when an instant-read thermometer inserted into the thickest part but away from the bone of a breast and thigh reads 165°F when checked a few times over 3 minutes.

Let the chicken rest for 20 minutes. Carve or use poultry shears to cut the chicken into serving portions (cut large breasts in half, if desired).

In a small bowl, make a finishing sauce by mixing together the remaining ½ teaspoon of spice mix, remaining ¼ cup of oil, the reserved ¼ cup of uncooked herb stuffing, and the lemon juice and drizzle it over the chicken.

Serve the chicken warm or at room temperature along with the herb stuffing.

MAKE IT IN ADVANCE: *The chicken can be roasted up to 1 day in advance. To store, remove the herb stuffing from the chicken and refrigerate separately along with the finishing sauce ingredients. Do not assemble the herb finishing sauce until ready to serve.*

PICKLE-BRINED CHICKEN TWO WAYS

Each recipe serves 4 to 6

Pickle brine is the special ingredient for a duo of succulent chicken dishes perfect for Shabbat dinners. A quart bottle of kosher-style pickles (with or without garlic and/or dill, sour or half sour, whole or halves) usually has about 2 cups of brine. For the best results, use brine from pickles cured with only salt, water, and seasonings. This produces lactic acid and the fermentation gives these pickles their distinctive salty and sour flavor. They are in the refrigerated section of the supermarket. Pickle brine made with vinegar, available in shelf-stable jars, is a good alternative. Do not use the brine from sweet pickles. To give the chicken a spicy kick, serve with a side of Z'hug (page 213) or Harissa (page 214).

ROAST CHICKEN IN PICKLE BRINE

½ cup plus 2 tablespoons pickle brine

2 tablespoons pickle jar seasonings, optional

1 teaspoon chopped garlic plus ¼ cup peeled whole garlic cloves

2½ to 3 pounds bone-in, skin-on chicken thighs

2 tablespoons olive oil plus extra for greasing the baking pan

1 cup thinly sliced onions

¼ teaspoon ground black pepper

¼ teaspoon paprika

3 tablespoons chopped fresh dill

In a large glass or stainless-steel container, mix together ½ cup of pickle brine, brine seasonings (if using), and 1 teaspoon of chopped garlic. Place the chicken thighs in the container, cover with plastic wrap, and marinate, turning the chicken often, for at least 1 hour or place in the refrigerator for up to 24 hours.

Preheat the oven to 400°F. Grease a 9-by-13-inch baking pan with olive oil.

Scatter the sliced onions and ¼ cup of whole garlic cloves in the baking pan. Remove the chicken from the marinade and place the pieces on the onions, skin side up. Discard the marinade. In a small bowl, mix together the remaining 2 tablespoons of pickle brine, 2 tablespoons of olive oil, black pepper, and paprika and drizzle the mixture evenly over the chicken.

Bake for 45 minutes, basting occasionally with the pan juices, or until the chicken is cooked through but still juicy. The chicken is ready when the juices run clear after you cut into the thickest piece. An instant-read thermometer should read 175°F when checked multiple times over 3 minutes. To serve, sprinkle with dill and scatter the onions and garlic over the chicken.

OVEN-FRIED PICKLE-BRINED CHICKEN

½ cup pickle brine
2 tablespoons pickle jar seasonings
2½ to 3 pounds bone-in chicken thighs
Vegetable oil spray
2 large eggs, beaten
½ cup all-purpose flour
¼ teaspoon paprika

¼ teaspoon ground black pepper
¼ teaspoon salt
¼ teaspoon dried dill or 1 teaspoon fresh
  minced dill
1 cup unseasoned breadcrumbs,
  panko-style breadcrumbs, or matzo meal
4 to 6 lemon wedges
Pickled Red Onions (page 165), optional

In a glass or stainless-steel container, mix together the pickle brine and the pickle jar seasonings. Add the chicken and turn the pieces until they are coated. Cover with plastic wrap and marinate, turning the chicken pieces often, for at least 1 hour or refrigerate for up to 24 hours. Drain and discard the marinade and pat dry the chicken with paper towels.

Preheat the oven to 400°F. Spray a rimmed baking sheet with cooking spray.

Place the beaten eggs in a shallow bowl. In another shallow bowl, mix together the flour, paprika, pepper, salt, and dill. Add the breadcrumbs to a third similar bowl.

Dip one chicken thigh into the egg, turn to coat it evenly, and let the excess egg drip back into the dish. Dredge the chicken in the flour mixture, making sure to coat evenly and shaking any excess back into the bowl. Dredge in the bread crumbs until evenly coated, shaking any excess back into the bowl. Place the chicken, skin side up, on the baking sheet. Repeat with the remaining chicken thighs. Spray the tops of the chicken with cooking spray.

Bake for 25 minutes. Spray the chicken again with cooking spray and bake for 20 to 25 minutes, or until the juices run clear when you cut into the thickest piece. An instant-read thermometer should read 175°F when checked multiple times over 3 minutes. Let the chicken rest for 10 minutes. Serve with the lemon wedges and Pickled Red Onions (if using) on the side.

MAKE IT SHABBAT:

STARTER/APPETIZER: *Green salad with Tahini Dressing (page 220)*

MAIN COURSE: *Roast Chicken in Pickle Brine or Oven-Fried Pickle-Brined Chicken*

SIDE DISH: *Charred Greens (page 163)*

ACCOMPANIMENT: *Oven-Baked Garlic Fries (page 157)*

BREAD: *Friday Night Challah (page 204)*

DESSERT: *Flourless Chocolate Berry Cake (page 178)*

LAYERED CHICKEN AND RICE PLOV

Serves 8

A plov (sometimes called plof) is the star of Central Asian Jewish cuisine. A showstopper of a rice dish full of subtle flavors and moist chicken, it is served for Shabbat, holidays, and special occasions. it has roots in Central Asia's Silk Road past, a time when it was a major crossroads of camel caravans and traders from as far away as India.

Central Asia encompasses the countries that are between Afghanistan, Russia, China, and the Caspian Sea. In the twentieth century, these countries (Kazakhstan, Kyrgyzstan, Tajikistan, Turkmenistan, and Uzbekistan) were part of the Soviet Union. In addition to the Bukharan Jews (also known as Bukharian Jews or Bukhari Jews) who have lived in the region for millennia (migrating at the invitation of the Persian king after the fall of Babylon), European Jews fleeing the Holocaust made their homes there, as well as those expelled by Stalin. There was an influx of Persian Jews in the nineteenth century. Many of these Jews have now migrated to Israel or elsewhere.

Plov somewhat resembles Persian, Middle Eastern, and Indian pilafs, pilaus, and biriyanis. The one made by the Bukharan Jews is layered and traditionally ends the Shabbat dinner. I've tinkered with tradition here in several ways, making it a one-pot main dish while keeping it a centerpiece for a Friday night dinner.

2 cups white basmati rice

1¾ teaspoons salt, divided

¼ teaspoon crumbled saffron threads

3½ cups boiling water

3 pounds boneless, skinless chicken thighs, cut into 1-inch pieces

¾ teaspoon ground black pepper, divided

2 tablespoons vegetable oil, plus more if needed

4 cups thinly sliced onions

½ pound carrots, cut into 1-inch matchsticks

½ teaspoon ground cinnamon

½ teaspoon ground turmeric

½ cup finely chopped fresh dill or cilantro, divided

½ pound green beans, cut into 1-inch pieces

4 cups chopped fresh spinach or chard

3 tablespoons Pomegranate Molasses (page 212) or purchased

MAKE IT SHABBAT:

STARTER/APPETIZER: *Gefilte Fish with Smashed Tomato Topping (page 118)*

MAIN COURSE: *Layered Chicken and Rice Plov*

SIDE DISH: *California Hakol Salat (page 130)*

BREAD: *Friday Night Challah (page 204)*

DESSERT: *Fruit Juice Sorbet (page 191) or fruit salad*

Rinse the rice in several changes of water until the water runs clear. Drain. In a large heatproof bowl, mix together the rice, 1 teaspoon of salt, the saffron, and boiling water. Let soak for at least 1 hour.

In a large bowl, toss the chicken with ½ teaspoon of salt and ½ teaspoon of black pepper.

In a 6-quart pot, heat the vegetable oil over medium-high heat. Add the onions and sauté until the onions begin to soften, 7 to 10 minutes. Add the carrots and sauté until they begin to soften, about 10 minutes, adding another drizzle of oil if the pot seems dry.

Stir in the cinnamon, turmeric, remaining ¼ teaspoon of salt, remaining ¼ teaspoon of black pepper, and ¼ cup of dill and sauté for 1 minute. Add the chicken, lower the heat to medium and cook, stirring occasionally, for 12 minutes.

Layer the green beans evenly over the chicken and vegetables. Layer the spinach over the green beans. Carefully pour the rice mixture with the water into the pot. Do not stir or mix in with the other ingredients. Cover and bring to a simmer. Lower the heat to medium-low and simmer until all the water is absorbed and the rice is tender, about 45 minutes. (While the rice is cooking, open the lid as little as possible but check periodically to make sure the pot has not dried out. Add water, a little at a time, as needed.) Turn off the heat and let the pot sit, covered, for 10 minutes.

Uncover, place a rimmed platter on top of the pot and carefully flip over the pot onto the platter. The plov should turn out with the vegetables and chicken on top. Use a spatula to smooth it back into shape if needed. Serve the plov on the platter, garnished with the remaining ¼ cup of dill, and drizzled with pomegranate molasses.

MAKE IT IN ADVANCE: *Make the plov in a Dutch oven or other ovenproof pot up to 3 days in advance and keep it in the pot (or alternatively, transfer it to a large casserole or baking pan). Cover and refrigerate. To serve, sprinkle the top with a little water. Cover and reheat in a 350°F oven for 30 to 40 minutes (from room temperature), or until it's warmed through. Invert the pot onto a serving platter and garnish as instructed above.*

TURKEY WITH TAHINI SAUCE IN A SWEET POTATO CRUST

Serves 4

This dish combines Middle Eastern ingredients with American leftovers. The technique is adapted from those used to make sinaya (sometimes spelled synia or siniyah), a dish with Palestinian roots that's usually made with ground lamb mixed with tahini sauce over a layer of eggplant. This recipe gives new life to leftover turkey and baked sweet potatoes from Thanksgiving for a unique Shabbat dinner the day after the holiday. If you don't have leftover turkey or sweet potatoes, use any cooked chicken, or make the Za'atar Roast Turkey (page 108).

Vegetable oil for the baking pan
1 large (12-ounce) sweet potato or 1½ cups peeled, baked (or boiled), and mashed sweet potato
3 tablespoons olive oil, divided, plus more for the baking pan
2 cups chopped onion
2 tablespoons minced garlic
½ teaspoon salt
½ teaspoon dried oregano
½ teaspoon plus ⅛ teaspoon paprika
½ teaspoon ground cumin
½ teaspoon ground cinnamon
¼ teaspoon ground cloves
4 cups shredded cooked turkey, at room temperature
4 tablespoons Pomegranate Molasses (page 212) or purchased, divided
Tahini Sauce (page 210)
3 tablespoons chopped fresh flat-leaf parsley

MAKE IT SHABBAT:

STARTER/APPETIZER: *Charred Eggplant Dip (page 131) with vegetable sticks*

MAIN COURSE: *Turkey with Tahini Sauce in a Sweet Potato Crust*

SIDE DISH: *Leftover Thanksgiving vegetables or Charred Greens (page 163) and leftover cranberry sauce*

BREAD: *Friday Night Challah (page 204) with za'atar*

DESSERT: *Fruit Juice Sorbet (page 191) made with cranberry juice*

If you need to cook the sweet potato, preheat the oven to 375°F. Scrub the potato well, prick it all over with a fork, and place it on a baking sheet. Bake for 30 minutes and start checking for doneness at 10-minute intervals, until a fork goes through it without any resistance. Let sit until cool enough to handle, remove the peel, and mash. Can be made up to 3 days in advance and stored in an airtight container in the refrigerator. Return to room temperature before using.

Preheat the oven to 375°F. Grease an 8-by-8-inch baking pan.

Spread the sweet potato evenly over the bottom of the baking pan and set aside.

In a large skillet, heat 2 tablespoons of olive oil over medium-high heat. Add the onions and sauté, stirring occasionally, until softened, 7 to 10 minutes. Add the garlic and sauté, stirring occasionally, until golden, 1 to 2 minutes. Stir in the salt, oregano, ½ teaspoon of paprika, the cumin, cinnamon, and cloves and sauté for 1 minute. Add the turkey, 1 tablespoon of olive oil, and 3 tablespoons of pomegranate molasses and stir until the ingredients are well distributed.

Layer the turkey mixture evenly over the sweet potato. Spoon the tahini sauce over the top to cover and sprinkle with the remaining ⅛ teaspoon of paprika.

Bake for 30 to 35 minutes, or until the tahini is slightly browned and the ingredients are heated through.

Serve hot, warm, or at room temperature. Just before serving, drizzle with the remaining 1 tablespoon of pomegranate molasses and sprinkle with the parsley.

The world of tahini

Tahini is so much more than ground sesame seeds. Whether it is called tahina, rasi, tachina, tahin, ardeh, t'hine, tashi, or any other name, this thick paste of ground sesame seeds plays an enormous role in Middle Eastern, Arab, North Africa, Near Eastern, Turkish, and Mediterranean culinary traditions. It is the key component of Tahini Sauce (page 210) which is used on falafel, vegetables, or fish or as a dip. It's used in recipes as diverse as hummus, sinaya, casseroles, salads and salad dressings, baked goods, halvah (a tahini-based candy), and even tahini milk shakes.

To make tahini paste, sesame seeds are soaked in water and crushed, separating the outer hull from the inside kernel. The kernels are then toasted and ground. (Untoasted kernels are used for raw tahini) Much like peanut butter, the oil separates from the solids after the tahini settles, so it must be stirred to blend thoroughly before measuring and using. Unhulled sesame seeds are used to make a more intense and darker sesame butter.

The oldest recorded mention of tahini is an Arab cookbook from the 1200s. It wasn't until the 1960s that tahini paste became widely available in the United States. Look for it online, in specialty, kosher, and Middle Eastern markets, and in the international aisles of supermarkets. Check the expiration dates and buy the freshest you can. Look for 100 percent sesame seeds in the ingredients and choose brands without salt or additives. Choose either raw (milder and paler) or toasted (stronger and somewhat darker) tahini for the recipes in this book. If you think you will go through a container within a few months, store it at room temperature. For longer shelf life, store it in the refrigerator. Bring to room temperature before using.

POMEGRANATE MOLASSES BRISKET

Serves 8

When I was growing up, for Shabbat most people I knew served either roast chicken or brisket. We always had my grandmother's braised brisket, which tasted best when she burnt the onions, which added much of the flavor and savoriness.

No need to burn the onions when you make this recipe. Its tangy, robust flavor makes this my family's favorite brisket recipe. The long, slow cooking method breaks down this tougher cut of meat, and the pomegranate molasses gives it a tart sweetness that melds well with the rich beef. Leftovers can be used in dishes as varied as simple sandwiches or one of my favorites, Brisket Fried Rice (page 41).

I especially like how using Pomegranate Molasses (page 212), a Sephardic and Mizrahi ingredient, is combined with brisket, an American Ashkenazi staple. Cooking large cuts of brisket on their own and not as part of a stew or soup was not that common in Eastern Europe. It took New World prosperity and a new focus on meat as a main ingredient to make brisket a cut of meat to showcase and create a quintessentially Jewish food and a Shabbat and holiday table staple.

Even if this is your first brisket ever, by following this recipe you will have a tender, luscious result. Be sure to read How to Brisket (page 40) before buying and preparing the brisket. And like most briskets, this one tastes even better made in advance, which makes it ideal for a more relaxing Shabbat dinner.

For directions on how to make the brisket in the oven, see the instructions for the Red Wine Pot Roast (page 114).

1 (4- to 5-pound) beef brisket or boneless chuck roast

¾ teaspoon salt, divided

¾ teaspoon ground black pepper, divided

½ teaspoon paprika

½ teaspoon ground cumin

4 tablespoons vegetable oil, divided

4 cups chopped onions

2 tablespoons minced garlic

1 cup (¼-inch slices) carrots

1 (28-ounce) can diced tomatoes, with its liquid

½ cup plus 2 tablespoons Pomegranate Molasses (page 212) or purchased

2 tablespoons tomato paste, divided

2 tablespoons brown sugar

1 tablespoon fresh lemon juice

3 tablespoons chopped fresh flat-leaf parsley, cilantro, and/or mint, for garnish

3 tablespoons pomegranate seeds, optional

MAKE IT SHABBAT:

STARTER/APPETIZER: *Hawaij Vegetable Soup (page 104) with Matzo Balls (page 199)*

MAIN COURSE: *Pomegranate Molasses Brisket*

SIDE DISH: *North African Carrot Salad (page 164) and/or a green salad with Lemon, Garlic, and Za'atar Dressing (page 219)*

ACCOMPANIMENT: *Couscous or Potato Latkes (page 158)*

BREAD: *Friday Night Challah (page 204)*

DESSERT: *Turkish Coconut Pudding (page 190)*

Trim the brisket of excess external fat, leaving a ¼-inch cap on top and place it on a plate. In a small bowl, mix together ½ teaspoon of salt, ½ teaspoon of pepper, paprika, and cumin and rub the mixture on all sides of the brisket.

In a large heavy pot, or Dutch oven, heat 2 tablespoons of oil over medium-high heat. Sear the brisket on all sides until well browned, 5 to 7 minutes a side. If the piece of brisket is too big for the pan, cut the meat in half and sear it in batches. Transfer the brisket to the plate and set aside.

Add the remaining 2 tablespoons of oil to the pot. Add the onions and sauté, stirring up any browned bits from bottom of the pot, until softened, 5 to 7 minutes. Add the garlic and sauté until golden, 1 to 2 minutes. Add the carrots and sauté for 1 minute. Add the tomatoes with their liquid, ½ cup of pomegranate molasses, 1 tablespoon of tomato paste, the brown sugar, and the remaining ¼ teaspoon of salt and ¼ teaspoon of pepper. Stir well, bring the mixture to a simmer, and add the brisket, fat side up, along with any accumulated juices from the plate.

Cover the pot with a lid or aluminum foil and lower the heat to medium-low to keep it at simmer. Cook for 3 to 4 hours, basting with the liquid every 30 minutes and turning the meat in the liquid every 60 minutes. If the liquid begins to evaporate, add ½ cup of water. Start testing for doneness at 3 hours. The brisket is ready when a dinner fork can slide through the meat without any resistance. Transfer the meat to a plate and let rest for at least 20 minutes before shredding or cutting it against the grain (see How to Brisket, page 40) into ½-inch slices (at this point, I recommend chilling the uncut brisket and sauce separately overnight if you can, which will improve the flavor of the meat and make it easier to cut).

Once the brisket is removed, add the lemon juice, remaining 1 tablespoon of tomato paste, and the remaining 2 tablespoons of pomegranate molasses to the pot and stir to combine. Simmer, uncovered, over medium-low heat, stirring occasionally, until the liquid is reduced by about half or until thick enough to use as a sauce, 10 to 15 minutes. Taste and adjust the seasonings by adding more salt, lemon juice, and/or brown sugar, if desired. The sauce should be on the tangy side of sweet and sour. Keep the sauce warm to serve immediately with the brisket or chill it separately in an airtight container.

If serving immediately, arrange the brisket on a platter, spoon a few tablespoons of sauce over the top, and garnish with parsley and pomegranate seeds (if using). Serve the remaining sauce on the side.

If reheating, skim the fat off the chilled sauce, if desired. Reheat the sauce in a large pot over medium heat. Once it's simmering, add the chilled brisket and reheat, stirring gently. Serve as above.

MAKE IT IN ADVANCE: *Brisket can be made up to 5 days in advance and refrigerated in an airtight container. To freeze, shred or cut the cooled meat into thin slices (see Going Against the Grain on page 40) and store in an airtight container with the sauce for up to 3 months.*

How to brisket

What is brisket? It's the hard-working muscle from the cow's chest that has lots of connective tissue. A whole brisket can weigh more than 14 pounds, but they are usually sold in smaller sections of 3 to 6 pounds each. A whole brisket consists of two layers, or cuts, of meat separated by a layer of fat. Most briskets are sold separated but not all stores carry both cuts. Both are delicious, though each meaty layer has its champions.

The first cut or flat cut is roughly square or rectangular, has less internal marbling, and is beloved by some Jewish grandmothers as the healthier selection. Others prefer the second cut or point cut. It is more irregular in shape, often with a peak or cap of meat (called the deckle) and fat on the top, beloved by other Jewish grandmothers as the most delicious option. The grain of the meat is coarser in the second cut and it is more succulent with more internal fat. It stays moister during cooking.

Some stores do not separate the two layers; they simply cut to the desired weight. If your brisket is more than 4 inches thick and has a horizontal dividing line of fat, you have a section of whole brisket. Cut along the fat fault line and cook the pieces side by side or on top of each other because the sections will cook at different rates.

Fat adds taste and flavor, but too much fat can make the finished dish greasy. Not enough fat and your brisket will be dry and tasteless. All cuts of brisket have a layer of fat on top, with the point cut having more. Use a sharp knife to pare down the external fat so there is no more than ¼ inch on top. (Once the brisket is cooked and chilled you can scrape away excess fat from the meat and sauce, if desired.)

If brisket is difficult for you to find at the store or it's too expensive, use an equal amount of boneless beef chuck roast. Chuck roast is the traditional meat used for pot roast (which is the term for braising a large section of meat with some liquid) and it makes a tasty and more widely available substitute. Chuck roast also needs long and slow cooking. While it tends to have less external fat than the brisket, any excess should be trimmed as instructed in the recipe.

HOW MUCH TO BUY: Brisket shrinks when it cooks, so the general rule is ½ pound raw per person. If you purchased your brisket with the fat untrimmed, there will be additional weight loss. Once it's cooked, if it doesn't look like enough to feed your crowd, try shredding the meat instead of slicing it, which seems to extend the servings.

HOW LONG TO COOK: The cooking time depends on many factors, from what cut of brisket you are using and its thickness, to what the cow ate and how tender you want the cooked beef. My family prefers it so soft and tender it practically falls apart when you try to slice it, so I simmer longer. Others prefer it more intact. Either way, cook it until a dinner fork inserted in the meat can easily glide through.

GOING AGAINST THE GRAIN: If you are cutting slices instead of shredding your brisket (or chuck roast), you need to cut the meat perpendicular to the way the fibers are arranged, otherwise the meat will be tough to chew. This is called cutting against or across the grain. In many cases, the direction of the meat fibers will angle or change throughout a piece of brisket, so you may need to adjust as you cut to be sure you are still cutting against the grain. Thinner slices are better than thicker, which is why I recommend waiting to slice the meat until after it is chilled because the meat will be easier to cut.

BRISKET FRIED RICE

Serves 4

I once attended a banquet celebrating the relationship between China and Israel. Organizers promised food reflecting both traditions, but the resulting menu just alternated between Chinese and Israeli specialties. What I craved was a mash-up of the flavors and cuisine, so I came up with this fried rice.

The flavor of the fried rice depends on well-seasoned and well-sauced meat, so the Pomegranate Molasses Brisket (page 38) with its sweet-tart, full flavor is a perfect choice, but any braised beef works well. Shred the meat from Spicy Beef Tzimmes (page 69), or try the fried rice with saucy braised or stewed poultry such as Pulled Turkey with Pomegranate Molasses (page 65).

This is one of the dishes I change up all the time depending on what vegetables I have in the house and my mood, so feel free to substitute or add vegetables as you see fit. It's a great use for defrosted, frozen leftover brisket.

MAKE IT SHABBAT:

STARTER/APPETIZER: *Fruit and Salad Rolls (page 136)*

MAIN COURSE: *Brisket Fried Rice*

SIDE DISH: *Iraqi-Israeli Vegetable Pickles (page 166) and/or Vegetable Salad Rolls (page 138)*

BREAD: *Friday Night Challah (page 204)*

DESSERT: *Fruit Juice Sorbet (page 191) with Twice-Baked Lemon Cookies (page 185)*

2 tablespoons vegetable oil
½ teaspoon minced ginger
2 teaspoons minced garlic
¼ teaspoon crushed red pepper, optional
½ cup chopped carrots
½ cup chopped celery
½ cup shelled fresh green peas or frozen
2 cups shredded or slivered cooked brisket or pot roast
2 to 3 tablespoons sauce from meat, optional
3 cups cooked long-grain white rice, at room temperature
½ teaspoon salt
¼ teaspoon ground black pepper
¼ cup thinly sliced green onions
1 teaspoon sesame oil
2 tablespoons chopped fresh cilantro

In a 12-inch skillet or wok, heat the oil over high heat. Add the ginger, garlic, and crushed red pepper (if using) and cook, stirring frequently, until the garlic is golden, 1 to 2 minutes. Add the carrots and celery and cook, stirring, for 3 minutes. Add the peas and cook, stirring, for 1 minute. Add the brisket and sauce (if using) and cook, stirring frequently, until hot, 3 to 5 minutes.

Add the rice and cook, stirring and breaking up any clumps in the rice, until heated through, 3 to 5 minutes. Add the salt, black pepper, and green onions and stir until combined. Taste, and add more salt and/or black pepper, if desired.

Serve hot, drizzled with sesame oil and sprinkled with cilantro.

STUFFED CABBAGE MEATLOAF

Serves 4

While my Grandma Anna wasn't known for her cooking, she made a tasty meatloaf and her stuffed cabbage was stellar. Both dishes provided the inspiration for this recipe, which is a giant stuffed cabbage roll. I wanted all the flavors of stuffed cabbage but I didn't want to do all the work. The tangy sweet-and-sour raisin sauce replicates the one my grandmother made. The sauce is also tasty on cooked grains and makes a nice accompaniment for roasted or grilled chicken or fish. Make two meatloaves if you are doubling the recipe.

MAKE IT SHABBAT:

STARTER/APPETIZER: *Chicken Soup with Matzo Balls (page 196)*

MAIN COURSE: *Stuffed Cabbage Meatloaf*

SIDE DISH: *Lemon, Za'atar, and Garlic Dressing (page 219) over sliced cucumbers and tomatoes or green salad*

ACCOMPANIMENT: *Rice, egg noodles, or mashed potatoes*

BREAD: *Friday Night Challah (page 204)*

DESSERT: *Bundt Cake with Black and White Bundt Glazes (page 180)*

FOR THE SWEET-AND-SOUR SAUCE

½ cup raisins
1 (8-ounce) can tomato sauce
1 tablespoon sugar
¼ teaspoon ground ginger
⅛ teaspoon salt
⅛ teaspoon ground black pepper
2 tablespoons apple cider vinegar
¼ cup diced tomatoes

FOR THE STUFFED CABBAGE

1 pound ground beef
1 cup unseasoned breadcrumbs or matzo
   meal
1 large egg, beaten
½ cup finely chopped onions
2 teaspoons minced garlic
½ teaspoon salt
½ teaspoon ground black pepper
¼ teaspoon paprika
¼ teaspoon dried oregano
2 tablespoons tomato paste
6 large green cabbage leaves
3 tablespoons vegetable oil, divided
3 large hard-boiled eggs, peeled

TO MAKE THE SWEET-AND-SOUR SAUCE

Place the raisins in a small bowl, add hot water to cover, and let soak for 20 minutes. Drain the raisins and transfer them to a small saucepan. Add the tomato sauce, sugar, ginger, salt, and black pepper and bring to a simmer, stirring occasionally, over medium-low heat. Continue to cook, stirring occasionally, for 10 minutes. Add the vinegar and diced tomatoes and cook until very thick but pourable, an additional 10 minutes. Taste, adjust the salt, and add sugar and/or vinegar as needed to get the sauce as sweet or sour as you like. Set aside.

TO MAKE THE STUFFED CABBAGE

In a large bowl, mix together the ground beef, breadcrumbs, beaten egg, onions, garlic, salt, pepper, paprika, oregano, and tomato paste until just combined (do not overmix). Let rest for 10 minutes.

Bring a large pot of water to a boil over high heat. Immerse the cabbage leaves in the boiling water, cover, lower the heat to a simmer, and cook until the leaves are just pliable, 3 to 4 minutes. Using tongs, remove the leaves, rinse with cold water, and pat dry. Transfer to a plate and set aside. The leaves will be very pliable. Trim off any hard or very fibrous stem ends.

Preheat the oven to 350°F. Grease a large rimmed baking sheet with 1 tablespoon oil. Place the 2 largest cabbage leaves in the center of the baking pan, stem end to stem end.

Mound half of the meatloaf mixture into an 8-by-4-inch loaf shape in the middle of the 2 cabbage leaves. Using the back of a spoon or your fingers, shape a 1-by-1-inch channel lengthwise in the middle of the meat. Press the whole hard-boiled eggs into the channel, spacing them evenly. Mound the remaining meat mixture over the top, completely covering the eggs. Drape 2 or 3 cabbage leaves over the meatloaf, filling in any gaps with the remaining leaves. Fold up the cabbage leaves from the bottom of the meatloaf to enclose it completely. Brush the cabbage-wrapped meatloaf with 1 tablespoon of oil.

Bake for 40 to 50 minutes, brushing the cabbage with the remaining tablespoon of oil after 20 minutes, or until the meatloaf is cooked through, firm to the touch, and an instant-read thermometer inserted a few inches into the meatloaf (inserted from the side to avoid the eggs) registers 160°F. Let the meatloaf sit for 20 minutes. Transfer the meatloaf to a serving platter and top with a few tablespoons of the sweet-and-sour raisin sauce. Using a large serrated knife, gently cut the meatloaf into slices. Serve with extra sauce on the side.

MAKE IT IN ADVANCE: *The recipe can be made 1 day in advance. Store the meatloaf and sauce separately in the refrigerator, wrapping the meatloaf tightly in plastic wrap.*

EGGPLANT OVERFLOWING WITH LAMB

Serves 6 to 8

Eggplant is the most versatile of vegetables, and combining it with lamb could be one of my favorite ways to serve it. This was inspired by a filled eggplant I first had in Turkey, but the flavors are Middle Eastern as well. The rich lamb is tempered by the onions, garlic, tomatoes, and fresh herbs (dill is especially good with lamb), and its eggplant container becomes silky soft and delectable as it bakes. The recipe also works well with ground beef or a combination of beef and lamb. Serve drizzled with Tahini or Tahini Sauce (page 210) and Pomegranate Molasses (page 212) and sprinkled with fresh herbs. Like most stuffed vegetable dishes, this one does have a lot of steps, but the entire dish can be made ahead and reheated just before serving.

2 eggplants (each about 1 pound)
4 cups very thinly sliced onions
1 teaspoon salt
1 teaspoon ground sumac
5 tablespoons olive oil, plus more if needed
1 tablespoon minced garlic
1 pound ground lamb
2 cups chopped fresh tomatoes or
  1 (14½-ounce) can diced tomatoes,
  drained
2 tablespoons tomato paste
1 teaspoon paprika
½ teaspoon ground cumin
½ teaspoon ground black pepper
⅛ teaspoon sugar
⅓ cup finely chopped fresh dill
⅓ cup finely chopped fresh mint
⅔ cup finely chopped fresh flat-leaf parsley
¼ cup fresh lemon juice

FOR THE GARNISHES

3 tablespoons tahini or Tahini Sauce
  (page 210)
3 tablespoons Pomegranate Molasses (page
  212) or purchased or silan (see page 25)
¼ cup chopped fresh dill, mint, and/or flat-
  leaf parsley

MAKE IT SHABBAT:

STARTER/APPETIZER: *California Hakol Salat (page 130)*

MAIN COURSE: *Eggplant Overflowing with Lamb*

SIDE DISH: *Iraqi-Israeli Pickled Vegetables (page 166)*

ACCOMPANIMENT: *Bulgur, couscous, or rice*

BREAD: *Friday Night Challah (page 204) with za'atar topping or flatbreads*

DESSERT: *Raisin and Almond Twirls (page 187)*

Trim any leaves off the eggplant, leaving the stems intact. Cut the eggplants in half lengthwise. Using a paring knife or a vegetable peeler, remove 3 long strips (¾ to 1 inch wide) of eggplant peel from each half, starting at the stem end and leaving the peel intact between strips, creating a striped pattern. (Removing the peel in strips allows the eggplant to retain its shape and still be able to absorb the pan juices). Cut a bit off the rounded bottom of the eggplant to stabilize it, if needed. Using a large soup spoon, hollow out the eggplants, leaving about ½ inch of flesh and being careful not to pierce the skin. Chop the scooped-out eggplant pieces and measure out 2 cups to use for the filling. (Reserve the remaining eggplant for another use, such as adding it to Freekah Pilaf, page 152, or sautéing with the peppers in the Mostly Make-It-Ahead Shakshouka, page 100.)

In a large bowl, toss together the onions, salt, and sumac until evenly coated. Set aside.

Preheat the oven to 425°F.

In a large skillet, heat 1 tablespoon of olive oil over medium-high heat. Add the garlic and sauté until golden, 1 to 2 minutes. Add the chopped eggplant and sauté until it begins to soften and turn golden, about 3 minutes. Add a little more olive oil if the pan seems dry. Add the lamb and sauté, breaking it up with a spoon, until just browned, about 3 minutes. Remove the lamb and eggplant with a slotted spoon and add it to the bowl with the seasoned onions. Add the tomatoes, tomato paste, paprika, cumin, pepper, sugar, dill, mint, parsley, and lemon juice to the lamb and onions in the bowl and mix well.

Spoon the filling into each eggplant half, mounding more on top, and covering the surface of the eggplant to the edges.

Place the filled eggplants, filling side up, in a 9-by-13-inch baking pan. Drizzle the remaining 4 tablespoons of olive oil over the tops. Pour water into the baking pan until it comes ½ inch up the sides of the eggplants. Loosely cover the baking pan with aluminum foil and bake for 65 to 75 minutes, spooning the cooking liquid over the tops every 15 minutes, until the eggplant shells are very soft but not collapsing and the lamb is cooked through. Add more water if needed as the eggplants cook. Spoon the liquid over the tops one more time and transfer them to a serving platter. Drizzle the eggplants with the tahini and pomegranate molasses. Sprinkle with chopped dill and serve hot or warm.

MAKE IT IN ADVANCE: *Make the recipe as instructed up to 2 days in advance and do not garnish. Cover the baking pan with aluminum foil and refrigerate. Reheat in a 350°F oven until warmed through, about 20 minutes. Remove the foil, brush with the pan liquid, and bake for 10 additional minutes.*

ROAST SALMON WITH CITRUS-HONEY SAUCE

Serves 4 to 6 as a main course, or 8 to 10 as a starter

During my childhood, I thought Jews mainly ate two types of fish—gefilte (served with horseradish) and lox (served with bagels and cream cheese). One of the joys of being a grownup and cooking for myself was discovering the meaty, clean taste of fresh salmon. Salmon is the most popular fresh fish in the U.S. for a reason. It's mild tasting, widely available, good for you, and very versatile. For the best taste and to support the environment, choose wild or sustainably raised salmon.

In this recipe, the spices and mint mesh with the citrus and honey sauce, making it perfect for a Shabbat dinner when you want big flavor without a lot of fuss. The optional Sichuan peppercorns, the dried husks of the seeds of several species of prickly ash, add a mild, pleasant tingle. They are available in spice stores, Asian and specialty markets, as well as online. Crush them lightly in a mortar and pestle or with a meat tenderizer mallet before using. If you are worried about their intensity, start with ½ teaspoon and add more if desired.

Dishes with honey are traditional during the fall holidays and a way to wish for a sweet New Year at Rosh Hashanah. Fish are also said to be lucky and are often part of Shabbat and holiday menus.

⅓ cup fresh orange juice, blood orange juice, or tangerine juice
½ cup light-colored honey
½ teaspoon dried mint
¼ teaspoon salt
¼ teaspoon cayenne pepper or paprika
¼ teaspoon ground black pepper
½ to 1 teaspoon Sichuan peppercorns, lightly crushed, optional
Vegetable oil for the baking sheet
1½ to 2 pounds salmon fillet
6 tablespoons thinly sliced green onions

MAKE IT SHABBAT:

STARTER/APPETIZER: *Vegetable Salad Rolls (page 138)*

MAIN COURSE: *Roast Salmon with Citrus-Honey Sauce*

SIDE DISH: *Steamed green beans*

ACCOMPANIMENT: *Tahini Mashed Potatoes (page 156) or rice*

BREAD: *Friday Night Challah (page 204) with sesame seed topping*

DESSERT: *Mango and Cardamom Mini Cheesecakes (page 184)*

In a small bowl, mix together the orange juice, honey, mint, salt, cayenne, black pepper, and crushed Sichuan peppercorns (if using) to make a marinade. Set aside half of the marinade to use later for the sauce.

Grease a rimmed baking sheet with oil. Place the salmon, skin side down, in the pan and brush the top of the salmon with some of the marinade. Let sit for at least 30 minutes or up to 60 minutes, brushing often with the marinade.

Preheat the oven to 350°F.

While the fish is marinating, pour the reserved marinade into a small saucepan over medium heat and bring to a boil. Lower the heat to low and simmer, uncovered, stirring occasionally, until the liquid is reduced by two-thirds, 15 to 20 minutes. Taste, and adjust the salt and other seasonings, if desired. Set the sauce aside.

Brush or spoon the remaining marinade over the salmon. Roast for 15 to 20 minutes, basting with the pan juices after 10 minutes, until the salmon is cooked to the desired doneness. For fully cooked fish, it should read 145°F when an instant-read thermometer is placed in the thickest part of the fillet. The flesh should be opaque all the way through but still be very moist.

To serve, transfer the salmon to a platter and spoon the sauce over the fish. Sprinkle with green onions and serve warm, at room temperature, or chilled.

MAKE IT IN ADVANCE: *The fish and sauce can be made up to 2 days ahead and refrigerated separately in airtight containers.*

Fish as a part of Jewish cuisine

Fish are a symbol of fertility and prosperity. They are also seen as lacking in sin, protected from evil, and connected to creation. The Talmud (ancient rabbinic writings that interpret the Torah) also says eating fish is one way to show delight in Shabbat. This is why, for more than a thousand years, Shabbat dinners have often included fish.

For Jews from Eastern Europe, that fish might be gefilte fish (minced fish with eggs and seasonings poached in fish stock). Gefilte Fish with Smashed Tomato Topping (page 118) is a modern version. Chopped herring with onions in wine sauce in another common dish. For Libyan Jews, it might be a dish similar to Fish in Spicy H'raimi-Style Tomato Sauce (page 48). Although the recipes vary, serving fish is a connection that honors the Shabbat tradition.

FISH IN SPICY H'RAIMI-STYLE TOMATO SAUCE

Serves 4 or 6 as a main course, or 8 to 10 as a starter

H'raimi is fish cooked in a spicy tomato sauce and it's a traditional component of a Friday night dinner in Libya (where the inspiration for this version is from) and throughout North Africa. The dish has become popular in Israel and Italy where many Libyan Jews have immigrated.

While it is usually served in small portions as a first course, my interpretation makes the dish a main course and adds carrots and red bell peppers. The dish calls for white fish cut into thick fillets or steaks, but I've also used thick fillets of salmon with excellent results.

The dish goes by many names (chraime, hraimeh, and aharaimi being just a few) and ingredients can vary greatly from home to home. Some cooks include onion, some rely on fresh hot peppers, others on hot paprika or cayenne pepper, and some add caraway in addition to the cumin. For a vegan version made with tofu, please see the variation following the recipe. The fish and sauce can be served warm, at room temperature, or even chilled.

2 tablespoons olive oil

1½ cups chopped onion

2 teaspoons finely chopped garlic

2 to 3 teaspoons seeded, finely chopped fresh jalapeños or serrano chiles (see Note)

1½ teaspoons paprika or hot (sharp) paprika

1 teaspoon ground cumin

½ teaspoon ground caraway, optional

½ teaspoon salt

1½ cups (¼-inch slices) carrots

1½ cups chopped red bell pepper

2 tablespoons tomato paste

2 tablespoons fresh lemon juice

2 cups chopped fresh tomatoes or 1 (14½-ounce) can chopped tomatoes, with juices

1½ cups water

1½ pounds cod, halibut, sea bass or other mild, firm-fleshed fish fillets, any bones removed

½ cup chopped fresh cilantro or flat-leaf parsley, divided

MAKE IT SHABBAT:

STARTER/APPETIZER: *Mushroom-Eggplant Hummus Bowls (page 149)*

MAIN COURSE: *Fish in Spicy H'raimi-Style Tomato Sauce*

SIDE DISH: *Sautéed spinach and/or green salad with North African Dressing (page 219)*

ACCOMPANIMENT: *Yellow Rice (page 160)*

BREAD: *Friday Night Challah (page 204) or flatbread*

DESSERT: *Flourless Chocolate Berry Cake (page 178)*

Heat the oil in a Dutch oven or a large, deep skillet with a lid over medium-high heat. Add the onion and sauté until softened and starting to brown, 5 to 7 minutes. Add the garlic and sauté until golden, 1 to 2 minutes. Add the jalapeños (2 teaspoons for a milder dish, 3 for a spicier one) and sauté for 1 minute. Add the paprika, cumin, caraway (if using), salt, carrots, and bell peppers and sauté for 1 minute. Add the tomato paste, lemon juice, tomatoes with their juices, and water. Stir well and bring the mixture to a simmer. Lower the heat to medium-low, cover, and simmer, stirring occasionally, until the vegetables have begun to soften, 10 to 15 minutes.

Cut the fish into portions, depending on whether you are serving it as a first course or a main dish. Nestle the fish pieces into the sauce in the Dutch oven and spoon some of the sauce over the top. Cover, return to a simmer, and cook until the fish is just cooked through, 10 to 20 minutes. (The timing will vary depending on type and thickness of the fish.) The fish is done when it flakes when cut at the thickest point, is no longer translucent, and is very moist. It should read 145°F when an instant-read thermometer is placed in the thickest part of the fillet. Remove the fish from the sauce and transfer to a rimmed serving plate. Cover lightly with aluminum foil to keep warm.

Return the sauce to a simmer and cook over medium-low heat until the sauce has reduced by half, about 15 minutes. Taste and add more salt and/or paprika, if desired. Stir in half the cilantro and cook for 1 minute. Ladle the sauce over the fish and garnish with the remaining cilantro.

Serve the fish and sauce warm, at room temperature, or cold. If using cold, taste again before serving and add more salt if needed.

NOTE: *Traditionally, red chiles are used in this dish, but green jalapeños or serranos work well. Red versions are riper and hotter.*

VARIATION: *Tofu in Spicy H'raimi-Style Tomato Sauce—Substitute 1½ pounds firm tofu for the fish. Drain and rinse the tofu and pat dry with paper towels. Place a clean kitchen towel on a plate. Place the tofu on the kitchen towel and top with another towel. Top with a second plate. Place a weight on top of the plate, such as large can of tomatoes, and press the tofu for 20 minutes. Pat dry the tofu with paper towels again. Cut the tofu into 2-inch-wide slices. Add the tofu to the sauce at the same time the fish would have been added. Spoon the sauce over the tofu, cover, and simmer until heated through, 10 to 15 minutes. Transfer the tofu to a serving plate and follow the recipe as instructed.*

MAKE IT IN ADVANCE: *The recipe can be made up to 2 days in advance. Store the fish or tofu in the sauce in an airtight container and refrigerate.*

winter

WITH THE COMING OF WINTER

in the Northern Hemisphere, the lights and warmth of Shabbat take on special meaning, as does the food with its comforting emphasis on soups, stews, and heartier dishes.

Warm belly and soul with Matzo Ball and Pozole Chicken Soup (page 60), which mixes Eastern European and Latin American traditions; Ethiopian Spiced Pot Roast (page 73), a Kramer family favorite combining American braised beef with the spices of the Beta Israel Jews; steamy Winter Borscht with Lamb (page 76) based on a recipe from a Russian Holocaust survivor; and my Spice Trade Fish Stew (page 78), which channels Yemeni Jewish flavors.

WINTER HOLIDAYS AND SPECIAL DAYS

The shifting Hebrew calendar means that winter roughly aligns with the last of Kislev and the months of Tebet, Shevat and part of Adar (or in years with a leap month, Adar I).

The eight nights of Hanukkah shine this season. The word "Hanukkah" means "dedication," and the holiday commemorates the determination of the Jews in Judea to overthrow oppressive invaders, the retaking of the sacred Temple, and the miracle of a limited oil supply lasting

eight days during the rededication of the restored Temple. The holiday also marks the end of the ancient olive harvest and may have originally been based on Sukkot, the fall harvest festival.

Foods fried in oil are traditional for Hanukkah (and for the Shabbat during Hanukkah). Accompany the tangy sweetness and fragrant spices of Pulled Turkey with Pomegranate Molasses (page 65) with crispy fried Potato Latkes (page 158), a traditional Hanukkah favorite for Jews of Eastern European descent. Tender Leek-and-Mint Fritters alongside succulent Oregano Roast Chicken (page 62), and fried South Indian fish cakes with tangy Coconut-Cilantro Chutney (page 120) are good choices. For dessert, try the Challah Fritters with Sweet Tahini Sauce (page 188).

Dairy foods are another Hanukkah tradition. Try the Mushroom and Cheese Strudels (page 98), Falafel Pizza with Feta and Herbs (page 102) or the Spinach and Dill Phyllo Pies (page 126). Mango and Cardamom Mini Cheesecakes (page 184) make a festive dairy-based dessert.

For many American Jews, eating Chinese food on Christmas or Christmas Eve has become a ritual. Try Sweet-and-Sour Fish (page 89) or the Brisket Fried Rice (page 41).

Some families celebrate two winter holiday traditions, and Friday Night Tamales (page 71) filled with Spicy Beef Tzimmes (page 69) recognizes that. A riff on the Mexican tradition of tamales at Christmas, the dish starts with a spicy variation of tzimmes, an Eastern European fruit and vegetable stew, and then steams it wrapped in traditional Mexican tamale dough (adapted to meet Jewish dietary laws).

Tu B'Shevat, or the New Year of the Trees, has become an ecological and environmental holiday, but it began as a way to decide when to tax fruit trees. Rabbis and sages transformed the holiday from administrative to mystical, creating home-based celebrations honoring the different qualities of fruit and how they reflect human traits and beliefs.

Sephardic and Mizrahi Jews kept the custom with a wide assortment of fruits, but in cold and frigid Eastern Europe, fruit choices were limited, so Ashkenazi Jews observed the holiday by eating dried fruit. Another holiday custom is to eat foods based on the Seven Species named in the Torah—wheat, barley, pomegranates, olives, figs, dates, and grapes. Some recipes to try for the holiday include the Carrot Curry Tzimmes (page 56), Spicy Beef Tzimmes (page 69), Freekah Pilaf (page 152), Pomegranate Molasses Brisket (page 38), or Sweet-and-Tart Silan-Roasted Carrots with Lentils (page 24).

The Jewish calendar is lunar-based adjusted for the solar year seven times in nineteen years when there is a leap month added to the Hebrew calendar. This adds a second month of Adar (or Adar II). When it is a leap year, Purim moves to Adar II, and instead of late February or early March it is celebrated in late March.

Purim is a holiday of joy, celebration, and triumph, but also one of dark and dangerous secrets. It celebrates Queen Esther and her relative Mordecai foiling the evil vizier Haman's plot to harm the Jews in ancient Persia. Wearing costumes, attending carnivals, creating plays, reading the "official" story from the Book of Esther, donating money, and sending food presents to others are just some of the customs associated with the holiday.

Symbolic foods include ones with fillings (representing the hidden nature of much of the story) and vegetarian dishes, since Esther was said to only eat legumes and other foods that didn't violate Jewish dietary laws in the palace of the king. Try Middle East–inspired Peppers Stuffed with White Beans, Bulgur, Chard, and Tomatoes (page 54) drizzled with a garlic and lemon sauce, or the spicy Carrot Curry Tzimmes (page 56) influenced by the food ways of Jews from Eastern Europe and the Bene Israel who settled on the Konkan coast of Western India.

It is considered good luck to not only eat sweets at Purim but to share them with at least two others by delivering gifts called mishloach manot. Raisin and Almond Twirls (page 187) with its fruit-and-nut filling, and sturdy Twice-Baked Lemon Cookies (page 185) are two good candidates for holiday desserts or gift giving.

PEPPERS STUFFED WITH WHITE BEANS, BULGUR, CHARD, AND TOMATOES

Serves 4

This all-in-one dish is packed with vegetables, beans, and bulgur and combines some of my favorite flavors and textures in a tasty make-ahead Shabbat dinner entrée, particularly around Sukkot and Purim, when filled and vegetarian foods are symbolic connections to the holidays. The flavors are Middle Eastern and Near Eastern, and the aromas of cumin, paprika, and turmeric will pervade your kitchen. The lemony garlic sauce is inspired by toum, a Lebanese staple. It adds creaminess and another layer of flavor. Substitute plain yogurt for a milder option.

MAKE IT SHABBAT:

STARTER/APPETIZER: *Charred Eggplant Dip (page 131) with Matzo Crackers (page 208)*

MAIN COURSE: *Peppers Stuffed with White Beans, Bulgur, Chard, and Tomatoes*

SIDE DISH: *Bitter Herbs Salad (page 116)*

BREAD: *Friday Night Challah (page 204)*

DESSERT: *Chocolate and Cookie Truffles (page 186)*

FOR THE SEASONED TOMATO SAUCE

2 (8-ounce) cans tomato sauce
1 tablespoons olive oil
½ teaspoon paprika
½ teaspoon sugar
¼ teaspoon salt
¼ teaspoon ground black pepper

FOR THE STUFFED PEPPERS

8 large red, yellow, or orange bell peppers
½ cup water
2 tablespoons olive oil, plus more for the baking pan
1½ cups chopped onion
1 tablespoon minced garlic
1 cup chopped carrots
¾ cup chopped celery
2 cups Vegetable Broth (page 197) or purchased plus more if needed
1 teaspoon ground cumin
1 teaspoon paprika
¼ teaspoon ground turmeric
½ teaspoon salt
½ teaspoon ground black pepper
¼ teaspoon crushed red pepper
2 cups packed chopped chard
1 (15-ounce) can small white beans, drained and rinsed
1 (14½-ounce) can diced tomatoes, drained
1 cup cooked bulgur or couscous
¼ cup Garlic Sauce (page 210) or plain dairy or non-dairy yogurt

TO MAKE THE SEASONED TOMATO SAUCE

In a medium bowl, stir together the tomato sauce, olive oil, paprika, sugar, salt, and pepper. Set aside.

TO MAKE THE STUFFED PEPPERS

Cut about ¼ inch of the tops off the peppers. If the peppers wobble when you stand them up, cut a thin slice off the bottom, being careful not to pierce the shell. Remove the seeds and discard. Chop the pepper tops and set aside. Pour the water into a microwave-safe baking pan as large as will fit into your microwave. Place the peppers upright in the dish. (You might need to microwave in 2 batches.) Microwave on high until the peppers are tender, 5 to 8 minutes. Drain.

Preheat the oven to 350°F. Grease a large baking pan big enough to hold the peppers upright.

In a large skillet, heat the olive oil over medium-high heat. Add the onion and sauté until softened, 5 to 7 minutes. Add the garlic and sauté until golden, 1 to 2 minutes. Add the carrots, celery, and the reserved chopped bell pepper and sauté for 2 minutes. Add the vegetable broth, cumin, paprika, turmeric, salt, black pepper, and crushed red pepper, stir to combine, and bring to a simmer. Lower the heat to medium-low and cook, stirring occasionally, until the carrots begin to soften, about 10 minutes.

Add the chard and beans and cook, stirring frequently, until the chard is wilted and the liquid is reduced but not completely evaporated. Stir in the tomatoes and the bulgur. The mixture should be wet but not too liquid. If it is dry, add more broth, a little at a time, as needed. If it is too wet, cook for a few more minutes until the liquid reduces.

Spoon the mixture into the bell peppers and place them in the baking pan, open side up. Spoon 2 to 3 tablespoons of the tomato sauce on top of each of the peppers, covering the filling. Loosely cover with aluminum foil and bake for 30 minutes. Uncover and bake for another 10 to 20 minutes, or until the tomato sauce is bubbling and the filling is heated through.

To serve, arrange 2 stuffed peppers on each of 4 plates. Drizzle with the garlic sauce and serve hot or warm.

MAKE IT IN ADVANCE: *The peppers, without garlic sauce, can be made 1 day in advance, covered with plastic wrap in the baking pan, and refrigerated.*

CARROT CURRY TZIMMES

Serves 4 to 6

This recipe combines a spiced carrot dish from India's Bene Israel community with an Ashkenazi tzimmes (fruit and vegetable stew). How spicy your tzimmes is depends on how much cayenne pepper you use and how much heat your garam masala packs. This makes a wonderful vegan main course or it can be used as a side dish with Shawarma Chicken (page 110) or Yemeni Grilled Chicken (page 141). I like to serve purchased hot or spicy lime pickle and/or mango chutney on the side. Both Indian condiments are available in some supermarkets, specialty stores, and Indian and other international grocers.

MAKE IT SHABBAT:

STARTER/APPETIZER: *Fruit and Salad Rolls (page 136)*

MAIN COURSE: *Carrot Curry Tzimmes*

SIDE DISH: *Green salad with Whole Lemon Dressing (page 218)*

ACCOMPANIMENT: *Basmati rice*

BREAD: *Flatbreads*

DESSERT: *Mango and Cardamom Mini Cheesecakes (page 184)*

2 tablespoons vegetable oil
1 teaspoon brown, black, or yellow mustard seeds
1 teaspoon cumin seeds
2 teaspoons garam masala or curry powder
1 teaspoon ground cardamom
⅛ teaspoon ground cloves
¼ teaspoon cayenne pepper
2 cups chopped onions
1 teaspoon finely chopped garlic
½ teaspoon salt, divided
½ teaspoon ground black pepper
1 pound carrots, cut into ½-inch rounds
1 pound sweet potatoes, peeled and cut into ½-inch chunks
1 cup dried apricots
½ cup raisins
2 cups Vegetable Broth (page 197) or purchased
1 large ripe banana, mashed
1 (15-ounce) can chickpeas, drained and rinsed
½ cup chopped fresh cilantro or flat-leaf parsley, divided
½ cup plain dairy or non-dairy yogurt
Silan (see page 25) optional
Coconut-Cilantro Chutney (page 120), optional

In a large heavy pot or Dutch oven, heat the oil over medium-high heat. Add the mustard and cumin seeds and sauté until sizzling, about 1 minute. Stir in the garam masala, cardamom, cloves, and cayenne and sauté for 1 minute. Add the onions and sauté until softened, 5 to 7 minutes.

Add the garlic and sauté until golden, 1 to 2 minutes. Add ¼ teaspoon of salt, black pepper, and carrots and sauté for 10 minutes. Add the sweet potatoes, apricots, and raisins and stir until covered in oil and seasonings.

Add the broth and banana and bring to a simmer. Add the chickpeas and return to a simmer. Cover, lower the heat to medium-low, and simmer, stirring occasionally, until the carrots and sweet potatoes are tender but not falling apart, 30 to 40 minutes.

Remove the cover and simmer uncovered (raising the heat if necessary), until the liquid is mostly evaporated and syrupy, about 10 minutes. Taste and stir in the remaining ¼ teaspoon salt and ¼ cup of cilantro.

To serve, ladle the stew into bowls and top each with a dollop of yogurt and a sprinkling of the remaining ¼ cup of cilantro. Drizzle with silan (if using) and top with the Coconut-Cilantro Chutney (if using).

MAKE IT IN ADVANCE: *Tzimmes can be made up to 3 days in advance and refrigerated in an airtight container.*

The Bene Israel

One of several Jewish groups in India, the Bene Israel are centered around Mumbai. They trace their ancestry to shipwrecked survivors who landed on the Konkan coast. The survivors were said to be shipwrecked traders or refugees fleeing from Antiochus Epiphanes, the king whose rule led to the revolt of the Maccabees, Jewish independence, and celebration of Hanukkah. For Shabbat, they enjoy special flatbreads made with coconut milk and sugar.

WHOLE ROASTED CAULIFLOWER

Serves 4 as a main course, or 6 to 8 as a side dish or starter

Ever since I had my first whole roasted cauliflower in Israel I have been in love with it as a starter, main course, or side dish. I like to drizzle lots of sauces on the roasted cauliflower and sprinkle on an abundance of fresh chopped herbs and red onions, making the dish look like a feast on a platter. Try it with any of the marinades listed in the recipe or just improvise; the technique is what makes it work.

There are real differences in cooking times due to the freshness and size of your cauliflower. A large, dense cauliflower will take much longer than a smaller one, so test for doneness rather than just going by time.

1 large or 2 small heads of cauliflower (about 2 pounds total)

¾ to 1 cup marinade such as Za'atar marinade (page 108), Yemeni marinade (page 141), or Pomegranate Molasses marinade (page 143)

½ teaspoon paprika

2 tablespoons olive oil, optional

3 tablespoons Tahini or Tahini Sauce (page 210)

3 tablespoons, amba (see page 135) or Yellow Curry Sauce (page 211), optional

2 tablespoons Pomegranate Molasses (page 212) or purchased or silan (see page 25)

¼ cup chopped fresh herbs, such as cilantro, dill, mint, and/or parsley or a combination

3 tablespoons chopped red onions

Z'hug (page 213) or Harissa (page 214), optional, for serving

MAKE IT SHABBAT:

STARTER/APPETIZER: *Spinach and Dill Phyllo Pies (page 126)*

MAIN COURSE: *Whole Roasted Cauliflower*

ACCOMPANIMENT: *Tuna Freekah Salad (page 153)*

BREAD: *Friday Night Challah (page 204), pita, or flatbreads*

DESSERT: *Sweet Tahini Sauce (page 188) over vanilla ice cream*

Prep the cauliflower by trimming the base so it will sit flat. Remove any leaves.

Line a rimmed baking sheet with parchment paper or aluminum foil. Set the cauliflower on the prepared pan, stem down, and lightly brush marinade over the entire head, turning it over to cover completely. Lightly drip the marinade into any crevices between the florets. Let the cauliflower sit, stem side up, for 20 to 30 minutes.

Preheat the oven to 425°F.

Brush the top and sides of the cauliflower heavily with marinade again, place it stem side down on the baking sheet, and put it in the oven. Tent loosely with aluminum foil. Roast for 30 minutes, or until a dinner fork can easily pierce the cauliflower but will not glide all the way through (if not, cover with foil and continue to roast, checking every 15 minutes).

Brush the pan juices or leftover marinade all over the cauliflower (use olive oil if there is not enough liquid available for basting). Sprinkle with paprika and roast, uncovered, for 20 to 30 minutes more, until browned and soft through to the core when pierced with a dinner fork.

Let the cauliflower rest for a few minutes, then drizzle with tahini, amba (if using), and pomegranate molasses and sprinkle with the herbs and red onions. Cut the cauliflower into sections and serve with z'hug (if using).

NOTES: *To reduce roasting time, you can microwave the marinated cauliflower(s) in a glass dish with ¼ cup of water. Tent with wax paper and microwave on high until a dinner fork can pierce the vegetable(s) but cannot glide all the way through, 5 to 6 minutes. Roast it, stem side down, without the foil tent, and reduce the roasting time to about 30 minutes, or until browned and tender throughout.*

MAKE IT IN ADVANCE: *The roasted cauliflower, without garnishes, can be wrapped tightly and refrigerated for up to 3 days.*

MATZO BALL AND POZOLE CHICKEN SOUP

Serves 4 to 6 as a main course, or 8 as a starter

The food ways of the Jews in Mexico incorporate local ingredients with those of both Ashkenazi and Sephardic dishes and inspired this hearty soup, perfect as a dinner main course or starter.

Matzo balls (knaidlach) are dumplings made from matzo meal (ground-up matzo). They first appeared in Jewish food about the same time as bread-based dumplings began being added to soups and stews in Germany, Austria, and France. Originally a feature of Ashkenazi Passover meals, they have been adapted by many Jewish cultures and are often given a local twist or are combined with other regional flavors in soups or stews.

Pozole is a traditional, long-cooked soup or stew from Mexico made with hominy (corn that has been treated with an alkaline solution). Canned hominy is available in many supermarkets and Mexican groceries.

Since canned hominy already has added salt, be sure to taste and add salt at the end of the cooking time. For a milder soup, either seed the jalapeños or skip them altogether. If hominy is not available, use 2 (15-ounce) cans of drained and rinsed chickpeas.

8 cups Chicken Broth (page 194)
1 pound boneless, skinless chicken thighs
2 cups chopped onion
1 tablespoon chopped garlic
½ teaspoon ground black pepper
5 cups ½-inch mixed vegetable chunks, such as sweet potato, potato, carrots, butternut squash, turnip, or cauliflower
1 cup (½-inch pieces) chopped red, orange, or yellow bell pepper
1 teaspoon finely chopped jalapeño, optional
1 (30-ounce) can hominy corn, drained and rinsed
8 large or 16 small cooked Jalapeño and Cilantro Matzo Balls (page 200), at room temperature
1½ cups chopped tomatoes, divided
1 cup fresh or frozen corn kernels
3 cups chopped spinach
½ teaspoon salt
¼ cup chopped fresh cilantro
¼ cup chopped green onions
¼ cup thinly sliced radishes
4 to 6 lemon or lime wedges
Salsa or Z'hug (page 213), optional

MAKE IT SHABBAT:

STARTER/APPETIZER: *Real Deal Chopped Chicken Liver (page 202) with Matzo Crackers (page 208)*

MAIN COURSE: *Matzo Ball and Pozole Chicken Soup*

BREAD: *Tortillas or Friday Night Challah (page 215)*

DESSERT: *One-Pan Banana Bread (page 183)*

In a large pot, bring the chicken broth to a simmer over medium heat (do not let it boil). Add the chicken, cover, and lower the heat to medium-low. Simmer until the chicken is just cooked through, 15 to 20 minutes. Using a slotted spoon or tongs, transfer the chicken to a bowl and set aside to cool.

Return the broth to a simmer. Add the onion, garlic, black pepper, and mixed vegetables, cover, and cook until the vegetables just begin to soften, about 15 minutes. Add the bell pepper and jalapeño (if using), cover, and simmer until the mixed vegetables are tender enough that the outsides can be pierced with a fork but there is still some resistance in their centers, 10 to 20 minutes.

Shred the chicken. Raise the heat to medium, add the chicken, hominy, and matzo balls to the soup, and bring it to a gentle simmer. Lower the heat to low, cover, and cook for 20 minutes. Add 1 cup of the chopped tomatoes, the corn, and the spinach and simmer until the spinach is wilted and the matzo balls are heated through, about another 5 minutes. Add the salt. Taste and add more salt and black pepper, if desired.

Serve topped with the remaining ½ cup chopped tomatoes, the cilantro, the green onions, and radishes or place the garnishes in individual bowls and pass them at the table so diners can make their choice. Squeeze lemon juice into the soup and stir before eating. Pass the salsa to stir in (if using).

VARIATION: *Make It Vegetarian—Use Vegetable Broth (page 197). Omit the chicken. Add 3 cups cooked chickpeas (or two 15-ounce cans of chickpeas, drained and rinsed) when adding the hominy.*

MAKE IT IN ADVANCE: *The chicken broth and matzo balls can be made ahead, stored in airtight containers, and refrigerated for up to 5 days or frozen for up to 3 months.*

Judaism in Mexico

There are an estimated 50,000 Jews in Mexico, most descended from Ashkenazi immigrants from Eastern Europe or Sephardic immigrants from the former Ottoman Empire who arrived from the late nineteenth century through the middle of the twentieth century. The two groups maintain their separate religious organizations and practices, but the food ways have mingled and both cuisines have been influenced by local ingredients.

The earliest Jewish immigrants arrived in the sixteenth century and were Conversos, Jews who converted to Christianity to escape the inquisitions in Spain and Portugal. Some of the descendants of these immigrants practiced Judaism in secret or had family traditions that were rooted in Judaism.

OREGANO ROAST CHICKEN WITH LEEK-AND-MINT FRITTERS

Serves 4 to 6

These recipes were inspired by a Greek-Jewish grandmother. Her grand-daughter shared memories of the dishes her grandmother cooked and her descriptions were so tempting, I had to improvise my own versions. They have now become Shabbat mainstays for me. The chicken is juicy and fragrant with the aromas of oregano and lemon. I like to fry the fritters while the chicken is roasting. The fried fritters are a great option for Hanukkah and are also served at Rosh Hashanah because the Hebrew word for leeks sounds like the word for foiling your enemies, a common wish for the New Year.

MAKE IT SHABBAT:

STARTER/APPETIZER: *Green salad with Kalamata olives, chopped tomatoes, and red onions with Tahini Dressing (page 220)*

MAIN COURSE: *Oregano Roast Chicken with Leek-and-Mint Fritters*

ACCOMPANIMENT: *Freekah Pilaf (page 152)*

BREAD: *Friday Night Challah (page 204)*

DESSERT: *Raisin and Almond Twirls (page 187)*

FOR THE CHICKEN

6 lemons
¼ cup olive oil, plus extra for the baking pan
¼ teaspoon crushed red pepper
¼ teaspoon ground black pepper
½ teaspoon salt
3 tablespoons minced fresh oregano or 1 tablespoon dried
2 teaspoons minced garlic
¼ cup water
3 to 4 pounds bone-in, skin-on chicken breast halves, larger pieces cut in half

FOR THE FRITTERS

3½ to 4 pounds leeks (about 6 large), trimmed, rinsed, and finely chopped
1 teaspoon minced garlic
½ teaspoon salt
¼ teaspoon ground black pepper
⅛ teaspoon crushed red pepper
4 large eggs, beaten
¼ cup matzo meal or plain bread crumbs
¼ cup minced fresh mint
Vegetable oil for frying
4 to 6 lemon wedges

TO MAKE THE CHICKEN

Zest 3 of the lemons and reserve for garnish. Juice all 6 lemons. In a large bowl, whisk together ¾ cup of the lemon juice (save any additional for another use), olive oil, crushed red pepper, black pepper, salt, oregano, garlic, and water. Add the chicken, turn the pieces to cover them in the marinade, and cover the bowl with plastic wrap. Place the bowl in the refrigerator and marinate for 1 hour, turning the pieces in the marinade every 20 minutes.

Preheat the oven to 450°F. Grease a large baking pan or roasting pan with olive oil.

Place the chicken, skin side up, in the baking pan. Pour the marinade over the chicken and roast for 35 to 45 minutes, basting the chicken with the pan juices every 15 minutes, until the juices run clear when you cut into the thickest piece. The chicken is ready when an instant-read thermometer inserted in a breast reads 165°F after checking several times over 3 minutes.

Let the chicken sit for 10 minutes.

TO MAKE THE FRITTERS

Place the leeks in a medium saucepan over medium heat, add enough water to cover, and bring to a simmer. Lower the heat to medium-low and simmer until very soft, about 7 to 10 minutes. Transfer the leeks to a strainer and drain, pressing out as much liquid as possible.

In a medium bowl, mix together the leeks, garlic, salt, black pepper, and crushed red pepper. Add the egg, matzo meal, and mint and stir until combined. Let the batter rest for 10 minutes. The batter will be loose, but should hold together when cooked. If it's too loose, add matzo meal by the teaspoon and mix until the batter is no longer runny.

Heat ¼ inch of vegetable oil in a large skillet over medium-high heat until a drop of batter sizzles immediately on contact with the oil.

Stir the batter. Gently drop ¼ cup of batter into the hot oil and flatten it slightly with a spatula. Repeat with more batter, making sure not to crowd the pan. Fry the fritters in batches until golden brown, about 2 minutes on each side. Drain the fritters on paper towels. Adjust the heat as needed so the fritters brown and don't burn. Add more oil as needed.

TO SERVE

Place the chicken in the center of a platter and surround with fritters and lemon wedges. Garnish the chicken and fritters with the lemon zest and serve with the pan juices.

MAKE IT IN ADVANCE: *The chicken can be cooked up to 2 days in advance and the fritters can be made 1 day in advance. Store in airtight containers in the refrigerator.*

Jewish life in Greece

Jews have lived in Greece for more than two millennia and many of their customs come from Romaniote or Middle Eastern Jewish traditions. Other customs were adopted after the influx of Sephardic Jews after 1492.

Two Greek Shabbat customs are shared by other Sephardic communities. One is to light wicks that are floating in olive oil instead of traditional candles for Shabbat and holidays. The other is to serve slow-cooked eggs, known as huevos haminados, before or after the Friday night dinner.

One way to make the eggs is to save the skins from yellow or brown onions as you use them. Once you have the skins from about 10 onions, place 12 room-temperature large eggs in a single layer in a large deep pot and top them with the onion skins. Sprinkle a few teaspoons of black tea leaves over the top. Pour in enough water to cover by several inches. Add 1 tablespoon white vinegar and 1 tablespoon olive oil and bring to a boil over medium-high heat. Cover, lower the heat to medium-low, and simmer for 5 hours. Add more water as needed to keep the eggs covered. Submerge the eggs in an ice water bath until cooled. Refrigerate unpeeled eggs for up to 7 days.

PULLED TURKEY WITH POMEGRANATE MOLASSES

Serves 4 to 6

Think of this recipe as a Middle-Eastern sweet-and-sour turkey pot roast. The turkey is shredded and served in its cooking sauce. The tangy sauce pairs wonderfully with a side of crispy fried latkes, mashed potatoes, or pasta. This recipe can be served as multicultural street tacos in corn tortillas with Pickled Red Onions (page 165), chopped tomatoes, and chopped fresh cilantro. It makes a good alternative filling for Friday Night Tamales (page 71), too.

1¼ teaspoons salt, divided
¾ teaspoon ground black pepper, divided
¼ teaspoon cayenne pepper
½ teaspoon ground cumin
½ teaspoon ground cinnamon
⅛ teaspoon ground allspice
3 pounds bone-in turkey thighs
2 tablespoons vegetable oil, plus more if needed
2 cups chopped onions
1 tablespoon minced garlic
1 (15-ounce) can crushed tomatoes
4 tablespoons Pomegranate Molasses (page 212) or purchased, divided
3 tablespoons brown sugar, divided, plus more if needed
¾ cup Chicken Broth (page 194) or purchased, or water
1 tablespoon tomato paste
Fresh lemon juice, optional

MAKE IT SHABBAT:

STARTER/APPETIZER: *Whole Roasted Cauliflower (page 58)*

MAIN COURSE: *Pulled Turkey with Pomegranate Molasses*

SIDE DISH: *Charred Greens (page 163)*

ACCOMPANIMENT: *Potato Latkes (page 158)*

BREAD: *Friday Night Challah (page 204)*

DESSERT: *Challah Fritters with Sweet Tahini Sauce (page 188)*

(recipe continues)

In a small bowl, mix together 1 teaspoon of salt, ½ teaspoon of pepper, cayenne, cumin, cinnamon, and allspice. Remove and discard the skin from the turkey thighs. Rub the spice mixture on all sides of the thighs, place them on a rimmed platter, and let sit for 20 minutes at room temperature.

In a Dutch oven or large, heavy pot with a lid, heat the 2 tablespoons of oil over medium-high heat. Working in batches, brown the turkey thighs on all sides, about 7 minutes per side. Place the browned thighs on the platter and set aside.

Add more vegetable oil to the Dutch oven, if needed, add the onions and sauté until soft, scraping up any browned-on bits from the bottom of pan, 5 to 7 minutes. Add the garlic and sauté until golden, 1 to 2 minutes. Stir in the remaining ¼ teaspoon of salt, and remaining ¼ teaspoon of black pepper. Lower the heat to medium, add the crushed tomatoes, 3 tablespoons of pomegranate molasses, 1 tablespoon of brown sugar, and chicken broth, and bring to a simmer, stirring well. Add the browned turkey, meaty side up, plus any accumulated juices. Try to fit the turkey thighs side by side, but stack them slightly to fit if necessary. Spoon the sauce over the thighs and bring it to a simmer. Cover and simmer over medium-low heat for 30 minutes.

Turn over the turkey thighs (and rotate the position if stacked), spooning the sauce over the tops. Cover and simmer until cooked through, 20 to 25 minutes more. An instant-read thermometer should read 165°F after multiple checks in the meaty part of the thickest thigh over 3 minutes. Transfer the thighs to a platter and let rest for 20 minutes.

Add the tomato paste, the remaining 2 tablespoons of brown sugar, and remaining 1 tablespoon of pomegranate molasses to the sauce in the Dutch oven and bring to a simmer. Cook, stirring often, until the sauce is a little thicker than spaghetti sauce, 10 to 15 minutes. Taste and add salt, if needed. If the sauce is too sour, add brown sugar by the teaspoon as needed. If it is too sweet, add lemon juice by the teaspoon as needed. Keep the sauce warm or reheat when ready to use.

Use two forks or your hands to shred the turkey and discard the bones. Add the turkey to the sauce and stir occasionally, until the meat is reheated. If the sauce gets too thick, add 1 or 2 tablespoons of water. Serve immediately.

MAKE IT IN ADVANCE: *This can be made up to 3 days in advance and stored in an airtight container in the refrigerator.*

TURKEY-STUFFED POTATOES IN LIBYAN-INSPIRED TOMATO SAUCE

Serves 4 as a main course, or 8 as a starter

The complex and fragrant spice mix transforms a stuffed baked potato from simple to sublime. It is an untraditional take on a classic dish of fried, filled potato slices stewed in a sauce.

The recipe (or parts of it) can be done in advance. The flavors of the spices, based on the traditional bzar spice mix of cinnamon, nutmeg, turmeric, cardamom, and cloves, elevate the potatoes into a festive entree. Use leftover bzar for seasoning meatballs, soups, chicken, or even stewed or roasted fruit.

Leftover Bzar spice mix can be stored in an airtight container away from direct sunlight for up to a year.

MAKE IT SHABBAT:

STARTER/APPETIZER: *Charred Eggplant Dip with Tahini (page 131) with vegetable sticks*

MAIN COURSE: *Turkey-Stuffed Potatoes in Libyan-Inspired Tomato Sauce*

SIDE DISH: *Green salad with Lemon, Za'atar, and Garlic Dressing (page 219)*

BREAD: *Friday Night Challah (page 204)*

DESSERT: *Fruit salad or Fruit Juice Sorbet (page 191)*

FOR THE BZAR SPICE MIX

1 teaspoon ground black pepper
1 teaspoon ground cinnamon
1 teaspoon ground nutmeg
1 teaspoon ground turmeric
1 teaspoon ground cardamom
½ teaspoon ground cumin
½ teaspoon ground cloves

FOR THE STUFFED POTATOES

8 small russet or Idaho baking potatoes
   (about 4 ounces each), scrubbed
3 tablespoons olive oil, divided
½ cup minced onion
2 tablespoons minced garlic
½ teaspoon salt
¼ teaspoon paprika or cayenne pepper
1 pound ground dark meat turkey
1 tablespoon tomato paste
½ cup chopped fresh cilantro
½ cup chopped fresh flat-leaf parsley
1 large egg, beaten

FOR THE SAUCE

2 tablespoons olive oil
2 cups chopped onion
2 tablespoons minced garlic
½ teaspoon salt
2 cups chopped bell peppers
1 (28-ounce) can crushed tomatoes
2 tablespoons tomato paste
1 cup Chicken Broth (page 194) or purchased, plus more if needed
2 large tomatoes, each cut into 8 wedges
3 tablespoons chopped fresh cilantro

(recipe continues)

TO MAKE THE SPICE MIX

In a small bowl, mix together the black pepper, cinnamon, nutmeg, turmeric, cardamom, cumin, and cloves. Set aside 4 teaspoons for this recipe.

TO MAKE THE STUFFED POTATOES

Preheat the oven to 450°F.

Prick the potatoes on all sides with a fork and place them on a baking sheet. Bake, turning occasionally, for 40 to 50 minutes, or until a fork meets just a slight resistance in the center. Let sit for 10 minutes.

Make a 1-inch-deep cut the long way into each potato, making sure not to cut through the ends. Squeeze the potato to open it wide. Scoop out 1 tablespoon of potato from each one, place it in a bowl, and mash with a fork.

In a 12-inch skillet, heat the oil over medium-high heat. Add the onion and cook until softened, 5 to 7 minutes. Add the garlic, 2 teaspoons of bzar spice mix, salt, and paprika and sauté for 1 to 2 minutes. Add the turkey and brown, breaking up any clumps, about 5 minutes. Add the tomato paste and stir to combine. Stir in the cilantro and parsley.

Remove from the heat. Mix together the reserved potato and egg, and stir it into the turkey. Divide the filling equally between the potatoes and press it into each one.

TO MAKE THE SAUCE

In a large Dutch oven, heat the oil over medium heat. Add the onions and sauté until light brown, 7 to 10 minutes. Add the garlic, remaining 2 teaspoons of the bzar spice mix and salt, and sauté for 1 to 2 minutes. Add the bell peppers and sauté until they begin to soften, about 5 minutes. Stir in the crushed tomatoes, tomato paste, and chicken broth and bring to a boil. Lower the heat to medium-low, add the tomato wedges, and simmer, stirring well.

Nestle the potatoes in a single layer in the sauce. Spoon the sauce over the filling. Cover and simmer, spooning sauce over the potatoes every 10 minutes, until the filling is firm and the potatoes are heated through, 30 to 40 minutes.

The sauce should resemble a thin pasta sauce. If it's too thin, transfer the potatoes to a large platter and cover them with foil. Simmer the sauce until it's reduced. If it's too thick, add broth or water until it reaches the desired consistency.

TO SERVE

Arrange 1 or 2 potatoes on each plate. Spoon the sauce over the potatoes, garnish with cilantro, and serve hot, warm, or at room temperature.

MAKE IT IN ADVANCE: *The stuffed potatoes and sauce can be made up to 2 days ahead. Refrigerate the filled potatoes and sauce separately.*

SPICY BEEF TZIMMES

Serves 6 to 8

"Tzimmes" (sim-ess) is a Yiddish word with two meanings. The first is a thick, vegetarian or meat stew filled with root vegetables and dried fruit. The other usage is slang for making a big deal over something. And this recipe is worth making a big deal over. It's rich and full of Mexican and Eastern European flavors accented by the fruity, smoky, heat of chipotle peppers. It works as a great main course over noodles or rice and it's also an excellent filling for the Friday Night Tamales (page 71).

Like many braised meat dishes, this stew is best made ahead to give its deep, rich flavor a chance to really develop and because of its long cooking time. Serve it for Friday night dinner for 6 to 8, or use half and freeze the remaining amount to use for future tamale making.

3 pounds boneless chuck roast or brisket, fat trimmed, and cut into 1-inch cubes

1 teaspoon salt, divided

½ teaspoon ground black pepper, divided

2 tablespoons vegetable oil, plus more if needed

1 large onion, halved and thinly sliced

2 teaspoons minced garlic

1 to 2 canned chipotle peppers (see Note, page 70) minced

¼ teaspoon cayenne pepper, optional

2 cups (½-inch slices) carrots

½ cup roughly chopped dried apricots

½ cup roughly chopped pitted dried prunes

1 cup Chicken Broth (page 194) or purchased plus more if needed

2 tablespoons tomato paste

1 cup (1-inch cubes) sweet potatoes (peeling optional)

3 tablespoons chopped fresh cilantro or flat-leaf parsley for garnish

MAKE IT SHABBAT:

STARTER/APPETIZER: *Matzo Ball and Pozole Soup (page 60)*

MAIN COURSE: *Spicy Beef Tzimmes*

SIDE DISH: *Green salad with Whole Lemon Dressing (page 218)*

ACCOMPANIMENT: *Rice*

BREAD: *Friday Night Challah (page 204) or tortillas*

DESSERT: *Challah Fritters with Sweet Tahini Sauce (page 188)*

(recipe continues)

Place the meat in a large bowl and toss with ¼ teaspoon of salt and ¼ teaspoon of black pepper. In a Dutch oven or large, heavy soup pot, heat the vegetable oil over medium-high heat. Working in batches, brown the beef on all sides until browned, 8 to 10 minutes. Transfer the beef to a rimmed plate.

Add a little more oil to the pot if it seems dry. Add the onions and sauté, stirring up any browned bits with a spoon, until the onions begin to soften, 5 to 7 minutes. Add the garlic and sauté until golden, 1 to 2 minutes. Add the remaining ¾ teaspoon of salt, remaining ¼ teaspoon of black pepper, chipotle peppers, cayenne (if using), carrots, apricots, and prunes and sauté for 1 minute. Add the broth, stir to combine, and bring to a simmer. Stir in the tomato paste until dissolved and return to a simmer. Add the browned beef and any accumulated juices and bring to a simmer. Cover, lower the heat to medium-low, and simmer, stirring occasionally, for 1 hour.

Stir in the sweet potatoes, cover, and simmer, stirring occasionally, until a fork can glide easily through the beef, 1 to 2 hours. If the pot becomes dry, add more liquid as needed. The sauce should be thick and not at all watery. Taste and adjust the seasoning, if needed. Garnish with the cilantro and serve hot.

NOTE: *Canned chipotle peppers are packed in adobo sauce and have a smoky heat. They are usually available in 4-ounce cans in the international section of many supermarkets, Mexican and Latin American groceries, and online. Take out the chiles you need with the sauce clinging to them and chop. Store any remaining peppers and sauce in an airtight glass container and refrigerate for up to 3 months. Use them in soups, stews, even in omelets or Mostly Make-It-Ahead Shakshouka (page 100); anywhere a splash of smoky heat would be appreciated.*

MAKE IT IN ADVANCE: *This can be made ahead, stored in an airtight container, and refrigerated for up to 3 days or frozen for up to 3 months.*

FRIDAY NIGHT TAMALES

Serves 4 as a main course

I wanted a recipe to reflect interfaith traditions during the winter holiday season. Dawn Kepler, director of Building Jewish Bridges, told me about a Mexican-American grandmother who made kosher tamales (a Christmas Eve tradition for many) for her Jewish grandchildren at Hanukkah. That sparked this recipe, which is filled with Spicy Beef Tzimmes (page 69). I've also made tamales with Pulled Turkey with Pomegranate Molasses (page 65), and a spiced-up version of Carrot Curry Tzimmes (page 56).

Assembling the tamales is a fun group project. Add 1 hour to the prep time to give enough time to soak the corn husks. You'll need challah or other bread for the blessings, but the tamales do not need any bread to fill out the dinner.

Look for corn husks and masa harina in the international sections of grocery stores or in Mexican and Latin American markets.

20 (8-inch) dried corn husks (about half a 6-ounce bag)

3 cups Spicy Beef Tzimmes (page 69)

1¾ cups masa harina

¾ teaspoon salt

1 cup plus 2 tablespoons boiling water

½ cup plus 2 tablespoons chilled rendered chicken fat (schmaltz) or vegetable shortening

1 teaspoon baking powder

1¼ cups Chicken Broth (page 194) or purchased

Salsa, Z'hug (page 213), or Harissa (page 214), optional

MAKE IT SHABBAT:

STARTER/APPETIZER: *Charred Eggplant Dip with Roasted Tomatoes and Jalapeño (page 132) with vegetable sticks*

MAIN COURSE: *Friday Night Tamales*

SIDE DISH: *Green salad with Lemon, Za'atar, and Garlic Dressing (page 219)*

DESSERT: *Fruit Juice Sorbet (page 191) made with lemon or mango juice*

(recipe continues)

Bring a large pot of water to a boil. Turn off the heat, add the husks, and place a plate on top to keep them submerged. Let sit for 1 hour. Chop the tzimmes into ½-inch pieces and set aside.

Drain the husks and select 12 of the biggest and most intact for filling. Tear one of the remaining husks into 12 long strips about ¼-inch wide for tying the tamales. Save the remainder of the husks to line the steamer.

In a large bowl, mix together the masa harina and salt. Add the hot water and stir with a wooden spoon until well combined. The mixture will have big clumps.

In another large bowl, combine the chicken fat and baking powder and, using an electric hand mixer on high, beat until light and fluffy, about 1 minute.

With the mixer on medium, add the seasoned masa harina to the fat and baking powder in 3 batches, mixing well in between. The mixture will be crumbly. Add ½ cup of broth and beat until incorporated. Add ¼ cup of broth and beat again until incorporated. Repeat, adding the broth, ¼ cup at a time, until the dough is soft, holds its shape, and is not sticky. You may not need all the broth.

Using the 12 intact corn husks you set aside, open one up and place it flat on a work surface with the narrower end down. If the corn husks are less than 8 inches wide or split, overlap two of them using the soaked husks reserved for the steamer. Place ¼ cup of masa dough in the center of the husk and press it into a 4-inch square, leaving ¾-inch margins on both sides and a 1 ½-inch margin at the bottom.

Spoon 2½ tablespoons of the chopped filling in a strip about 1½ inches wide in the middle of the masa, making sure it doesn't go all the way to the edges. Lift the long sides of the husks and bring them together to push the dough together and seal in the filling. Pat the dough together to repair any cracks. Bring the long sides together again and roll them around the tamale to enclose it. Flip over the stuffed husk so the seam is facing up. Fold up the pointy end and, using one of the torn husk strips, secure the flap by tying it into a knot just tight enough to hold the corn husk wrapper closed. Repeat with the rest of the filling and husks.

Pour several inches of water in a large deep pot. Place a bamboo steamer or a steamer rack inside. Line the steamer with one or two reserved corn husks. Place the tamales in the steamer, standing upright, with the folded bottoms down. If needed, place an upside-down heatproof cup or bowl in the steamer to help the tamales stay upright. Cover with one or two of the remaining soaked husks. Cover with a lid or foil. Bring the water to a boil over high heat.

Lower the heat to low and steam the tamales for about 1½ hours, keeping the water at a simmer and adding more water as needed, until the husk peels away from the tamale dough easily. Let rest for a few minutes before serving with salsa (if using).

MAKE IT IN ADVANCE: *The tamales can be wrapped individually in their corn husks in plastic wrap or aluminum foil and refrigerated for up to 2 days or frozen for up to 3 months.*

ETHIOPIAN SPICED POT ROAST

Serves 6 to 8

My mother was a fearless cook, diving into recipes, ingredients, and cuisines that were new to her. Pot roast was one of her specialties, and I've followed her lead into more adventurous flavors.

Here I use berbere, an Ethiopian spice mix consisting primarily of chile peppers, cumin, cardamom, ginger, and fenugreek, in a very untraditional way. Berbere is available online and at specialty, spice, and African markets. If you can't find it, try Basically Berbere (page 215), which is a close substitute. Since berbere varies in heat, start with a lesser amount and add more if desired. Berbere usually flavors a wot (also spelled wat), or stew, which often includes hard-boiled eggs, which I have incorporated into the recipe.

Like all pot roasts, this one tastes best when it's made at least 1 day in advance. (The recipe can also be made with brisket.) Most Ethiopian meals are eaten with injera, a flatbread made with fermented teff (a gluten-free whole grain) batter. Find injera at some African and other international markets, and some Ethiopian restaurants sell it to go. Diners wrap up bits of meat, salad, and vegetables in sections of injera instead of using a fork. Substitute other flatbreads or serve with bulgur or other grains.

1 (3- to 4-pound) boneless beef chuck roast or brisket
1 to 2 tablespoons berbere or Basically Berbere (page 215)
1 teaspoon brown sugar
½ teaspoon ground cardamom
1 teaspoon ground black pepper
1 teaspoon salt
2 tablespoons vegetable oil, plus more if needed
2 cups chopped red onion
1 tablespoon minced garlic
1 teaspoon minced fresh ginger
2 tablespoons tomato paste
½ cup dry red wine or water
1 (28-ounce) can diced tomatoes
8 hard-boiled eggs, peeled

MAKE IT SHABBAT:

STARTER/APPETIZER: *Gefilte Fish with Smashed Tomato Topping (page 118)*

MAIN COURSE: *Ethiopian Spiced Pot Roast*

SIDE DISH: *Green salad with North African Dressing (page 219)*

ACCOMPANIMENT: *Rice, couscous, or bulgur*

BREAD: *Injera, flatbreads, or Challah Pull-Apart Rolls (page 206)*

DESSERT: *Raisin and Almond Twirls (page 187)*

(recipe continues)

Trim the meat of excess fat, leaving a covering of about ¼-inch thick of fat if using brisket (see How to Brisket, page 40). Transfer the meat to a plate and set aside.

In a small bowl, mix together the berbere, brown sugar, cardamom, black pepper, and ½ teaspoon of salt. Rub the mixture over all sides of the meat. Set aside any extra spice mix. Let the meat sit for 30 minutes.

In a large, heavy pot, heat the oil over medium-high heat. Sear the meat on all sides until browned, 5 to 7 minutes a side. Transfer to the plate.

Add a little more oil to the pot if it seems dry. Add the onions and sauté, making sure to stir up any browned bits on the bottom of the pan, until they begin to soften, 5 to 7 minutes. Add the garlic and ginger and sauté until the garlic is golden, 1 to 2 minutes. Stir in any remaining berbere and sauté for 1 minute. Add tomato paste, wine, and tomatoes with their juices and bring to simmer.

Return the meat and any accumulated juices to the pot and spoon the sauce over the top of the meat. Return to a simmer, cover, lower the heat to medium-low, and simmer until the meat is tender and a dinner fork can easily pierce the beef, 2 to 4 hours, making sure to spoon the pan sauce on top of the beef every 30 minutes and turn the meat over every 60 minutes. If the pan liquid begins to evaporate, add water, ¼ cup at a time, as needed. Transfer the meat to the plate.

Prick the eggs lightly all over with a fork and place them in the sauce. Bring to a simmer and cook for 5 minutes, turning them often in the sauce. Transfer the eggs to a bowl. Continue simmering the sauce for another 10 to 15 minutes, until it's thicker than pasta sauce but still liquid. Taste, and add ½ teaspoon of salt, if desired. Add more berbere, if desired. (If adding more berbere, simmer for a few more minutes to temper the spice.)

If making a day in advance (which I recommend), refrigerate the meat, sauce, and eggs separately in airtight containers. Once cold, scrape off any fat from the top of the sauce, if desired. Cut the meat across the grain into slices (see Going Against the Grain, page 40) or shred it. Transfer the sauce to a large pot over medium-low heat and bring it to simmer. Add the meat and reheat thoroughly, adding the eggs a few minutes before serving to heat through.

If serving immediately, keep the sauce warm and let the meat cool for at least 20 minutes before cutting into slices or shredding. Return the meat and eggs to the pot and reheat as above.

MAKE IT IN ADVANCE: *The pot roast can be made up to 5 days in advance without the eggs and refrigerated in an airtight container. To freeze, combine the sliced or shredded meat with the sauce in an airtight container and freeze for up to 3 months. Do not freeze the eggs.*

The Jews of Ethiopia

Economic and political conditions caused nearly all Ethiopian Jews to migrate (mostly to Israel) starting in the 1980s. The largest group is known as the Beta Israel, which spread over more than five hundred villages in northern and northwestern Ethiopia. There they followed traditions that developed from their interpretation of the Torah during their long separation from other Jewish communities. Their holy book, the Orit, was written in Ge'ez, a classical Ethiopian language now mostly used for Ethiopian Christian and Jewish liturgy. In Ethiopia, the community observed dietary laws, Shabbat, biblical holidays, and other traditional Jewish practices that they continue now in Israel.

Community life in Ethiopia revolved around the synagogue, and Shabbat remains a central focus of Beta Israel life. Beta Israel observance of biblical laws meant no heating of food during the Sabbath, so all meals were prepared in advance. In Ethiopia, honeyed mead or local beer was used instead of grape wine for Kiddush, and a special blessing was said before eating dabo, small, round yeasted wheat rolls cooked in a round pan and served on Shabbat instead of injera, the flatbread traditionally eaten with most meals.

Today, there are more than 125,000 Ethiopian Jews in Israel; about 8,000 remain in Ethiopia, many waiting to emigrate.

WINTER BORSCHT WITH LAMB

Serves 8 as a main course, or 12 or more as a starter

Pola Silver, of blessed memory, was born in Odessa in the Ukraine and escaped to Uzbekistan in Central Asia during the Holocaust only to be thrown in jail and then rescued by the man who later became her husband. She lived a long and productive life in Oakland, California, where she was known for devotion to friends and family, her generosity, and her cooking.

She called this dish simply Russian Borscht and served it topped with slices of boiled, peeled potatoes. I had the opportunity to learn how to make it with her. Her version was made with chuck roast, short ribs, or both. I prefer it with lamb and made a few other changes, including adding some untraditional garnishes. I recommend using plastic gloves whenever you work with beets to avoid staining your hands.

14 cups water

1½ pounds boneless lamb shoulder, cut into 1-inch cubes

1 meaty lamb shank

2 pounds beets (weight without greens), scrubbed, trimmed, and each cut in half

2 cups chopped onion

2 carrots, grated or shredded

1 pound white potatoes, peeled and cut into 1-inch cubes

1 teaspoon salt

¼ teaspoon ground black pepper

1½ teaspoons sugar, plus more if needed

1 small head cabbage, chopped or shredded

1 (14½-ounce) can diced tomatoes

¼ cup apple cider vinegar, plus more if needed

4 tablespoons chopped fresh flat-leaf parsley, divided

4 tablespoons chopped fresh dill, divided

OPTIONAL GARNISHES

Boiled, peeled potatoes, sliced

Hard-boiled eggs, peeled and cut into halves or quarters

Tahini Sauce (page 210)

Garlic Sauce (page 210)

Chopped fresh tomatoes

Chopped green onions or chives

Steamed or raw grated beets

Sautéed and chopped beet greens or chard

Matzo Balls (page 199)

Grated lemon zest

Lemon wedges

MAKE IT SHABBAT:

STARTER/APPETIZER: *Mushroom-Eggplant Hummus Bowls (page 149)*

MAIN COURSE: *Pola's Russian Borscht with Lamb*

BREAD: *Friday Night Challah (page 204) with salt topping*

DESSERT: *Twice-Baked Lemon Cookies (page 185)*

In a large pot, bring the water to a simmer over medium-high heat. Add the lamb cubes and shank and simmer, skimming off any foam or scum, for 10 minutes. Add the beets, lower the heat to medium-low, cover, and simmer for 1 hour. Remove the beets, rub off the peels, and let cool. Shred or dice the cooked beets.

Simmer the lamb until the cubes have started to become tender, about 30 minutes. A fork should begin to pierce the lamb but the meat should not yet be soft most of the way through. Add the beets, onion, carrots, potatoes, salt, pepper, and sugar and stir well. Cover, return to a simmer, and cook until the lamb cubes are tender, about 30 minutes.

Add the cabbage and the tomatoes with their juices and stir. Cover and simmer until the cabbage is very soft, about 20 minutes longer.

Remove the shank and use two forks to shred any meat off the bone. Return the meat to the pot, cover, and bring the soup back to a simmer. Remove the pot from the heat. Stir in the vinegar. Taste. Add more sugar and/or add more vinegar, a little at a time, if needed. The soup should have a nice balance of sweet and tart. Taste and add more salt, if desired. Stir in 1 tablespoon of the parsley and 1 tablespoon of the dill. Cover and let stand for 10 minutes. Serve warm, topped with the remaining 3 tablespoons of parsley and dill and any desired garnishes.

MAKE IT IN ADVANCE: *Can be made up to 3 days in advance and stored, before adding the parsley or dill, in an airtight container in the refrigerator or frozen for up to 3 months.*

SPICE TRADE FISH STEW

Serves 8

The spicy side of Jewish cooking is an ancient tradition, going back to when Jews played a role in the spice trade and Yemen was a commercial crossroads. A key ingredient in Yemeni Jewish cooking is a spice mix called hawaij (or hawayij), which means "what is needed." There are several types of hawaij spice mixes, and the recipes change depending on the cook and region, but the basic version for soup, made with turmeric, cumin, black pepper, and cardamom, is the one I used in this book. It can be hard to find in stores, but it is available online, or use my homemade alternative: Instant Almost Hawaij (page 216).

The stew is on the soupy side and I like it served in bowls over Yellow Rice (page 160).

2 tablespoons olive oil

1½ cups chopped onion

4 garlic cloves, minced

3 cups chopped red bell peppers

1 teaspoon paprika

1 teaspoon hawaij for soup or Instant Almost Hawaij (page 216)

½ teaspoon salt

½ teaspoon ground black pepper

¼ teaspoon dried oregano

6 cups chopped kale, divided

2 cups chopped tomato

1 (28-ounce) can crushed or puréed tomatoes

1 cup Vegetable Broth (page 197) or purchased, plus more if needed

1 to 2 tablespoons Z'hug (page 213), plus more for serving

3 pounds cod or other firm white fish fillets, cut into 2-inch pieces

½ cup chopped fresh flat-leaf parsley, divided

½ cup chopped fresh cilantro, divided

6 cups Yellow Rice (page 160) or plain, cooked rice

MAKE IT SHABBAT:

STARTER/APPETIZER: *Almost Homemade Hummus (page 96) with vegetable sticks*

MAIN COURSE: *Spice Trade Fish Stew*

SIDE DISH: *Green salad with North African Dressing (page 219)*

ACCOMPANIMENT: *Yellow Rice (page 160)*

BREAD: *Challah Pull-Apart Rolls (page 206)*

DESSERT: *Turkish Coconut Pudding (page 190)*

In a Dutch oven or a large deep pot, heat the olive oil over medium-high heat. Add the onion and sauté until softened, 5 to 7 minutes.

Add the garlic and sauté until golden, 1 to 2 minutes. Add the bell peppers, paprika, hawaij, salt, black pepper, and oregano and sauté until the peppers begin to soften, 3 to 5 minutes. Add half of the kale and sauté until wilted, about 5 minutes. Stir in the remaining kale and sauté until all the kale has wilted, 7 to 10 minutes longer.

Add the chopped tomatoes, canned crushed tomatoes with their juices, broth, and z'hug and bring to a simmer. Add the fish and return to a simmer. Add ¼ cup of the parsley and ¼ cup of the cilantro and stir to combine. Cover and lower the heat to medium-low, and simmer until the fish is tender, flakes when cut with a knife, and is no longer translucent, 5 to 10 minutes, adding more broth as needed to keep the fish almost covered.

To serve, divide the rice among individual bowls. Ladle the stew on top. Garnish each bowl with a sprinkle of the remaining parsley and cilantro and serve hot. Pass more z'hug at the table. Alternatively, using a slotted spoon, transfer the fish pieces to a plate. Simmer the pan sauce over low heat until reduced to the consistency of a thin pasta sauce. Spoon the rice onto a platter, top with the fish, and spoon the sauce generously over the top, reserving some to pass at the table. Garnish with the parsley and cilantro. Pass more z'hug and the remaining sauce at the table.

MAKE IT IN ADVANCE: *The fish stew can be made up to 1 day in advance, stored in an airtight container, and refrigerated. To serve, gently reheat, covered, on the stovetop over medium-low heat.*

The Jews of Yemen

The Yemeni (or Yemenite) Jewish community is one of the oldest in the world and is full of traditions, history, and flavors that live on in a diaspora that centers on Israel.

Some believe the first Jews in Yemen were sent by King Solomon to mine for precious metals. Historical records show that Jews have lived in Yemen for more than two millennia and included a ruling Jewish kingdom. By the ninth century, the country was controlled by waves of Islamic rulers, which in some eras led to discrimination, hardship, and violence.

Yemeni Jews (or Teimanim) began migrating to what was then Palestine in 1881, with most of the country's then 55,000 Jews arriving in Israel in 1949 and 1950. Today, only a handful of elderly Jews remain in Yemen.

Jewish Yemeni cuisine was frugal but full of spices, reflecting the area's long role in the ancient spice trade (in which Jewish merchants played a part). The cuisine is centered on flatbreads, soups and stews, legumes, bulgur, the hot sauce known as Z'hug (page 213), and a fenugreek relish often served with grated tomatoes.

Yemeni Jewish life centered on its synagogues, and the communities were very pious. Friday before Shabbat was a special transition time with its own foods and customs. For Shabbat, dinner might include a chicken or meat stew seasoned a spicy and peppery mix known as hawaij (see page 78). Many Yemeni have a custom of eating fruit between the blessing of the wine (kiddush) and the bread (Hamotzi) before beginning their Friday night dinner.

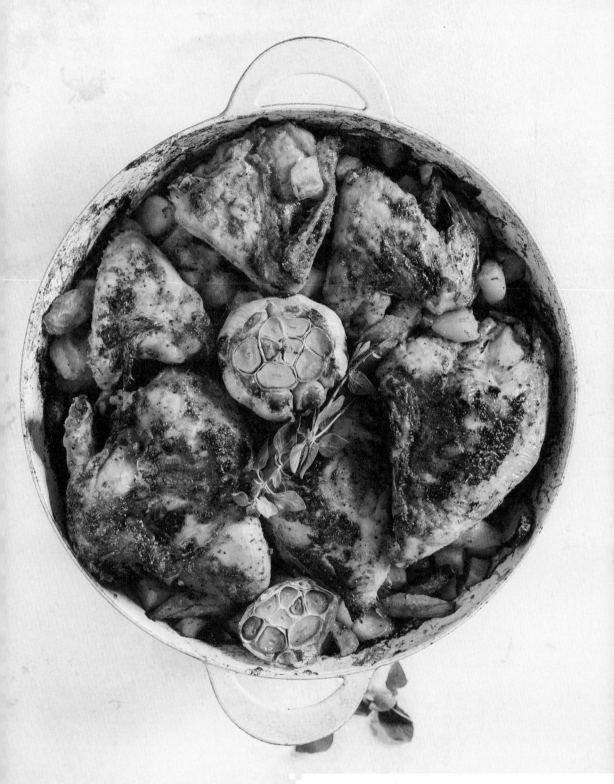

SPICE-RUBBED CHICKEN ON ROOT VEGETABLES pg. 28

POMEGRANATE MOLASSES BRISKET pg. 38   **POTATO LATKES** pg. 158

ROAST SALMON WITH CITRUS-HONEY SAUCE pg. 46

MATZO BALL AND POZOLE CHICKEN SOUP pg. 60

SPICE TRADE FISH STEW pg. 78

MUSHROOM AND CHEESE STRUDEL pg. 98

FALAFEL PIZZA WITH FETA AND HERBS pg. 102

CHICKEN AND VEGETABLE TAGINE pg. 106

SWEET-AND-SOUR FISH

Serves 4

For many American Jews, it's a Christmas Eve tradition to go out for Chinese food. I don't remember doing that growing up, but I have fond memories of going to the local Chinese restaurant whenever my grandparents came to visit. As an adult, my friends and I enjoyed many a Christmas Eve together eating Chinese food and seeing a movie. Now, I tend to stay in and cook my own Asian food.

Sweet-and-sour sauce was a childhood favorite and is still one I enjoy, although now I'm likely to toss in chile flakes or ground Sichuan peppercorns and make it much more sour than sweet.

This recipe was shaped by two experiences. The first was a cooking school class I took in Shanghai, where Chef Jing used ketchup as the main ingredient of an overseas-style sweet-and-sour sauce. The second was at a talk by a Jewish woman whose family emigrated from Russia to Manchuria and lived in Shanghai in the 1930s and 1940s. She spoke enthusiastically about her favorite restaurant in Shanghai. I tracked down a 1930s-era English-language menu from the restaurant and among its offerings was a fish dish that reminded me of the sweet-and-sour sauce I made with Chef Jing.

FOR THE SWEET-AND-SOUR SAUCE

¼ cup plus 1 teaspoon sugar
¼ cup distilled white vinegar
¼ cup ketchup
1 tablespoon soy sauce or gluten-free tamari sauce
1 cup water

FOR THE FISH

1½ pounds thick rock cod or cod fillets or other non-oily white fish
1 teaspoon salt
2 large eggs, beaten
4 tablespoons cornstarch, divided
1 tablespoon water
Vegetable oil for frying
2 tablespoons minced garlic
¼ cup plus 2 tablespoons thinly sliced green onions, divided
2 cups (1-inch pieces) green, red, yellow, and/or orange bell pepper
2 medium tomatoes cut into 8 wedges each

MAKE IT SHABBAT:

STARTER/APPETIZER: *Fruit and Salad Rolls (page 136)*

MAIN COURSE: *Sweet-and-Sour Fish*

SIDE DISH: *Sautéed chopped spinach*

ACCOMPANIMENT: *Rice*

BREAD: *Friday Night Challah (page 204) with sesame seed topping or flatbreads*

DESSERT: *Fresh fruit*

(recipe continues)

TO MAKE THE SWEET-AND-SOUR SAUCE

In a saucepan over medium heat, combine the sugar, vinegar, ketchup, soy sauce, and water. Cook, stirring occasionally, until the sugar is dissolved and the mixture is heated through, about 5 minutes. Taste, and add more vinegar, ketchup, soy sauce, or sugar until the sweet-and-sour taste is to your preference. Set aside.

TO MAKE THE FISH

Rinse and pat dry the fish with paper towels. Sprinkle with salt. Cut the fish into 1½-inch pieces.

In a large bowl, whisk the eggs with 3 tablespoons of the cornstarch until well blended. Add the fish pieces and turn gently to coat thoroughly.

In a small bowl, mix the remaining 1 tablespoon cornstarch with the water. Set aside.

Line a plate with paper towels. Add ½ inch of oil to a wok or 1 inch of oil to a large, heavy skillet and heat on high. When a drop of cornstarch and egg batter sizzles when added to the hot oil and begins to brown, add about one-third of the battered fish pieces, making sure they are not crowded or stuck together. Fry, turning with metal tongs as needed, until golden brown on all sides, 3 to 4 minutes. The fish is done when it is opaque and cooked through when you cut into one piece. Using the tongs, transfer the fish to the paper towel–lined plate. Remove any loose bits left in the pan and repeat with the remaining fish, adding oil if needed and reheating the oil to a sizzle between batches.

Turn off the heat and let the oil cool slightly. Carefully pour out and safely dispose of all but 2 tablespoons of the oil. Return the wok to the burner over medium-high heat. Add the garlic and stir-fry until golden, 15 to 25 seconds, being careful not to let it burn. Add ¼ cup of the green onions and peppers, raise the heat to high, and stir-fry until the peppers begin to soften, 3 to 5 minutes. Add the tomato wedges and stir-fry until they begin to soften, 1 to 2 minutes.

Pour the sweet-and-sour sauce into the wok and bring to a boil. Stir the reserved cornstarch mixture and slowly drizzle it into the wok, stirring constantly, until the sauce thickens and coats the back of the spoon. Add the fried fish and stir until it is coated with the sauce. Lower the heat to medium-high and cook, stirring constantly, until the fish is heated through. Garnish with the remaining 2 tablespoons green onions and serve immediately.

VARIATION: *Pineapple—Chef Jing used pineapple instead of tomatoes. Replace half or all of the tomatoes with fresh or canned pineapple chunks. Add to the sauce with the fish.*

VARIATION: *Spicy—Toss in 1 teaspoon of minced jalapeño or serrano chiles or ¼ to ½ teaspoon crushed red pepper when adding the green onions. Or when serving, pass ground or crushed Sichuan peppercorns or chile oil.*

MAKE IT IN ADVANCE: *Sweet-and-sour sauce can be made 1 day in advance, refrigerated and reheated. The fish is best made immediately before serving.*

Jews in India and China

Throughout the Jewish diaspora, there have been Jewish communities in India and China, many originating because of trade opportunities. The Silk Road and the Spice Route were overland and maritime conduits for spices, gems, and other goods. They ran from China and India through Central Asia and North Africa (both of which had Jewish communities) to the Middle East and southern Europe.

About 1,400 years ago, Jewish traders known as the Radhanites took control of the east-west trade and dominated it for 300 years. But, Jews traded long before (starting with the Phoenicians) and after them as well. Jewish communities along the 4,000-miles of camel caravans and merchant shipping lanes became middlemen, providing traders with business partners, credit, a common language, and shared traditions. Among the best-known Jewish settlements were those in what is now called Kochi in southern India and in Kaifeng, then the capital of China.

The Jews in Kochi, known as the Cochin Jews, arrived more than a thousand years ago to trade black pepper. They were later joined by Sephardic Jews fleeing Iberia. Another community was founded in Chennai by Sephardic Jewish coral and diamond traders in the 17th century.

The largest and oldest of the Indian communities is the Bene Israel. Their ancestry goes back two millennia to their arrival on the Konkan coast after a shipwreck. (For more on the Bene Israel, see page 57.) They were once called "Saturday oil pressers," since they closed their oil production businesses on Shabbat. They adopted local food ways adapted for Jewish dietary laws, and they observed many Jewish holidays and traditions.

Today, migration to Israel and elsewhere has reduced their numbers from 67,000 to 5,000, centered in Mumbai. Among the other Jewish groups in India, the Baghdadi Jews from Iraq and Syria are the best known. They arrived in India in the 18th century, settling around Mumbai and Kolkata, and created a trading network throughout Asia. One of the most important of these was in Shanghai, where the community began in the 19th century. It was an observant community that adapted Iraqi dishes and served kosher versions of British and Chinese specialties.

The first Jews in China were Babylonians and Persians who became cotton manufacturers in Kaifeng in the 9th century. The community was identifiably Jewish until the mid-19th century. Even after assimilation they kept a few traditions, including not eating pork. Today, some of their 500 descendants have begun to explore their Jewish roots.

About 20,000 Russian Jews settled in Harbin, in China's northernmost province. They moved to the Manchurian fishing village to escape pogroms and the Russian revolution. Most of the Harbin Jews left after the 1931 Japanese occupation of China, with about a fourth settling in Shanghai, a port on China's central coast, already home to 500 families in the Iraqi Jewish community.

In the 1940s, World War II brought 20,000 Eastern European Holocaust refugees to Shanghai. Living conditions were atrocious, but the Japanese occupiers saved them from the Nazis. After the war and the rise of Communism, both communities left China.

spring

THE JEWISH MONTHS THAT CORRESPOND TO SPRING

in the Northern Hemisphere are associated with renewal, harvests, and rebirth, and the Shabbat menus reflect that with many dishes that are lighter or vegetable-centric.

Many of the season's recipes work as light main courses or appetizers and starters. Dishes such as smooth and earthy Almost Homemade Hummus (page 96) and bright and cheery Mostly Make-It-Ahead Shakshouka (page 100) with tomatoes, bell peppers, and eggs are versatile choices.

Start spring Shabbat dinners off with Hawaij Vegetable Soup (page 104), which gets its color and flavor from lively Yemeni spices, or Falafel Pizza with Feta and Herbs (page 102). For more substantial meals, Shawarma Roast Chicken (page 110) brings home the flavors of a shawarma, gyro, or doner kebab—the Rice Pilaf on page 161 is the perfect accompaniment—or try the Make-Ahead Meatballs (page 112), which can be adapted for Passover, and use them to complement sauces, soups, and stews year-round.

SPRING HOLIDAYS & SPECIAL DAYS

In no other season is the impact of the lunisolar calendar felt as much as in Spring. In a leap year, the second month of Adar (Adar II) is observed, adding a thirteenth month to the calendar (pushing Purim into spring from winter). Adar's symbol is the fish, considered good luck, so I like to serve fish during Adar, perhaps the South Indian–Inspired Fish Cakes (page 120) with a tart and bright Cilantro-Coconut Chutney.

Besides part of Adar I and possibly Adar II, spring brings Nisan, Iyar, and part or all of Sivan.

Nisan is the first month of the Hebrew calendar and when we celebrate the eight-day holiday of Passover (seven days in Israel) in March or April.

Passover (or Pesach) rituals and customs vary by personal observance and beliefs, but there are some basics. Products made from grains that are leavened (allowed to rise through fermentation or yeast) are forbidden and are to be gathered up and disposed (nowadays many donate to food banks) or arranged to be ceremoniously sold and not used until redeemed from the buyer. The first two nights of Passover there are home services called Seders (meaning order of service), which tell the story of Israel's redemption and release from slavery and journey across the Red Sea from Egypt into the desert and freedom. The Seders' symbolic foods include matzo, an unleavened flatbread, fresh spring greens (karpas) to dip in sour or salty liquid to remember the affliction of slavery, bitter herbs (maror), such as horseradish or chicory, to recall oppression, charoset, a fruit and nut dip meant to be reminiscent of mortar used in building the pyramids, a roasted lamb shank bone (zeroa) to represent the protection of God and the Temple sacrifices, and a roasted egg (beitzah), a symbol of sacrifice but also of life, mourning, and rebirth.

Passover dinners take place in the middle of the Seder (where the story of the Exodus is retold) and often include a soup such as the classic Chicken Soup with Matzo Balls (page 196), a fish course such as the Gefilte Fish with Smashed Tomato Topping (page 118), and a main course such as the Red Wine Pot Roast (page 114) or Roast Salmon with Citrus-Honey Sauce (page 46), along with a salad and side dishes and a dessert. Flourless Chocolate Berry Cake (page 178) is a good choice for dessert.

For a Passover Shabbat, try the Grilled Lamb Chops with Bitter Herbs Salad (page 116) or Chicken and Vegetable Tagine (page 106) served with quinoa.

Another significant holiday in May or June is Shavuot in Sivan. Shavuot marked the end of the barley harvest and the beginning of the wheat, but became associated with the giving of the Torah on Mount Sinai and the Ten Commandments.

The Mushroom and Cheese Strudels (page 98) combine two Shavuot traditions— foods shaped like Torah scrolls and those made with dairy. There are many symbolic explanations for dairy foods being associated with the holiday, but one simple reason is that spring is when milk and other dairy products are plentiful. Try the Spinach and Dill Phyllo Pies (on page 126) and the Mango and Cardamom Mini Cheesecakes (page 184). Tuna Freekah Salad (page 152), made from smoky roasted grains, connects to the wheat harvest, since freekah is made from young, green wheat.

ALMOST HOMEMADE HUMMUS

Makes about 3 cups

I've always liked hummus, the chickpea and sesame seed purée that is a staple of Middle Eastern and Arabic food, but it wasn't until I ate it in Israel, Palestine, and Jordan that I began to understand how it is really an essential food, and one that I could make fresh at home.

With its protein-packed, relatively inexpensive, and local ingredients, hummus is an important component to a meal in this region, not just a party dip. Its earthy flavor, with a tang of lemon and hint of garlic, makes it a tasty canvas to showcase a variety of toppings, such as in the Lamb Hummus Bowls and its vegan Mushroom-Eggplant variation (pages 148 and 149), as well as a creamy side dish or a filling snack or starter. Customize it by swirling with olive oil or Tahini Sauce (page 210), sprinkling with finely chopped cilantro or parsley, and/or dusting with sumac or paprika.

This recipe makes a smooth hummus that still has a bit of texture from the chickpeas and is a compromise between convenience and tradition. To make this completely from scratch, replace the canned chickpeas with 3 cups home-cooked.

2 (15-ounce) cans chickpeas, drained and rinsed
1 to 2 teaspoons minced garlic
½ cup extra-virgin olive oil
⅓ cup tahini, plus more if desired
⅓ cup fresh lemon juice, plus more if desired
¼ teaspoon salt, plus more if desired
⅓ cup very cold water, plus more as needed

MAKE IT SHABBAT:

STARTER/APPETIZER: *Almost Homemade Hummus with Pita*

MAIN COURSE: *Spinach and Dill Phyllo Pies (page 126)*

SIDE DISH: *Green salad with North African Dressing (page 219)*

ACCOMPANIMENT: *Rice Pilaf (page 161) with Chopped Tomato Salad (page 162)*

BREAD: *Pita or Friday Night Challah (page 204)*

DESSERT: *Raisin and Almond Twirls (page 187)*

Put ¼ cup of the chickpeas in a bowl and set aside.

TO MAKE WITH AN IMMERSION BLENDER

In a large, deep bowl, combine the remaining chickpeas, the garlic (use 1 teaspoon for a hint of garlic, 2 teaspoons for a stronger flavor), and the olive oil. Blend until as smooth as possible. Add the tahini, lemon juice, salt, and cold water and blend, scraping down the sides of the bowl as needed, until creamy. Add more water a little at a time if needed to achieve the desired consistency. Taste and adjust the salt, tahini, and lemon juice, if desired. Blend well. Serve topped with the reserved chickpeas.

TO MAKE WITH A FOOD PROCESSOR

In the bowl of a food processor, combine the remaining chickpeas, the garlic (use 1 teaspoon for a hint of garlic, 2 teaspoons for a stronger flavor), and the olive oil and process until smooth, scraping down the sides of the bowl as needed. Add the tahini, lemon juice, and cold water and process until creamy, adding more water a little at a time if needed to achieve the desired consistency. Taste and adjust the salt, tahini, and lemon juice, if desired. Process until combined. Serve topped with the reserved chickpeas.

TO MAKE BY HAND

If you don't have a food processor or immersion blender, place the remaining canned chickpeas and their liquid in a saucepan and simmer over medium-low heat for 15 minutes, drain and rinse. In a large bowl, combine the remaining chickpeas, garlic (1 or 2 teaspoons, as desired), and olive oil and, using a potato masher, mash thoroughly. Stir in the tahini paste, lemon juice, and water and mash again until as smooth as possible. Add more water if desired. Taste and stir in more salt, tahini, or lemon juice, if desired. Serve topped with the reserved chickpeas. The hummus will not be as smooth but it will taste delicious.

MAKE IT IN ADVANCE: *Hummus can be made and refrigerated in an airtight container for up to 5 days.*

MUSHROOM AND CHEESE STRUDELS

Serves 4 to 6 as main course, or 8 to 10 as an appetizer

Purchased phyllo dough sheets are the key to these rich and savory vegetarian rolls. Phyllo sheets are available in most supermarkets in the frozen foods section and in Middle Eastern markets. If the phyllo is sold in thick or thin varieties, choose the thin style. Most boxes are simply labeled phyllo (and sometimes as filo or fillo) dough.

This recipe requires just 8 to 10 sheets, so if your phyllo comes with two sealed sleeves, you will only need one. Defrost frozen phyllo according to the package instructions. If it is refrigerated, bring it to room temperature. Phyllo dough is very forgiving. Small tears in one layer can be covered by the next. If two sheets are stuck together, just use it like it's one. Always make sure the unused sheets are covered with a clean kitchen towel while you work to prevent them from drying out. Extra sheets can be rewrapped and refrozen.

Be sure to lightly brush the layers with oil and not saturate. It's the very thin layers of fat between the sheets that help create the flakiness as the phyllo bakes. Too much and your pastry may get soggy or greasy. A very light spray of olive oil spray will work instead of brushing with oil.

2 tablespoons plus ½ cup olive oil, divided

2 tablespoons unsalted butter

2½ cups thinly sliced onions

2 teaspoons minced garlic

1 teaspoon za'atar or Za'atar in a Pinch (page 217)

½ teaspoon salt

1¼ teaspoons paprika, divided

¼ teaspoon ground black pepper

2 pounds mixed fresh mushrooms, chopped, such as button, cremini, and shiitakes

10 (13-by-17-inch) sheets phyllo dough, at room temperature

1 cup breadcrumbs

6 ounces Brie or Camembert, cut into ½-inch chunks and chilled

2½ cups shredded Swiss and/or Gruyère cheese

¼ cup chopped green onions or chopped fresh flat-leaf parsley

MAKE IT SHABBAT:

STARTER/APPETIZER: *Fish in Spicy H'raimi-Style Tomato Sauce (page 48)*

MAIN COURSE: *Mushroom and Cheese Strudels*

SIDE DISH: *North African Carrot Salad (page 164)*

ACCOMPANIMENT: *Rice Pilaf (page 61) with Chopped Tomato Salad (page 162)*

BREAD: *Friday Night Challah (page 204)*

DESSERT: *Chocolate and Cookie Truffles (page 186)*

In a 12-inch skillet, heat 2 tablespoons of olive oil and the butter over medium-high heat. Add the onions and sauté until softened, 5 to 7 minutes. Add the garlic and sauté until golden, 1 to 2 minutes. Stir in the za'atar, salt, ¼ teaspoon of paprika, and the black pepper.

Add the mushrooms to the skillet in batches, sturdier ones (such as shitake) first. Sauté until they begin to soften, then add softer ones (such as oyster) until all the mushrooms are tender and the liquid is the pan is evaporated. Let cool for 5 minutes.

Preheat the oven to 350°F. Line a large baking sheet with parchment paper.

Lay the phyllo sheets on a work surface and cover them with a clean cloth kitchen towel. (You'll need 8 sheets for the recipe. Use the extras in case any sheets are badly ripped and you need to patch.) Have ready the remaining ½ cup of olive oil (you probably won't use it all) and a pastry brush.

Place 1 sheet of phyllo flat on a clean, dry work surface with a long side closest to you. Very lightly brush the entire surface with oil. Place another phyllo sheet directly on top of the first one and lightly brush with oil. Repeat with the third sheet. Top with a fourth sheet. Sprinkle half the breadcrumbs on top, leaving a 1-inch margin all around. Starting 1 inch from the long side closest to you, spread one-fourth of the mushrooms in 2-inch-wide horizontal strip, leaving 1-inch margins on both short ends. Evenly scatter half the chilled Brie over the mushrooms. Top with another one-fourth of the mushrooms. Scatter ¾ cup of the shredded cheese over the mushrooms.

Fold in the short sides of the phyllo about 1 inch on either side over the filling. Starting at the long side closest to you, roll the phyllo and filling, compressing as you roll up to create a compact roll. Using two spatulas, transfer the strudel to the prepared baking sheet, seam side down, leaving room for a second strudel.

Repeat with the remaining phyllo and filling.

Lightly brush the tops and sides of the strudels with oil. With a sharp knife, cut the strudels a third of the way through into 6 to 8 slices.

Bake for 35 minutes, or until just golden. Scatter ½ cup shredded cheese on top of each strudel. Sprinkle each with ½ teaspoon of paprika. Bake for 10 to 15 minutes, or until light brown and the cheese is melted. Let cool for at least 10 minutes before cutting.

Cut the strudel into slices, following the premade cuts, garnish with the green onions, and serve warm or at room temperature.

MAKE IT IN ADVANCE: *The mushroom filling can be made up to 2 days in advance and refrigerated in an airtight container. Reheat making sure any liquid is evaporated before using.*

MOSTLY MAKE-IT-AHEAD SHAKSHOUKA

Serves 6 as a main course, or 12 as a starter

There is something cheery and fun about shakshouka, the North African dish of eggs cooked in a bright red tomato and pepper sauce. The word means "shaken" or "mixed up" in Tunisian slang. Its bold colors and flavors give this egg-based dish a place at the Shabbat dinner table as a satisfying vegetarian main dish.

To make it even more Friday-night friendly, I've adjusted the basic recipe to feed more and made it a mostly make-ahead meal. The sauce base is made in advance and the final shakshouka is baked rather than cooked on the stovetop.

The idea to make this ahead first came to me when I was at a small hotel in southern Israel and I noticed the owner kept a stockpile of her shakshouka base in the freezer. For a milder version, reduce the amount of jalapeño or cayenne.

FOR THE SHAKSHOUKA BASE

4 pounds fresh tomatoes, chopped, or 2 (28-ounce) cans diced tomatoes
2½ cups chopped onions
2 tablespoons minced garlic
4 cups chopped red or yellow bell peppers
1 small jalapeño pepper, finely chopped or ¼ teaspoon cayenne pepper, optional
2 tablespoons olive oil
¼ teaspoon ground black pepper
½ teaspoon salt
½ teaspoon paprika
¾ teaspoon ground cumin
1 tablespoon tomato paste, optional
1 (8-ounce) can plain tomato sauce, optional
¼ teaspoon sugar, optional
1 tablespoon fresh lemon juice, optional

FOR FINISHING AND SERVING

½ cup chopped fresh flat-leaf parsley, divided
12 large eggs, at room temperature
Tahini Sauce (page 210)
½ cup amba (page 135) or Yellow Curry Sauce (page 211), optional
Z'hug (page 213) or other hot sauce, optional

MAKE IT SHABBAT:

STARTER/APPETIZER: *Charred Eggplant Dip with Tahini (page 132) with vegetable sticks*

MAIN COURSE: *Mostly Make-It-Ahead Shakshouka*

SIDE DISH: *Whole Roasted Cauliflower (page 58)*

BREAD: *Friday Night Challah (page 204) or pita*

DESSERT: *Mango and Cardamom Mini Cheesecakes (page 184)*

TO MAKE THE SHAKSHOUKA BASE

In a large pot over medium-high heat, cook the tomatoes, stirring often, until they soften and release their liquid, 3 to 5 minutes. (If using canned tomatoes, add to the pot with their juices and bring to a simmer over medium-high heat.) Add the onions and garlic and cook, stirring often, until the onions soften, about 5 to 7 minutes. Add the bell peppers and jalapeño (if using), and sauté, stirring often, until the peppers begin to soften, about 10 minutes, adding water by the tablespoon if the vegetables begin to stick.

Add the olive oil, black pepper, salt, paprika, and cumin and bring to a simmer, stirring often. Cover and simmer until the vegetables are very soft, 10 to 15 minutes. The mixture should be like a thick pasta sauce. If the sauce is too thin, stir in the tomato paste and cook, stirring, for 3 to 5 minutes. If the sauce is too thick, add the tomato sauce and simmer until it reaches the desired consistency. Taste and add salt, sugar, or lemon juice, if desired.

At this point the shakshouka sauce can be used immediately or stored in an airtight container in the refrigerator for up to 5 days or frozen for up to 3 months.

TO FINISH AND SERVE

Preheat oven to 350°F.

Heat (or reheat) the sauce base in a large, covered pot over medium-high heat and bring to a simmer. Lower the heat to medium-low and simmer, stirring occasionally, until sauce is hot and bubbly, 15 to 20 minutes. Transfer the base to a 9-by-13-inch baking pan and stir in ¼ cup of the parsley.

Using a serving spoon, press the back of the spoon into the sauce to make 12 indentations. Break one egg into each indentation, being careful to keep the yolks intact. Spoon some of the tomato sauce over the egg whites.

Bake until the egg whites are opaque and the yolks are set but still jiggly and runny, 10 to 15 minutes. If the whites are cooking faster than the yolks, cover the pan loosely with aluminum foil and continue to bake until the yolks are cooked to the desired doneness.

Season the eggs with salt and pepper. Scatter the remaining ¼ cup parsley over the top. Drizzle with tahini sauce and amba, if using. Pass z'hug at the table, if desired.

VARIATION: *Less Mess Shakshouka—Mix the room-temperature base with ¼ cup chopped fresh parsley in a baking pan, cover with foil, and bake in a 450°F oven for 30 minutes, or until hot and bubbly. Remove the foil, create the 12 indentations, and add the eggs. Lower the heat to 350°F and bake according to the recipe instructions.*

FALAFEL PIZZA WITH FETA AND HERBS

Serves 4 as a main course, or 8 as a side dish

This pizza is like an inside-out falafel sandwich, with the chickpea batter made into a baked crust and served with traditional falafel sauces. Try it for a main course or appetizer. Be sure to give yourself enough time since the dry chickpeas soak for at least 12 hours and don't overload the pizza with too much sauce. Much of the work can be done in advance.

MAKE IT SHABBAT:

STARTER/APPETIZER: *North African Carrot Salad (page 164)*

MAIN COURSE: *Falafel Pizza with Feta and Herbs*

SIDE DISH: *California Hakol Salat (page 130)*

BREAD: *Friday Night Challah (page 204) with za'atar*

DESSERT: *Chocolate and Cookie Truffles (page 186)*

FOR THE FALAFEL CRUST

1⅓ cups dried chickpeas
1 teaspoon olive oil, plus more for greasing
1 cup chopped onion
1 tablespoon minced garlic
1 cup chopped fresh cilantro
1 cup chopped fresh flat-leaf parsley
1½ teaspoons salt
1 teaspoon ground cumin
½ teaspoon baking powder
Flour or gluten-free flour as needed

FOR THE PIZZA TOPPINGS

3 cups seeded and diced tomatoes, drained and patted dry
½ teaspoon dried mint
½ teaspoon dried oregano
½ teaspoon ground black pepper
¼ teaspoon salt
8 ounces drained and crumbled feta
¼ cup chopped green onions
1 teaspoon olive oil
¼ cup chopped fresh herbs (flat-leaf parsley, mint, cilantro and/or dill)

FOR THE PIZZA SAUCES (SELECT 2 OR 3)

2 tablespoons Tahini Sauce (page 210) or tahini
2 tablespoons amba (see page 135) or Yellow Curry Sauce (page 211)
2 tablespoons Z'hug (page 213) thinned with olive oil until pourable
2 tablespoons Garlic Sauce (page 210)

TO MAKE THE CRUST

Remove any debris from the chickpeas. Rinse the chickpeas, transfer them to a large bowl, and cover with several inches of water. Let soak for 12 hours at room temperature, adding more water if needed to keep them submerged. Place the chickpeas in a colander and rinse them under running water. Pat dry with a clean kitchen towel.

Preheat the oven to 400°F. Thoroughly oil the surface of a 12- or 13-inch round pizza pan or line a large rimmed baking sheet with parchment paper and lightly oil the paper.

Transfer the chickpeas to a food processor and pulse until they are in about ⅛-inch pieces, scraping down the sides of the bowl as needed. Add the onion, garlic, cilantro, parsley, salt, cumin, and baking powder. Pulse until evenly mixed, again scraping down the sides of the bowl as needed. The mixture should be fairly moist and stick together when compressed into a patty. If it's too dry, add 1 tablespoon of water at a time and pulse to combine after each addition. If the mixture is too wet, add flour 1 tablespoon at a time, pulsing to combine after each addition, until it sticks together but is still moist.

Transfer the mixture to the prepared pan. Use your hand to press the mixture all the way to the edges of the round pizza pan. If using a rectangular baking sheet, press the mixture out into an 8-by-12-inch rectangle. Score the crust into 8 wedges (For a rectangular crust, cut into 8 equal pieces.) Lightly brush the crust with 1 teaspoon of olive oil.

Bake for 10 to 15 minutes, turning the pan in the oven as needed to ensure that the crust browns evenly, until lightly browned and firm. Remove the pan from the oven.

Raise the oven temperature to 450°F. Slide a thin metal spatula under the crust to loosen it but leave it in the pan. Using the edge of the spatula, cut through the scored lines into wedges or pieces.

TO ASSEMBLE THE TOPPINGS

In a medium bowl, toss together the tomatoes, mint, oregano, black pepper, and salt and scatter the mixture over the crust. Top with the feta and green onions. Drizzle with the olive oil.

Bake for 12 to 14 minutes, until heated through and the cheese has begun to soften slightly and is just starting to brown. Scatter the chopped fresh herbs over the top. Choose two or three of the sauces and drizzle them lightly over the top of the crust. Do not overload the slices. Too much sauce will make the pizza soggy.

Serve immediately, cutting again along the scored lines to separate slices if necessary. This pizza is best eaten with a knife and fork.

HAWAIJ VEGETABLE SOUP

Serves 6 as a starter

This recipe, seasoned with the spice mix hawaij for soup, is vegan. The cardamom, turmeric, black pepper, and cumin-based spice mix is available in specialty, spice, and Middle Eastern markets. If you have trouble finding it, use the Instant Almost Hawaij (page 216), which is an approximation to the real thing.

I first discovered a beef-based version of this soup at a home-style Yemeni restaurant in Tel Aviv. The owner, a grandson of the founders, invited me to visit his kitchen and pointed out the giant containers of hawaij, broth, and paprika he used to create his wonderful soups. This inspired me to create a soup with similar seasonings but with a vegetable base. Matzo Balls (page 199) are an untraditional but great addition.

MAKE IT SHABBAT:

STARTER/APPETIZER: *Hawaij Vegetable Soup*

MAIN COURSE: *Whole Roast Chicken with Herbs (page 30)*

SIDE DISH: *Sweet-and-Tart Silan-Roasted Carrots with Lentils (page 24)*

DESSERT: *Flourless Chocolate Berry Cake (page 178)*

FOR THE SOUP

8 cups Vegetable Broth (page 197)
½ cup (½-inch slices) carrots
2 cups shredded green cabbage
½ cup (½-inch cubes) peeled turnip
1 cup (1-inch cubes) peeled potatoes
1 cup (1-inch) cauliflower florets
1 cup (1-inch cubes) peeled butternut squash or pumpkin
1 cup trimmed and quartered cremini or white button mushrooms
½ cup chopped leek
2 teaspoons hawaij for soup or Instant Almost Hawaij (page 216)
½ teaspoon paprika
¼ teaspoon salt
¼ teaspoon ground black pepper
1 cup (½-inch rounds) zucchini

FOR THE TOMATO GARNISH

3 medium tomatoes
¼ cup minced fresh cilantro or flat-leaf parsley
2 tablespoons finely chopped green onions
Z'hug (page 213) or minced jalapeños

TO MAKE THE SOUP

In a large pot or Dutch oven, bring the broth to a simmer over medium heat. Add the carrots, cover, and bring to a simmer. Lower the heat to medium-low and cook for 5 minutes. Add the cabbage, turnip, potatoes, cauliflower, butternut squash, mushrooms, leeks, hawaij, paprika, salt, and pepper and stir to combine. Bring to a simmer, cover, and adjust the heat as needed to keep it at simmer (do not let the soup boil). Cook, until the vegetables are just tender, but not cooked through, 20 to 30 minutes. Taste and add salt and pepper, if desired. Add the zucchini, return to a simmer, and cook, covered, until the zucchini is cooked through, 5 to 10 minutes.

TO MAKE THE TOMATO GARNISH

While the soup is simmering, grate the tomatoes on a box grater down to the tomato skin. Discard the skins. Set a colander over a bowl and strain the tomatoes. Stir the tomato liquid into the soup.

In a bowl, mix together the grated tomato solids, cilantro, and green onions.

To serve, ladle the soup into bowls, top each with 2 teaspoons of the tomato garnish, and serve hot, with the z'hug on the side.

MAKE IT IN ADVANCE: *The soup without garnishes can be made up to 2 days in advance and refrigerated in an airtight container.*

CHICKEN AND VEGETABLE TAGINE

Serves 6

This recipe was inspired by the wonderful stews of the Jews in Morocco and North Africa. It takes its name from the vessel in which the original stews are cooked, a tagine, which is a round clay casserole dish with a tall conical lid that captures steam and returns it to the stew. Most people don't have a tagine, so for this recipe I give instructions to cook the stew in a Dutch oven or a deep sauté pan. For a spicier dish, serve it with Harissa (page 214), Z'hug (page 213), or a purchased hot sauce.

2 tablespoon olive oil, plus more if needed
2 pounds boneless, skinless chicken thighs, cut into 1½-inch pieces
1 cup chopped onion
2 teaspoons minced garlic
½ teaspoon ground cinnamon
½ teaspoon paprika
¼ teaspoon ground black pepper
¼ teaspoon salt
2 cups (1-inch pieces) peeled sweet potatoes
1 cup (¼-inch slices) carrots
3 cups (1-inch pieces) peeled eggplant
1½ to 2 cups Chicken Broth (page 194) or Vegetable Broth (page 197) or purchased
3 cups chopped chard
2 cups chopped tomatoes
Cooked couscous, toasted pearl (Israeli) couscous, or quinoa, warmed
3 tablespoons chopped fresh flat-leaf parsley, mint, and/or cilantro
6 lemon wedges

MAKE IT SHABBAT:

STARTER/APPETIZER: *Fish in Spicy H'raimi-Style Tomato Sauce (page 48)*

MAIN COURSE: *Chicken and Vegetable Tagine Couscous*

SIDE DISH: *Green salad with North African Dressing (page 219)*

BREAD: *Challah Pull-Apart Rolls (page 206)*

DESSERT: *Raisin and Almond Twirls (page 187)*

In a Dutch oven or a large, deep sauté pan, heat the olive oil over high heat. Add the chicken, working in batches if necessary, and cook until browned, 5 to 7 minutes per side. Transfer the chicken to a rimmed plate or bowl.

Lower the heat to medium-high. Add more oil, if needed, add the onion, and sauté until it begins to soften and turn golden, 7 to 10 minutes. Add the garlic and sauté until golden, 1 to 2 minutes. Add the cinnamon, paprika, pepper, and salt and sauté for 1 minute. Add the sweet potatoes, carrots, and eggplant and sauté for 3 minutes. Add 1½ cups of broth and bring to a simmer. Cover, lower the heat to medium-low, and simmer for 10 minutes.

Add the chard and tomatoes, cover, and simmer for 10 minutes or until the carrots begin to soften.

Add the browned chicken and any accumulated juices. Simmer, uncovered, until the chicken is cooked through when cut into and the vegetables are fork-tender, 10 to 20 minutes. Add more broth, if needed. Taste, and add more salt or other seasonings, if desired.

Spoon the warm couscous into bowls and top with the stew. Sprinkle with the parsley and serve hot with lemon wedges on the side.

MAKE IT IN ADVANCE: *The stew can be made up to 3 days in advance, stored in an airtight container, and refrigerated.*

Jewish life in Morocco

Jewish life in Morocco began more than two millennia ago. Immigration continued through the centuries with the largest influx coming from Sephardic Jews escaping religious persecution after 1492. Descendants of the original Moroccan Jews, Sephardic Jews, and the Jews from the nomadic Berber tribes in the Atlas Mountains had distinct languages and practices that remained separate for generations.

Most Jewish food traditions mirrored local tastes and dishes, often substituting oil for butter. Foods from the North African, Mediterranean, and Arab cultures dominated with strong Sephardic influences. French influences often come into play since much of the country was under French rule from 1912 until 1956,

In the north, there was more Spanish influence and foods often had a spicy tomato and onion base. Elsewhere more subtly spiced stews (including tagines) and couscous dominated, with harissa added for kick. Preserved lemons, chickpeas, fava beans, almonds, dates, wheat, olives, vegetable salads, and flaky, savory pastries were part of these food ways.

Mimouna is probably the best known Moroccan Jewish celebration, observed the evening after the last day of Passover. Jews brought over gifts of Passover foods to their non-Jewish neighbors and received flour and starter dough for their first post-Passover bread. Special pancakes would be made from the new flour to serve their neighbors and other guests. As Moroccan Jews emigrated they brought Mimouna with them. In Israel it is now a public holiday.

In 1948, there were more than 250,000 Jews in Morocco. Most have now emigrated, mainly to Israel. About 2,500 Jews still live in Morocco.

ZA'ATAR ROAST TURKEY

Serves 4 or 5

Za'atar is my go-to herb-and-spice mixture when it comes to Middle Eastern cooking. It is a blend, usually with oregano, marjoram, thyme, sesame seeds, and sumac (a dried and ground tart berry), and is available in some grocery stores; in Middle Eastern, spice, and specialty stores; and online. There are many regional variations (and alternate spellings). If the za'atar you find comes in red or green varieties, select green for the recipes in this book. If it is unavailable, try the Za'atar in a Pinch (page 217).

MAKE IT SHABBAT:

STARTER/APPETIZER: *Chile, Ginger, and Spice Charred Eggplant Dip (page 131) with vegetable sticks*

MAIN COURSE: *Za'atar Roast Turkey*

SIDE DISH: *Tamarind Okra or Zucchini (page 168)*

ACCOMPANIMENT: *Yellow Rice (page 160)*

BREAD: *Friday Night Challah (page 204) or flatbreads*

DESSERT: *Challah Fritters (page 188) with chocolate sauce*

FOR THE ZA'ATAR MARINADE

½ cup olive oil plus extra for the pan
1 tablespoon minced garlic
2 tablespoons fresh lemon juice
1 teaspoon grated lemon zest
1 teaspoon za'atar or Za'atar in a Pinch (page 217)
¼ teaspoon salt
½ teaspoon dried mint
¼ to ½ teaspoon crushed red pepper
½ teaspoon ground sumac or 1 teaspoon minced lemon zest
¼ teaspoon ground cumin

FOR THE TURKEY

1 (2- to 3-pound) bone-in, skin-on turkey breast half
½ teaspoon paprika

TO MAKE THE MARINADE

In a small bowl, whisk together the olive oil, garlic, lemon juice and zest, za'atar, salt, mint, crushed red pepper, sumac, and cumin.

TO PREPARE THE TURKEY

Place the turkey breast in a snug-fitting pot or container that is taller than the turkey. Brush the turkey with marinade. Using your fingers, carefully separate the skin from the turkey (do not detach) and brush or rub the marinade under the skin. Pour the remaining marinade over the turkey, cover with plastic wrap, and marinate in the refrigerator for at least 1 hour and up to 1 day, turning the turkey and brushing it with marinade occasionally.

Preheat the oven to 450°F. Grease the roasting pan with olive oil.

Place the turkey breast skin side up in a roasting pan. Brush thoroughly with the marinade, sprinkle with paprika, and place it in the oven. Discard any leftover marinade.

Immediately lower the heat to 325°F and roast for 20 to 25 minutes per pound, or until an instant-read thermometer reads 160°F and the meat at the bone is just cooked and no longer pink. Baste occasionally with liquid from the pan or use additional olive oil. Remove from the oven, cover the pan with aluminum foil, and let sit for 20 minutes before carving into slices. The turkey will continue to cook while it rests and should reach 165°F.

MAKE IT IN ADVANCE: *The turkey can be roasted up to 2 days in advance, cooled, wrapped tightly in plastic wrap and refrigerated.*

SHAWARMA ROAST CHICKEN

Serves 4 to 6

Also known as gyros or doner kebab, the names for this style of roasted meat may vary, but it's a favorite around the world. Shawarma consists of slices of marinated lamb, beef, veal, turkey, or chicken stacked on top of each other and slowly spit-roasted on a vertical grill. Each portion is sliced off to order, which means every serving is a mixture of crisp edges and succulent meat. Making it at home never really appealed to me because it is hard to duplicate its unique textures, but then I tried using the traditional shawarma seasonings on whole, roasted chicken and was pleased with the combination of crispy skin and juicy chicken.

MAKE IT SHABBAT:

STARTER/APPETIZER: *Purchased Falafel with Tahini Sauce (page 210)*

MAIN COURSE: *Shawarma Roast Chicken*

SIDE DISH: *Iraqi-Israeli Vegetable Pickles (page 166)*

ACCOMPANIMENT: *Rice Pilaf (page 161) with Chopped Tomato Salad (page 162)*

BREAD: *Flatbreads or pita*

DESSERT: *Turkish Coconut Pudding (page 190)*

FOR THE SPICE RUB

1 tablespoon minced garlic
½ teaspoon ground cumin
½ teaspoon Diamond Crystal kosher salt or coarse sea salt (see page 17)
¼ to ½ teaspoon cayenne pepper, optional
¼ teaspoon ground sumac or 1 teaspoon minced lemon zest
¼ teaspoon paprika
¼ teaspoon ground cardamom
¼ teaspoon ground turmeric
¼ teaspoon ground black pepper
⅛ teaspoon ground allspice
⅛ teaspoon dried oregano
⅛ teaspoon ground cinnamon
3 tablespoons olive oil
2 tablespoons fresh lemon juice

FOR THE CHICKEN

1 (4- to 6-pound) roasting chicken
Olive oil, for basting, if needed
½ cup Chicken Broth (page 194) or purchased, or water

TO MAKE THE SPICE RUB

In a small bowl, mix together the garlic, cumin, salt, cayenne (if using, depending on desired heat level), sumac, paprika, cardamom, turmeric, black pepper, allspice, oregano, and cinnamon. Stir in the olive oil and lemon juice and set aside.

TO MAKE THE CHICKEN

Remove any gizzards or other innards that might be in the cavity of the chicken and discard them or save for another use. Wipe the inside of the chicken clean of any debris. Cut away any excess fat deposits at the neck or rear.

Place the chicken on a plate. Rub the inside and outside of the chicken with the spice rub. Do not truss the chicken. (It roasts more evenly if you don't.) Refrigerate the chicken for at least 1 hour or up to 1 day.

Preheat the oven to 400°F.

Pour the broth into a roasting pan and place a rack inside. Place the chicken on the rack, breast side down.

Turn the oven down to 350°F. Roast for 30 minutes. Brush or spoon the pan juices over the chicken. Using tongs and a large fork, carefully turn over the chicken so it is breast side up. Brush or spoon the pan juices over the chicken and roast, basting every 20 minutes (or use the olive oil if needed), for another 50 to 90 minutes depending on the size of the chicken.

The chicken is ready when an instant-read thermometer inserted in a breast and thigh reads 165°F after checking several times over 3 minutes. The juices should run clear when a thigh and breast are cut down to the bone. Let the chicken sit for 20 minutes. Carve slices or cut into serving portions and serve warm or at room temperature.

MAKE IT IN ADVANCE: *Can be roasted up to 2 days in advance and stored, well wrapped, in refrigerator.*

MAKE-AHEAD MEATBALLS

Makes about 28 meatballs; serves 6 to 8

These meatballs should be called my secret dinner time weapon. They are flavor-packed, freeze and reheat well, and can be used in so many different ways.

I always make the full recipe (or even double it) and freeze some and serve the rest for Friday night dinner. Use the meatballs as a starter or main course drizzled with Tahini Sauce (page 210) or serve with just about any sauce in this cookbook

Other great combos: Use a half-batch with the Peppers, Eggplant, and Onions in Tomato Sauce (page 201) or in place of the fish in the Fish in Spicy H'raimi-Style Tomato Sauce (page 48). Add a half batch to the Mostly Make-It-Ahead Shakshouka (page 100) when reheating the base, or to a pot of simmering Hawaij Vegetable Soup (page 104).

2 pounds ground beef
½ cup minced onion
2 tablespoons minced garlic
2 tablespoons tomato paste
½ teaspoon salt
½ teaspoon ground black pepper
½ teaspoon paprika
½ teaspoon dried oregano
¼ teaspoon ground cinnamon
¼ teaspoon cayenne pepper
2 large eggs, beaten
¼ cup plain bread crumbs or matzo meal
3 tablespoons vegetable oil

MAKE IT SHABBAT:

STARTER/APPETIZER: *Whole Roasted Garlic (page 218) with Matzo Crackers (page 208)*

MAIN COURSE: *Make-Ahead Meatballs (page 112) with Peppers, Eggplant, and Onions in Tomato Sauce (page 201)*

SIDE DISH: *Green salad with Lemon, Za'atar, and Garlic Dressing (page 219)*

ACCOMPANIMENT: *Pasta or mashed potatoes*

BREAD: *Friday Night Challah (page 204)*

DESSERT: *Twice-Baked Lemon Cookies (page 185)*

In a large bowl, mix together the beef, onion, garlic, tomato paste, salt, black pepper, paprika, oregano, cinnamon, and cayenne. Add the eggs and breadcrumbs and mix with your hands until just combined. Let rest 10 minutes. Using wet hands to avoid sticking, roll the mixture into 1½-inch balls.

Heat the oil in the skillet over medium-high heat. Cook the meatballs in batches, using tongs to turn them while they cook, until they are browned on all sides and cooked through, about 14 minutes. Drain the meatballs on a paper towel-lined plate.

MAKE IT IN ADVANCE: *The meatballs can be made up to 3 days in advance or frozen for up to 3 months.*

Meatballs and Jewish cuisine

Meatballs are found throughout the Jewish world. The small, round Sephardic meatball (albondiga, almondega, or boulette) came to Spain with the Moors from the Persians and was adopted by the Jews. It became a characteristic Jewish food usually made from lamb but also from beef, fish, or poultry pounded smooth in a mortar and pestle. For many Sephardic Jews meatballs remain an important part of Shabbat and holiday dinners by themselves or in sauces, soups or stews.

After expulsion and migration, the Jews, brought the concept with them as they settled through Europe and to the New World. Sephardim who settled in Ottoman lands kept their meatballs but also adapted them to make kebabs and meat-and-vegetable patties, much like the Jews of the Middle and Near East who also made dishes of lamb or beef pounded with bulgur known as kibbeh, kubbeh, or kubba.

Eastern European Jews have their own meatball history. The meatball, known as klop, kahklenten, or koklaten, was more of a bread dumpling with meat and was influenced by German dishes. Increased beef availability and the advent of the meat grinder (eliminating hand chopping) switched that ratio around. Meatballs are a favored Shabbat and holiday menu item. Ashkenazi meatballs, coarser in texture than the albondigas, are added to soups, stews, and sauces and are wrapped in cabbage leaves (stuffed cabbage).

RED WINE POT ROAST

Serves 6 to 8

This is my mother's pot roast, or at least the closest my sisters and I could come to re-creating it. It is a classic meat and potatoes comfort food, although since Mom and I loved mushrooms, I've added those to the pot as well. Like all pot roasts and braised meat dishes, it benefits from being made at least a day in advance and cut into slices when chilled.

1 (3-to-4 pound) boneless beef chuck roast or brisket

2 tablespoons plus ½ teaspoon soy sauce, divided

1 teaspoon salt, divided

¾ teaspoon ground black pepper

3 tablespoons vegetable oil, divided

2 cups chopped onion

1 tablespoon minced garlic

¼ teaspoon cayenne pepper, optional

½ teaspoon dried oregano

½ teaspoon dried rosemary

1½ cups red wine

¼ cup unsweetened apple juice

3 cups (1-inch slices) carrots

3 cups (1-inch chunks) new or red potatoes

2 cups sliced cremini or white button mushrooms

MAKE IT SHABBAT:

STARTER/APPETIZER: *Chicken Soup with Matzo Balls (page 196)*

MAIN COURSE: *Red Wine Pot Roast*

SIDE DISH: *Steamed asparagus and/or green salad with Lemon, Za'atar, and Garlic Dressing (page 219)*

ACCOMPANIMENT: *Pasta, egg noodles, or mashed potatoes*

BREAD: *Friday Night Challah (page 204) with everything topping*

DESSERT: *Bundt Cake with Black and White Glazes (page 180)*

Trim the chuck roast of excess surface fat and place on a rimmed plate. (If using brisket, leave a ¼-inch layer of fat on top. See How to Brisket on page 40.) Brush 2 tablespoons of soy sauce on all sides of the meat and sprinkle with salt and black pepper. In a Dutch oven or a large heavy soup pot, heat 2 tablespoons of oil over medium-high heat. Add the meat and cook until browned, 5 to 7 minutes per side. (Cut the meat in half against the grain if it's too large for the pot). Transfer the meat to the rimmed plate.

Add the remaining 1 tablespoon of oil to the Dutch oven. Add the onion and sauté, stirring up any browned bits with a spoon, until softened, 7 to 10 minutes. Add the garlic and sauté until golden, 1 to 2 minutes. Stir in the remaining ½ teaspoon of salt, remaining ¼ teaspoon of black pepper, the cayenne (if using), oregano, and rosemary and sauté for 1 minute. Add the wine and apple juice and bring to a simmer. Return the meat to the pan (if brisket, place fat side up) along with any juices (stack the meat if necessary) and bring to a simmer.

Add the carrots, cover, lower the heat to medium-low, and simmer, spooning the liquid over the meat every 30 minutes and turning the meat in the liquid every 60 minutes. (If the meat is stacked, switch the top and bottom pieces.) If the liquid evaporates, add more water. After 60 minutes, add the potatoes, cover, and simmer for another 60 minutes. Add the mushrooms, cover, and simmer until a dinner fork glides through the meat, 1 to 2 more hours.

Transfer the vegetables and meat to a rimmed plate. Add the remaining ½ teaspoon of soy sauce to the Dutch oven and simmer over medium heat until the liquid is reduced to the consistency of thin pasta sauce, 10 to 20 minutes. Taste and add more salt and black pepper, if desired.

Let the meat rest for at least 20 minutes before cutting across the grain into slices (see Going Against the Grain, page 40) or shredding. To serve, place the meat and vegetables on a serving platter and top with some of the sauce. Serve extra sauce on the side.

If making in advance, wrap the meat and place the sauce with vegetables in an airtight container and refrigerate for up to 3 days. To serve, cut the chilled meat against the grain into slices or shred. Remove the fat from the top of the chilled sauce, if desired. Bring the sauce and vegetables to a simmer over medium-low heat. Add the meat and cook until heated through.

VARIATION: *To Make Pot Roast or Brisket in an Oven—Preheat the oven to 325°F. Choose a heavy roasting pan or Dutch oven that is both stovetop and oven safe. Prepare as directed on the stovetop until the meat is in the pot and the liquid is simmering. Bake, covered (use aluminum foil if the pot does not have an oven-safe lid), for 3 to 4½ hours, following the recipe instructions.*

GRILLED LAMB CHOPS WITH BITTER HERBS SALAD

Serves 6

This recipe is inspired by the Passover customs of the Karaite Jews, a branch of Judaism founded in the eighth century that traditionally follows the Torah and not the rabbinic interpretations. Many of the Karaites lived in Egypt for centuries but were forced to leave after the wars with Israel and most now live in the United States.

The Karaites regard Shabbat as a day of joy and start Friday night prayers earlier to extend the day. In Egypt they would enjoy a glass of anise-flavored liquor with their Shabbat lunch. As the day ended, they would say blessings over wine and branches of myrtle or rue and greet each other in Arabic ("May your week be green") or in Hebrew ("May you have a good week").

Another Karaite Seder custom is to eat a "salad" of bitter herbs, which refers to the different greens used in the Seder service to symbolically represent the harshness of slavery under the Egyptians.

MAKE IT SHABBAT:

STARTER/APPETIZER: *Vegetable Soup (page 198) or Hawaij Vegetable Soup (page 104)*

MAIN COURSE: *Grilled Lamb Chops with Bitter Herbs Salad*

SIDE DISH: *Quinoa or rice*

BREAD: *Matzo or Matzo Crackers (page 208) or Friday Night Challah (page 204)*

DESSERT: *Flourless Chocolate Berry Cake (page 178)*

FOR THE LAMB

3 pounds bone-in lamb ribs or shoulder chops
¼ cup fresh lemon juice
¼ cup olive oil
¼ teaspoon ground cinnamon
¼ teaspoon salt
¼ teaspoon ground black pepper
⅛ teaspoon cayenne pepper
¼ cup minced fresh mint
2 teaspoons minced garlic

FOR THE BITTER HERBS SALAD

¾ cup (1-inch pieces) chopped fennel
2 tablespoons minced fennel fronds
1 cup (1-inch pieces) endive
2 cups (1-inch pieces) romaine lettuce
2 cups (1-inch pieces) chopped red leaf lettuce
1 cup (1-inch pieces) frisée or arugula
½ cup minced fresh flat-leaf parsley
½ cup minced fresh dill
About ½ cup Whole Lemon Dressing (page 218), plus more if desired
Matzo Crackers (page 208), or 3 sheets purchased matzo broken into 1-inch pieces

FOR SERVING

¼ cup Garlic Sauce (page 210) or Pomegranate Molasses (page 212) or purchased, optional
¼ cup chopped fresh mint or flat-leaf parsley

TO MAKE THE LAMB

Trim any excess fat from the lamb chops. In a small bowl, mix together the lemon juice, olive oil, cinnamon, salt, black pepper, cayenne pepper, mint, and garlic. Rub the mixture all over the lamb, cover, and refrigerate for at least 1 hour or up to 1 day. Bring the lamb to room temperature before grilling.

Prepare a grill for medium-high to high heat. Grill the lamb chops, turning occasionally, about 5 minutes per side, or until cooked to the desired doneness. Lamb will keep cooking for several minutes after being pulled from the grill, so it's best to slightly undercook. Transfer the lamb to a plate and cover with aluminum foil.

TO MAKE THE BITTER HERBS SALAD

In a large bowl, mix together the fennel, fennel fronds, endive, romaine lettuce, red leaf lettuce, frisée, parsley, and dill.

Just before serving, shake up the dressing, pour it over the salad, and toss until evenly coated. Add more dressing if desired. Add the matzo pieces and toss again.

TO SERVE

Transfer the lamb to individual plates and drizzle with Garlic Sauce (if using). Garnish with fresh mint. Serve with the bitter herbs salad on the side.

GEFILTE FISH WITH SMASHED TOMATO TOPPING

Makes 12 first-course portions

I grew up with bland gefilte fish out of jars, which I mostly appreciated as a vehicle for horseradish. This baked version is packed with flavors I associate with North African and Sephardic food and comes with a colorful garnish of cooked tomatoes and peppers, but you can just top it with horseradish (or do as I do and use both). I usually serve it as a starter or first course, but you can double the portion size for a main dish. For the best taste, use the freshest fish you can find. For a more Eastern European version, leave out the jalapeño, cumin, and turmeric. If you don't have a food processor, finely grate the onions and carrots and mince the vegetables and fish. This makes a great starter for Passover and other Jewish holidays. For some Jews, certain foods, including cumin, are considered kitniyot, foods that not prohibited by the Torah but are not allowed at Passover. If that's the case for you, simply omit the cumin in this recipe during the holiday.

MAKE IT SHABBAT:

STARTER/APPETIZER: *Baked Gefilte Fish with Tomato Topping*

MAIN COURSE: *Za'atar Roast Turkey (page 108)*

SIDE DISH: *North African Carrot Salad (page 164)*

ACCOMPANIMENT: *Tahini Mashed Potatoes (page 156)*

BREAD: *Friday Night Challah (page 204)*

DESSERT: *Fresh fruit salad*

FOR THE TOMATO TOPPING

2 tablespoons olive oil
2 cups thinly sliced onions, cut in half
2 to 3 tablespoons thinly sliced garlic
¼ teaspoon salt
⅛ teaspoon black pepper
¼ to 1 teaspoon cayenne pepper or paprika
2 cups (½-by 1-inch) yellow and/or red bell pepper pieces
2 cups small cherry or grape tomatoes
1 tablespoon fresh lemon juice
½ teaspoon sugar, optional

FOR THE GEFILTE FISH

Vegetable oil for the baking pan
1 medium onion, roughly chopped
3 large garlic cloves, roughly chopped
1 large carrot, roughly chopped
1 medium red bell pepper, quartered
1 small jalapeño or serrano chile, optional
1 large celery stalk, roughly chopped
½ cup fresh flat-leaf parsley
Zest and juice of 1 medium lemon
2 pounds boneless, skinless mild white fish fillets
1 teaspoon salt
1 to 2 teaspoons sugar
½ teaspoon ground cumin
½ teaspoon paprika
½ teaspoon dried oregano
½ teaspoon ground turmeric
¼ teaspoon ground black pepper
4 large eggs, beaten

FOR SERVING

2 to 3 cups arugula, watercress, or other greens
12 olives, for garnish
12 lemon wedges

TO MAKE THE TOMATO TOPPING

In a large skillet, heat the olive oil over medium heat. Add the onions and sauté until golden, 10 to 12 minutes. Add the garlic and sauté until golden, 1 to 2 minutes. Add the salt, black pepper, ¼ teaspoon of cayenne (use up to 1 teaspoon if you like it spicier), and the bell peppers and sauté until softened, 10 to 12 minutes. Add the tomatoes and sauté for a few minutes. Using a spatula, crush the tomatoes until they break apart. Continue to sauté until they are very soft, 10 to 15 minutes. Stir in the lemon juice and sauté until the liquid has mostly evaporated. Taste and add more salt, cayenne, lemon juice, and sugar, if desired. Set aside.

TO MAKE THE GEFILTE FISH

Preheat the oven to 350°F. Grease a 9-by-12-inch baking pan with vegetable oil.

Combine the onion, garlic, carrot, bell pepper, jalapeño (if using), celery, parsley, lemon zest, and lemon juice in the bowl of a food processor and process, scraping down the sides of the bowl, until finely chopped. Transfer the mixture to a large bowl.

Pat dry the fish and cut it into chunks. Place it in the food processor and process until it forms a coarse paste. You may need to work in batches. Transfer the fish to the bowl with the vegetables.

Add the salt, 1 teaspoon of sugar (use 2 teaspoons of sugar if you prefer it sweeter), cumin, paprika, oregano, turmeric, and black pepper and stir until well mixed. Add the eggs and stir until completely combined.

Add the fish mixture to the prepared baking pan, spreading it out and smoothing the top. Bake for 55 to 65 minutes, or until the fish is firm to the touch and beginning to pull away from the sides of the pan.

Let cool to slightly warm or room temperature (liquid on top will be reabsorbed), 30 to 45 minutes. Cut with a knife into 12 ovals or squares, or use a 2- to 3-inch cookie cutter to cut into rounds.

TO SERVE

Place the greens on a large serving platter. Arrange the gefilte fish over the greens and garnish each piece with a spoonful of the tomato topping and an olive with lemon wedges on the side.

MAKE IT IN ADVANCE: *The gefilte fish and sauce can be made up to 3 days ahead and stored separately. Let the fish cool in the baking pan, cover with aluminum foil, and refrigerate.*

SOUTH INDIAN–INSPIRED FISH CAKES WITH COCONUT-CILANTRO CHUTNEY

Serves 4 as a main course, or 8 as a starter

The Kerala region of southern India has been home to Jews for millenia, with local traditions placing the first Jews there during the time of King Solomon.

Jews thought to be descendants of seagoing traders centered around Kochi. They were joined after 1492 by Sephardic Jews seeking to escape persecution. Many eventually migrated to Israel, Canada, or the United States, but there are still Jews living in some of the area's villages.

The recipe was inspired by traditional dish recipes and the food I ate in Kerala. Coconut is used frequently in many dishes in southern India, and I use finely shredded or grated dried unsweetened coconut as a convenient replacement for fresh. Make just the chutney on its own and serve with grilled chicken or fish, or drizzle it over Middle Eastern Grilled Corn (page 134).

MAKE IT SHABBAT:

STARTER/APPETIZER: *Kerala Fish Cakes with Coconut-Cilantro Chutney*

MAIN COURSE: *Yemeni Grilled Chicken (page 141)*

SIDE DISH: *Iraqi-Israeli Vegetable Pickles (page 166)*

ACCOMPANIMENT: *Steamed rice*

BREAD: *Friday Night Challah (page 204) or flatbreads*

DESSERT: *Turkish Coconut Pudding (page 190)*

FOR THE COCONUT-CILANTRO CHUTNEY

1 cup finely grated or shredded dried unsweetened coconut
½ cup plus 2 tablespoons water, plus more if needed
1 small jalapeño, coarsely chopped
1 cup coarsely chopped cilantro leaves
1 teaspoon finely chopped fresh ginger
¼ packed cup coarsely chopped fresh mint
2 tablespoons tamarind concentrate or paste, or 2 tablespoons fresh lemon juice
1 teaspoon sugar
¼ teaspoon salt

FOR THE FISH CAKES

8 large garlic cloves, peeled
8 green onions, trimmed and cut into thirds
1 large jalapeño, coarsely chopped
1 (2-inch) piece fresh ginger, peeled and coarsely chopped
2 pounds chilled boneless, skinless red snapper or other mild white fish fillets, cut into 2-inch chunks
½ teaspoon ground coriander
½ teaspoon ground cumin
½ teaspoon ground cardamom
½ teaspoon salt
¼ teaspoon ground black pepper
¼ teaspoon ground turmeric
4 large eggs, beaten
¼ cup finely grated or shredded dried unsweetened coconut
2 tablespoons coconut oil plus more as needed

FOR SERVING

2 cups chopped tomatoes

TO MAKE THE COCONUT-CILANTRO CHUTNEY

In a bowl, combine the coconut with ½ cup of water and let sit for 5 minutes or until all the water is absorbed.

In a blender, combine 2 tablespoons of water, jalapeño, cilantro, ginger, and mint and blend until finely chopped. Add the soaked coconut, tamarind, sugar, and salt and blend, scraping down the sides of the jar as needed, until the ingredients are almost puréed, adding more water, 1 tablespoon at a time, if needed, just to help the ingredients blend. The chutney should be thin enough to pour but not too loose. Taste, and add sugar or salt, if desired. Set aside. The chutney can be made up to 1 day in advance, stored in an airtight container, and refrigerated.

TO MAKE THE FISH CAKES

Combine the garlic, green onions, jalapeño, and ginger in a food processor and pulse, scraping down the sides of the bowl as needed, until chopped. With the motor running, add the fish, one piece at a time, until very finely chopped and fully incorporated. Add the coriander, cumin, cardamom, salt, pepper, tumeric, eggs, and coconut and pulse, again scraping down the sides of the bowl as needed, until combined. Be careful to mix and not purée the ingredients.

Using wet hands, shape the mixture into 16 patties about 2½ inches in diameter and ½-inch thick. In a large skillet, heat the coconut oil over medium-high heat until very hot. A bit of batter dropped in should immediately sizzle. Add the fish cakes in batches and cook until browned and cooked through, 2 to 3 minutes on each side. Adjust the heat as necessary so it's hot enough for the next batch, adding more oil as needed. Transfer the fish cakes to paper towels to drain.

TO SERVE

Place the fish cakes on a large platter and top with the chopped tomatoes and chutney. Pass extra chutney at the table. The fish cakes can be served hot, warm, or at room temperature.

summer

THE CADENCE OF SHABBAT DINNERS CHANGES IN THE SUMMER.

Days are longer, so there can be more time to prepare; the weather is warmer, so lighter, cooler foods are appreciated; and dinners that can be grilled outdoors or cooked in advance rather than in the heat of the day are preferred.

Salad-based Shabbat menus appeal, so I included a Two-Salad Shabbat (page 128) pair of recipes here—one with a foundation of Israeli couscous and my version of hakol salat, or "everything salad," with a bounty of raw vegetables and greens. Both work for main courses or side dishes. The Fruit and Salad Rolls and Vegetable Salad Rolls (pages 136 and 138) wrap up seasonal produce in rice paper and give them an Asian spin with a soy-peanut dipping sauce.

Serve guests Charred Eggplant Dip (page 131) with pita triangles, Matzo Crackers (page 208), or vegetable sticks while they wait for the main course. The Yemeni Grilled Chicken (page 141), Lemongrass and Ginger Barbecued Flanken (cross-cut short ribs) (page 144), and Adana Burgers with Pomegranate Molasses Barbecue Sauce (page 150) are all great choices for outdoor grilling. Add a little zing and color to summer meals by serving Pickled Red Onions (page 165) or Iraqi-Israeli Vegetable Pickles (page 166) alongside them.

Serve Middle Eastern Grilled Corn (page 134) sprinkled with spices and herbs and drizzled with colorful sauces packed

with flavor and watch this side dish steal the show. Pair it with any of the grilled dishes, roast chicken, or Lamb Hummus Bowls (page 148) for a hearty full meal. The charred corn on the cob, a mash-up of Mexican and Middle Eastern street foods, also makes an unexpected but delicious starter.

Spinach and Dill Phyllo Pies (page 126) stuffed with greens, mint, and feta cheese are wonderful warm or at room temperature and can be made ahead as a main course, starter, or appetizer, while Fruit Juice Sorbet (page 191) makes a cooling summer desert.

SUMMER HOLIDAYS & SPECIAL DAYS

In the Northern Hemisphere, the season matches up with the last part of Sivan and the months of Tammuz, Av, and Elul. While summer is a time of pleasure, vacation, and enjoyment, Tammuz, Av, and Elul have periods of mourning, reflection, and spiritual preparation.

The day of deepest mourning is Tisha B'Av. The ninth of the month of Av (July or August) is a day of fasting and commem-

orates many tragedies, including the destruction of the First and Second Temples.
It is customary for observant Jews in the
Nine Days before the fast to not eat meat or
poultry, nor drink wine or grape juice.

One light spot is Tu B'Av, the fifteenth
day of the month of Av. Sometimes called
the Jewish Valentine's Day, it is a modern
revival of an old celebration of love and
weddings that marked the start of the
grape harvest. Join the celebration by
making someone you love a special dinner,
such as Skillet Paella with Chicken and
Sausage (page 139).

Elul (August or September) ushers in a
time of preparation for Rosh Hashanah and
Yom Kippur. In the synagogue, the shofar
(ram's horn) is blown to announce the
coming of the holidays. Individuals begin
looking inward to understand their actions
and outward to ask forgiveness of others.

SPINACH AND DILL PHYLLO PIES

Serves 4 to 6 as a main course, or 8 to 10 as an appetizer or starter

These herbaceous pies draw on Sephardic, Greek, and Turkish Jewish traditions of bourekas—flaky, baked savory small pastries. Instead of assembling individual pastries, I've made two larger ones to cut into slices and share as a main course or starter. Combining spinach with arugula, mint, and dill gives the pies the taste of just-picked wild greens. It's a very flexible recipe and you can substitute dandelion greens, watercress, chard, or just use additional spinach instead of arugula. For more on phyllo, see Mushroom and Cheese Strudels (page 98). Excess moisture is phyllo's enemy, so make sure to pat dry the feta, squeeze as much liquid out of the greens as possible, and brush the phyllo sheets only lightly with oil.

I've called for a couple extra phyllo sheets in case any are ripped or torn.

8 ounces feta cheese
2 tablespoons plus ¼ cup olive oil, plus more as needed
2 cups chopped red onion
2 teaspoons minced garlic
¼ cup thinly sliced green onions
1 teaspoon salt, divided
1 teaspoon black pepper, divided
¼ teaspoon cayenne pepper
½ teaspoon dried oregano, divided
½ teaspoon ground cumin, divided
½ teaspoon dried mint, divided
½ teaspoon cinnamon, divided
12 cups roughly chopped fresh spinach
4 cups roughly chopped arugula
2 large eggs, beaten
¼ cup chopped fresh mint
¼ cup chopped fresh dill
¼ teaspoon ground sumac or 1 teaspoon lemon zest
12 sheets (13-by-17-inch) phyllo dough, at room temperature
Plain Greek yogurt or Garlic Sauce (page 210), optional

MAKE IT SHABBAT:

STARTER/APPETIZER: *Whole Roasted Cauliflower (page 58)*

MAIN COURSE: *Spinach and Dill Phyllo Pies*

SIDE DISH: *Green Salad with Whole Lemon Dressing (page 218) and/or Israeli-Iraqi Vegetable Pickles (page 166)*

ACCOMPANIMENT: *Rice Pilaf (page 161) with Chopped Tomato Salad (page 162)*

BREAD: *Friday Night Challah (page 204)*

DESSERT: *Twice-Baked Lemon Cookies (page 185) and/or Fruit Juice Sorbet (page 191)*

Drain the feta if packed in brine and rinse it in cold water and pat dry with paper towels. Crumble the feta. Transfer to a bowl and set aside.

In a 12-inch skillet, heat 2 tablespoons of olive oil over medium-high heat. Add the onions and sauté until soft, 5 to 7 minutes. Add the garlic and green onions and sauté until the garlic is golden, 1 to 2 minutes. Stir in ½ teaspoon of salt, ½ teaspoon of black pepper, ⅛ teaspoon of cayenne, ¼ teaspoon of oregano, ¼ teaspoon of cumin, and ¼ teaspoon of cinnamon and sauté for 1 minute.

In a large bowl, toss the spinach and arugula. Add about one-third of the greens to the pan and cook, stirring constantly until just wilted, 1 to 2 minutes. Add the next third and continue to cook until those are wilted, 1 to 2 minutes. Add the remaining greens and cook until all the greens are wilted and bright green, another 3 to 5 minutes. Spread out the mixture on a rimmed platter and let cool for 10 minutes.

Squeeze out as much liquid as possible from the greens and transfer to a large bowl. Add the feta, eggs, the remaining ½ teaspoon salt, ½ teaspoon black pepper, ⅛ teaspoon cayenne, ¼ teaspoon oregano, ¼ teaspoon cumin, ¼ teaspoon cinnamon, the mint, dill, and sumac and stir to combine.

Preheat the oven to 350°F. Line 2 baking sheets with parchment paper. Lightly brush the parchment with some of the ¼ cup olive oil.

Lay phyllo sheets on a surface and cover with a damp kitchen towel. You will have 2 extra sheets to use if any tear or break.

To assemble the pies, think about the numbers of a clock face when placing the phyllo sheets on the baking sheet. Position the baking sheet with a long side closest to you. Lay out 1 phyllo sheet on the pan, with the short ends pointing to 3 o'clock and 9 o'clock. Brush the phyllo very lightly with olive oil. Center a second sheet with the short ends pointing to 12 o'clock and 6 o'clock. Brush the second phyllo sheet very lightly with olive oil. The third sheet should be positioned diagonally, with the short ends pointing at 1:30 and 7:30. Brush lightly with olive oil. Place the fourth sheet diagonally to point the short ends at 4:30 and 10:30. Do not oil.

Using a slotted spoon to reduce the chance of adding any liquid, place half of the filling in a 6-inch circle in the center of the phyllo. It should be about 1-inch deep. Fold up each side of phyllo to tightly wrap the filling, making sure to keep the phyllo package roughly round in shape. Lightly brush with olive oil. Place the fifth phyllo sheet on top of the wrapped round, centering it with the short ends pointing to 3:00 and 9:00. Tightly tuck the ends underneath the pie. Brush the top completely with olive oil.

Repeat for the second pie (you may need more olive oil). Bake both pans for 30 to 35 minutes, or until golden brown and slightly flaky. Let cool for at least 10 minutes.

Serve hot, warm, or at room temperature, with Greek yogurt (if using) at the table.

MAKE IT IN ADVANCE: *Bake up to 1 day in advance, let cool completely, cover with plastic wrap, and refrigerate. To reheat, brush the tops with olive oil and bake in a 350°F oven for 15 to 20 minutes, or until warm throughout.*

TWO-SALAD SHABBAT

Each salad makes 6 servings

When the weather turns warm, this duo of salads—one a filling pasta salad in a colorful and tangy dressing and the other full of crunchy vegetables—is the perfect Friday night dinner. Toasted pearl or Israeli couscous (called ptitm in Israel) is a small, round, extruded pasta about the size of tapioca pearl. Do not substitute traditional couscous; its tiny size and texture will not work in this salad. It's a good idea to use gloves when handling beets.

California Hakol Salat (page 130) is loosely based on the chopped vegetable salads from Turkey, Israel, and other Arabic and Middle Eastern countries. The dish reflects the bounty of ripe summer produce in California and is a variation on what Israelis call hakol salat or "everything salad." Pick a dressing from the ones suggested in the recipe, or dress it very simply with fresh lemon juice and olive oil.

ISRAELI COUSCOUS SALAD WITH BEET-TAHINI DRESSING

FOR THE BEET-TAHINI DRESSING

8 ounces cooked and peeled whole beets, drained if canned
¼ cup tahini
¾ cup fresh lemon juice, divided, plus more if desired
½ cup extra-virgin olive oil, divided
1 tablespoon minced fresh mint
1 teaspoon minced garlic
¼ teaspoon ground cumin
¼ teaspoon salt
⅛ teaspoon ground black pepper

FOR THE COUSCOUS SALAD

3 cups water
¾ teaspoon salt, divided
2 cups toasted pearl (Israeli) couscous
2 tablespoons extra-virgin olive oil
½ teaspoon ground black pepper
1 cup chopped carrots
1 cup chopped fennel root or celery
2 cups halved cherry tomatoes
¼ cup finely chopped fresh mint, plus 2 tablespoons for garnish
¼ cup finely chopped fresh flat-leaf parsley, plus 2 tablespoons for garnish
⅔ cup pitted and sliced Kalamata olives
8 ounces crumbled feta cheese

FOR SERVING

Arugula or other fresh greens

TO MAKE THE BEET TAHINI DRESSING

Cut the beets in quarters. Combine the beets, tahini, ½ cup of lemon juice, ¼ cup of olive oil, the mint, garlic, cumin, salt, and pepper in a food processor or blender and process until smooth and thick. While the motor is running, add the remaining ¼ cup lemon juice and remaining ¼ cup olive oil and process until incorporated. Taste and add salt and/or lemon juice, if desired. Set aside.

TO MAKE THE COUSCOUS SALAD

In a large pot, bring the water to a boil over high heat. Add ¼ teaspoon of the salt and the couscous, stir, and bring to a boil. Cover, lower the heat, and simmer until the couscous is tender but still firm to the bite, 8 to 10 minutes. Drain and transfer the couscous to a large bowl. Add the oil, ¼ teaspoon of salt, and the black pepper and toss until coated. Add the tomatoes, carrots, fennel, ¼ cup of mint, ¼ cup of parsley, the olives, and cheese and mix well. Taste, and add the remaining ¼ teaspoon salt, if desired.

TO ASSEMBLE THE SALAD

Just before serving, mix the beet-tahini dressing with the couscous salad. Place the dressed salad on a bed of arugula in a large serving bowl or on a rimmed platter. Garnish with the remaining 2 tablespoons each of mint and parsley.

MAKE IT IN ADVANCE: *The couscous and dressing can be stored separately in airtight containers and refrigerated for up to 3 days.*

MAKE IT SHABBAT:

STARTER/APPETIZER: *Fish (or Tofu) in Spicy H'riami-Style Tomato Sauce (page 48), chilled*

MAIN COURSE: *Two-Salad Shabbat*

BREAD: *Pita, flatbreads, or Friday Night Challah (page 204)*

DESSERT: *Mango and Cardamom Mini Cheesecakes (page 184)*

(recipe continues)

CALIFORNIA HAKOL SALAT

1 cup chopped red bell pepper
1 cup chopped green bell pepper
2 cups chopped cucumber
2 cups chopped tomatoes
1 cup chopped red onion
2 cups chopped, peeled jicama
½ cup chopped red radishes
2 cups chopped green beans
1 (15-ounce) can chickpeas, drained and rinsed

⅛ teaspoon salt
⅛ teaspoon ground black pepper
¼ cup finely chopped fresh mint
¼ cup finely chopped fresh flat-leaf parsley
¼ cup finely chopped fresh dill, optional
About 1¼ cups Lemon, Za'atar, and Garlic Dressing (page 219), North African Dressing (page 219), or Tahini Dressing (page 220)

In a large salad bowl, combine the red and green bell peppers, cucumber, tomatoes, red onion, jicama, radishes, green beans, and chickpeas and toss well. Add the salt and pepper and toss again.

Just before serving, add the mint, parsley, and dill (if using) and toss with half of the dressing. Add more dressing, if desired, tossing after each addition. Taste and add salt and pepper, if desired, and toss again.

CHARRED EGGPLANT DIP

Serves about 6

This is probably the most go-to and versatile recipe in the book. I make it several times a month, varying it by what I'm using it for (dip, appetizer, side dish, salad or even pasta or pizza topping).

I call this take on baba ghanoush—a famed Arab, Israeli, and Middle Eastern eggplant dish—"Charred Eggplant" because my favorite cooking method is to grill the whole eggplants until they are totally soft and the skin is burnt in places, but they can also be roasted in the oven or cooked on a stovetop grill pan. Make the eggplant dip with just salt, lemon, and garlic or add tahini paste and other ingredients for a creamier texture and different flavors. Serve with flatbreads and other accompaniments or put a big scoop on top of greens for a refreshing salad or starter.

2 pounds eggplants (2 to 3 medium)
Vegetable oil for the grill, optional
1 teaspoon minced garlic, plus more if desired
¼ teaspoon salt
2 tablespoons fresh lemon juice, plus more if desired
2 tablespoons chopped fresh cilantro or flat-leaf parsley
Flatbreads, pitas, raw vegetable sticks, or crackers for serving, optional

MAKE IT SHABBAT:

STARTER/APPETIZER: *Charred Eggplant Dip with Vegetable Sticks*

MAIN COURSE: *Roast Salmon in Citrus-Honey Sauce (page 46)*

SIDE DISH: *Charred Greens (page 163)*

ACCOMPANIMENT: *Rice Pilaf (page 161) with Chopped Tomato Salad (page 162)*

DESSERT: *One-Pan Banana Bread (page 183)*

(recipe continues)

Preheat the oven to 450°F. Cover a rimmed baking sheet with parchment paper or aluminum foil.

Using a fork, lightly prick holes in several spots all around the eggplants and place them on the prepared baking sheet. Roast for 20 minutes. Turn the eggplants and continue to roast until the eggplant is soft and collapsed into itself, and the skins are wrinkled and somewhat charred in spots, another 20 to 30 minutes (timing will depend on the shape and size of the eggplants). Let cool for 20 minutes on the baking sheet.

Alternatively, the eggplants can be prepared on a gas or charcoal grill. Do not prick holes in them. Oil the grill grates and grill over medium heat, turning often, until the eggplants are charred and soft.

Transfer the eggplants to a cutting board and cut in half lengthwise. Using a fork, scrape out the flesh down to the skins, discarding skins. Chop or mash the flesh until it's roughly puréed and transfer to a medium serving bowl along with any liquid. Stir in the garlic, salt, and lemon juice. Taste and add more garlic, salt, and lemon juice, if desired. Garnish with cilantro and serve with flatbreads or other accompaniments, if desired.

VARIATION: *Charred Eggplant Dip with Tahini—Increase the amount of minced garlic to 2 teaspoons and add ¼ cup tahini paste to the eggplant along with the lemon and salt.*

VARIATION: *Charred Eggplant Dip with Roasted Tomatoes and Jalapeño—When roasting or grilling the eggplant, also roast or grill a medium tomato and a whole medium jalapeño. The tomato and jalapeño should be soft and charred in 20 to 30 minutes (turn halfway through). Let cool slightly, remove the skins, chop, and stir them into eggplant along with the other ingredients. For a milder dip, leave out the jalapeño or only use half of the cooked pepper.*

VARIATION: *Charred Eggplant Dip with a Kick—Stir in 1 teaspoon or more of Z'hug (page 213), Harissa (page 214), or purchased hot sauce into the Charred Eggplant Dip or Charred Eggplant Dip with Tahini.*

VARIATION: *Chile, Ginger, and Spice Charred Eggplant Dip—Add 2 teaspoons minced jalapeño, 2 teaspoons grated fresh ginger, 2 teaspoons minced red onion, and 1 teaspoon ground turmeric to the Eggplant Dip with Tahini Variation. Stir well. For a milder dip, seed the jalapeño before using or use less.*

MAKE IT IN ADVANCE: *The eggplants (and the tomato and jalapeño) can be roasted or grilled up to 2 days in advance and refrigerated in an airtight container. The Charred Eggplant Dip and any of the variations can be made up to 1 day in advance. Cover the surface of the dip with plastic wrap and store in an airtight container in the refrigerator.*

An abundance of eggplant

It's hard to underestimate the importance of the eggplant to Jewish food. This large berry or fruit, eaten as a vegetable with a meaty taste and silken texture when cooked, was once known as "Jew's food" in Italy and "Jew's apple" in England.

Eggplant originated in Southeast Asia and has been cultivated in India for more than 4,000 years. By the fourth century it was available in Persia. Three centuries later the Persians were defeated by the Moors, who brought eggplant with them when they conquered Spain in the eighth century. Within 100 years, eggplants were being eaten in Europe beyond Spain and other Moorish strongholds.

Spanish Jews immediately saw the food's value as a replacement for meat in dairy meals, a way to stretch meat, and as a delicious ingredient on its own. Sadly, its popularity among them was used during the fifteenth and sixteenth centuries by Spanish inquisitors to accuse eggplant-eating Christian converts of not setting aside their Jewish ways.

Eggplant's versatility was also important in the development of Israel. Early Jewish settlers saw their Arab neighbors growing them in Palestine and began to cultivate eggplants themselves. It was one of the few crops that were plentiful in Israel's early years, and eggplant (called chatzilim in Hebrew), promoted by the government, soon became an essential food that could be grilled, roasted, fried, stewed, simmered, steamed, baked, chopped, puréed, mashed, stuffed, pickled, candied, and more.

MIDDLE EASTERN GRILLED CORN

Serves 4 to 8

I've eaten corn around the world, from the corn stews and pies of Chile and stir-fries in China, to fire-roasted whole corn in Laos and cups of heated canned corn from street stands in Jordan. But my favorite preparation is Mexican-style grilled corn, sprinkled with spices and drizzled with sauce. Here I've taken that idea and used Middle Eastern ingredients, resulting in a recipe full of texture and flavor with toppings that are spicy, creamy, and tart. Try the ones suggested here or improvise your own. It makes a fun appetizer, starter, side dish, or accompaniment. To make it vegan, choose non-dairy toppings.

MAKE IT SHABBAT:

STARTER/APPETIZER: *Hawaij Vegetable Soup (page 104)*

MAIN COURSE: *Za'atar Roast Turkey (page 108)*

SIDE DISH: *Green salad with Whole Lemon Dressing (page 218)*

ACCOMPANIMENT: *Middle Eastern Grilled Corn*

BREAD: *Friday Night Challah (page 204) or flatbreads*

DESSERT: *Raisin and Almond Twirls (page 187)*

FOR THE SPICE MIX

½ teaspoon salt
½ teaspoon ground black pepper
½ teaspoon paprika
½ teaspoon dried mint
½ teaspoon ground sumac

FOR THE CORN

4 large ears fresh corn on the cob with husks
1 tablespoon extra-virgin olive oil

FOR THE DRIZZLES
(CHOOSE 1 OR 2 CREAMY AND 1 TART)

Creamy:
1 to 3 tablespoons Tahini Sauce (page 210) or tahini
1 to 3 tablespoons plain yogurt
1 to 3 tablespoons Garlic Sauce (page 210)

Tart:
1 to 3 tablespoons amba (see page 135) or Yellow Curry Sauce (page 211)
1 to 3 tablespoons Pomegranate Molasses (page 212) or purchased
1 to 3 tablespoons silan (see page 25)

FOR THE HOT SAUCE (CHOOSE 1)

1 teaspoon Z'hug (page 213)
1 teaspoon Harissa (page 214)
1 teaspoon bottled hot sauce

FOR SERVING

½ cup crumbled feta cheese, optional
¼ cup chopped fresh cilantro or mint
¼ cup chopped green onion

TO MAKE THE SPICE MIX

In a small bowl, mix together the salt, black pepper, paprika, mint, and sumac and set aside.

TO MAKE THE CORN

Remove the silk from the corn, but leave the outer husks and stem on. Soak the corn in cold water for 20 minutes.

Heat a grill to medium-hot. With the husks closed over the corn cobs, grill the corn on all sides until the kernels can be easily pierced and are charred in places. (If a grill is not available, husk the corn and cook as desired.)

Pull down or remove the husks. Leave the stems on if desired. For smaller portions cut each corn cob in half. Brush each corn cob all over with olive oil. Rub the corn all over with the spice mix and place on a plate. Drizzle the tops with your choice of sauces and spoon or shake on the hot sauce. Sprinkle with feta (if using), cilantro, and green onions.

Serve immediately with lots of napkins.

About amba

Amba is a popular Israeli condiment made with fermented mango. It is yellow or yellowish orange or brown and adds a curry flavor and pleasant tartness. Traditionally it is served drizzled over falafel, sabich (fried eggplant), and shawarma pita sandwiches. It was adapted from local Indian pickled mangos by Iraqi Jews who had settled in India and then introduced back to Iraq. When Iraqi immigrants settled in Israel in the 1950s, they brought amba with them and its popularity spread.

Amba is available in smooth and chunky versions at some specialty, Middle Eastern, and kosher markets and online. Some spice markets sell amba powder with dried and ground sour mango and other seasonings. It can be mixed with yogurt or puréed with fresh fruit to give the taste and texture of amba. Since both amba and amba powder are hard to find, I developed Yellow Curry Sauce (page 211) to replicate the amba experience and to bring the condiment's color and vibrancy to a wide range of dishes.

FRUIT AND VEGETABLE RICE PAPER SALAD ROLLS

Each recipe makes 4 rolls

My mother-in-law always started her dinners with a fruit salad. After a trip to Southeast Asia, I was inspired, and transformed her chopped fruit salad into these rolls wrapped in rice papers. That made me remember another version of this recipe with vegetables that I had in a Thai street market, and it seemed fitting to include it here as well. Either of these would make a great appetizer, starter, or side dish. If you've never worked with rice papers before, try practicing with one or two first until you get the hang of it.

FRUIT AND SALAD ROLLS

FOR THE DIPPING SAUCE WITH PEANUTS

1½ tablespoons apple cider vinegar
1 tablespoon soy sauce
½ tablespoon vegetable oil
¼ teaspoon grated fresh ginger
⅛ teaspoon Chinese chile garlic sauce or Sriracha sauce
1½ teaspoons chopped green onions, white and green parts
2 tablespoons chopped roasted, salted, and skinless peanuts

or

FOR THE TAHINI–POMEGRANATE MOLASSES DIP

¼ cup tahini
1 tablespoon plus ½ teaspoon Pomegranate Molasses (page 212) or purchased

FOR THE ROLLS

1 large ripe banana
1 cup thinly sliced mango, divided
1 cup thinly sliced strawberries, divided
1 cup thinly sliced fresh pineapple spears, divided
1 cup chopped fresh mint, divided
4 (8½-inch) round rice paper wrappers
¾ cup packed chopped romaine lettuce
¼ cup grated fresh or dried unsweetened coconut, optional
¼ cup chopped fresh basil or Thai basil

MAKE IT SHABBAT:

STARTER/APPETIZER: *Fruit and Salad Rolls*

MAIN COURSE: *Mushroom-Eggplant Hummus Bowls (page 149)*

SIDE DISH: *Vegetable and Salad Rolls and/or Iraqi-Israeli Vegetable Pickles (page 166)*

BREAD: *Pita, flatbreads, or Friday Night Challah (page 204)*

DESSERT: *Raisin and Almond Twirls (page 187)*

TO MAKE THE DIPPING SAUCE WITH PEANUTS

In a small bowl, mix together the vinegar, soy sauce, oil, ginger, and chile garlic sauce. Set aside. Stir in the green onions and peanuts just before serving.

TO MAKE THE TAHINI-POMEGRANATE MOLASSES DIP

In a small bowl, mix together the tahini and 1 tablespoon of pomegranate molasses. Set aside. Just before serving, drizzle the remaining ½ teaspoon of pomegranate over the top and, using a dinner knife, swirl it through the dip so it looks marbleized.

TO MAKE THE ROLLS

Cut the banana crosswise, then cut each half into 4 long pieces. Set aside ¼ cup each of the mango, strawberries, pineapple, and mint.

Fill a small bowl with lukewarm water. Place a rice wrapper on a clean work surface. Dip a pastry or basting brush into the water. Brush the wrapper from edge to edge with water until it is very wet. Flip over the wrapper and repeat. Let the wrapper rest for 30 seconds.

Starting 1 inch from the left-hand edge, spread out one-quarter of the mango on the rice wrapper from top to bottom and to just past the midpoint. Top with one quarter of the strawberries, 3 tablespoons of lettuce, 2 banana slices, one quarter of the pineapple, 1 tablespoon of coconut (if using), 3 tablespoons of mint, and 1 tablespoon of basil.

Pull the left side of the wrapper up and over the filling with one hand while using your other hand to compress the filling into a tight log as you roll the wrapper over it. Continue rolling until the wrapper has sealed on itself. Transfer the roll to a serving platter seam side down. Repeat with the remaining rice paper wrappers.

TO SERVE

Finely dice the remaining fruit and scatter it over the rolls. Sprinkle with the remaining mint. Serve with your choice of sauces on the side.

(recipe continues)

VEGETABLE AND SALAD ROLLS

1½ tablespoons apple cider vinegar
1 tablespoon soy sauce
½ tablespoon vegetable oil
¼ teaspoon grated fresh ginger
⅛ teaspoon Chinese chile garlic sauce or
   Sriracha sauce
2 cups packed chopped kale
4 (8½-inch) round rice paper wrappers
1 cup thinly sliced red bell pepper

1 cup thinly sliced cucumber
16 green beans
1 cup grated carrot
1 cup grated raw beet
½ cup chopped green onions
½ cup chopped fresh basil or Thai basil
½ cup chopped fresh cilantro
Dipping Sauce with Peanuts (page 136)

In a large bowl, mix together the vinegar, soy sauce, oil, ginger, and chile garlic sauce. Add kale and stir to coat. Set aside.

Fill a small bowl with lukewarm water. Place a rice wrapper on a clean work surface. Dip a pastry or basting brush into the water. Brush the wrapper from edge to edge with water until it is very wet. Flip the wrapper and repeat. Let the wrapper rest 30 seconds.

Starting 1 inch from the left-hand edge, spread out ¼ cup of pepper strips from top to bottom and just past the midpoint. Top with ¼ cup of cucumber, ½ cup of kale, 4 green beans, 3 tablespoons of carrots, 3 tablespoons of beets, 2 tablespoons of green onions, 1½ tablespoons of basil, and 1½ tablespoons of cilantro.

Pull the left side of the wrapper up and over the filling with one hand while using your other hand to compress the filling into a tight log as you roll the wrapper over it. Continue rolling until the wrapper has sealed on itself. Transfer the roll to a serving platter seam side down. Repeat with the remaining rice paper wrappers.

Scatter the remaining carrots, beets, basil, and cilantro over the rolls. Serve with dipping sauce.

SKILLET PAELLA WITH CHICKEN AND SAUSAGE

Serves 6 to 8

This recipe is a history lesson in a pan. Rice was brought to Spain by the Moors, who ruled parts of what is now Spain for 700 years and are probably responsible for much of the Jewish world's preference for the grain.

Paella itself goes back to the nineteenth century, when farmers in Valencia (the home of this dish) cooked it over a fire for a midday meal. The name of both the metal pan and the dish itself are thought to come from "patella," a flat pan used by the Romans, who had previously conquered Spain; the word "paella" translates as "frying pan" in the Valencian language.

My take on paella has been adapted to be cooked indoors in a large skillet, no special pan needed. It even sometimes will produce a socarrat, the browned, crispy bottom rice that is beloved by all.

4 to 5 cups Chicken Broth (page 194) or purchased, divided

⅛ teaspoon crumbled saffron threads

1 pound boneless, skinless chicken thighs cut into 1½-inch pieces

½ teaspoon salt, divided

½ teaspoon ground black pepper, divided

½ teaspoon paprika, divided

½ teaspoon ground cumin, divided

4 tablespoons olive oil, divided

½ pound fresh sausage, such as chicken, turkey, beef, or lamb, cut into ½-inch slices

2 cups chopped onion

2 tablespoons minced garlic

¼ teaspoon crushed red pepper

1½ cups chopped carrots

1 cup chopped celery

3 tomatoes, 2 chopped and 1 cut into 8 wedges

½ cup chopped fresh flat-leaf parsley, divided

2 cups short-grain Valencia or other Spanish rice

½ cup dry white wine

8 asparagus spears or green beans, cooked but still crisp

¼ teaspoon smoked paprika

Garlic Sauce (page 210) or Tahini Sauce (page 210), optional

MAKE IT SHABBAT:

STARTER/APPETIZER: *Charred Eggplant Dip with a Kick (page 132) with vegetable sticks*

MAIN COURSE: *Skillet Paella with Chicken and Sausage*

SIDE DISH: *Green salad with Whole Lemon Dressing (page 218)*

BREAD: *Friday Night Challah (page 204)*

DESSERT: *Flourless Chocolate Berry Cake (page 178)*

(recipe continues)

In a medium saucepan, combine the chicken broth and saffron and bring to a simmer over medium heat. Turn off the heat, cover, and keep warm.

In a large bowl, combine the chicken, ¼ teaspoon of salt, ¼ teaspoon of black pepper, ¼ teaspoon of paprika, and ¼ teaspoon of cumin and toss until evenly coated.

In a 12-inch skillet, heat 2 tablespoons of oil over medium-high heat. Add the sausage and cook, stirring often until browned and half cooked through, 5 to 7 minutes. Transfer the sausage to a plate and set aside.

Add half the chicken to the pan and cook, turning the pieces occasionally, until browned and half cooked through, 10 to 12 minutes. Transfer to the plate with the sausage. Repeat with the remaining chicken.

Drain any liquid from the pan. Add 1 tablespoon of olive oil and heat for about 30 seconds. Add the onions and sauté until softened, 5 to 7 minutes. Add the garlic and sauté until golden, 1 to 2 minutes. Add the remaining ¼ teaspoon of salt, ¼ teaspoon of black pepper, ¼ teaspoon of paprika, ¼ teaspoon of cumin, the crushed red pepper, and the carrots and sauté for 5 minutes. Add the celery and sauté for 5 minutes.

Add the chopped tomatoes and ¼ cup of parsley and sauté for 1 minute. Stir in the remaining 1 tablespoon of olive oil and the rice, tossing until the rice is thoroughly coated in oil. Sauté for 1 minute, stir in the wine and 3 cups of broth and bring to a low boil, stirring often. Cook for 5 minutes, stirring well and adding more broth ¼ cup at a time as needed if the mixture gets dry. At this point, the rice will no longer be stirred.

Lower the heat to medium or medium-low to keep the liquid in pan at a simmer. Simmer for 15 to 20 minutes, moving the pan around on the burner if needed to maintain even heat and adding broth by the ¼ cup as needed. The rice will absorb the liquid as it cooks. If the rice seems to be drying out too fast in a particular spot, add a spoonful of broth.

The rice should be tender but pleasantly chewy in the center. The pan should not be dry and there should be some visible liquid. Add broth (or water if you have run out) so the rice is just wet.

Distribute the chicken and sausage evenly on the top of rice. Press lightly into the rice. Pour any accumulated meat juices over the rice. Cook for 5 minutes, adding ¼ cup of broth as needed to keep the rice slightly liquid. Arrange the asparagus and tomato wedges in a spoke pattern in the rice, adjusting the chicken or sausage to fit. Add ¼ cup of broth or water if the rice is dry. Sprinkle with smoked paprika.

Lower the heat to low, cover the paella pan tightly with aluminum foil (the pan's lid will not be a tight enough seal), and cook for 10 minutes. Most of the liquid should be absorbed and the chicken and sausage should be cooked through.

Remove the pan from the heat. Reseal the foil cover and let rest for 10 minutes.

Serve hot or warm, garnished with the remaining ¼ cup of parsley and drizzled with Garlic Sauce (if using).

YEMENI GRILLED CHICKEN

Serves 6 to 8

The Yemeni hawaij spice mix, with its notes of cumin and cardamom, is a great base for the chicken marinade as a shortcut for intense flavor. Using boneless thighs speeds up the cooking.

1 tablespoon Yemeni hawaij for soup or Instant Almost Hawaij (page 216)
½ cup olive oil
½ teaspoon salt
½ cup fresh lemon juice
3 tablespoons diced onion
1 tablespoon minced garlic
3 pounds boneless, skinless chicken thighs
Vegetable oil for the grill

MAKE IT SHABBAT:

STARTER/APPETIZER: *Fish in Spicy H'raimi-Style Tomato Sauce (page 48)*

MAIN COURSE: *Yemeni Grilled Chicken*

SIDE DISH: *Charred Greens (page 163) or Iraqi-Israeli Vegetable Pickles (page 166)*

SIDE DISH: *Rice Pilaf (page 161) with Chopped Tomato Salad (page 162)*

BREAD: *Challah Pull-Apart Rolls (page 206) or flatbreads*

DESSERT: *Chocolate and Cookie Truffles (page 186)*

In a large bowl, mix together the hawaij, olive oil, salt, lemon juice, onion, and garlic. Add the chicken to the marinade and turn it to make sure the chicken is fully coated. Cover with plastic wrap and marinate in the refrigerator for 1 hour, or up to 1 day, turning occasionally. Transfer the chicken to a plate, pour any leftover marinade in a saucepan, and bring to a boil over medium-high heat. Cover and boil for 5 minutes. Remove from the heat and set aside.

Brush the rack of an outdoor or indoor grill or a grill pan with oil. Heat to medium-high. Grill the chicken, turning occasionally and brushing it thickly with the heated marinade until the juices run clear when you cut into the thickest piece. An instant-read thermometer should read 165°F. Let rest 10 minutes before serving.

MAKE IT IN ADVANCE: *The chicken can be made up to 3 days in advance, stored in an airtight container, and refrigerated.*

TWO KEBABS

Each recipe serves 4

There is something about kebabs (or food on sticks, as my sons called them) that is appealing to both adults and children, so I've created two versions of the recipe for double the fun. These kebabs, with their Middle Eastern influences and a few Asian flavors, can be made outside on the grill or inside in a grill pan or an electric grill. The marinades also work well with tofu or fish. If using bamboo skewers, soak for 30 minutes before using.

ZA'ATAR KEBABS WITH VEGETABLES

1½ pounds boneless, skinless chicken thighs or breasts
1 cup olive oil
¼ cup fresh lemon juice
⅛ teaspoon cayenne pepper
⅛ teaspoon ground black pepper
¼ teaspoon salt
1 tablespoon za'atar or Za'atar in a Pinch (page 217)
1 tablespoon minced garlic

½ cup finely chopped onion
4 zucchini, cut into 1-inch pieces
1 red onion, cut into 1-inch pieces
2 red bell peppers, seeded and cut into 1-inch pieces
Vegetable oil for the grill
3 tablespoons chopped fresh flat-leaf parsley or cilantro
4 lemon wedges

Cut the chicken into 1½-inch chunks. In a large bowl, mix together the olive oil, lemon juice, cayenne, black pepper, salt, za'atar, garlic, and onion. Reserve ¼ cup of marinade for basting.

Add the chicken to the remaining marinade and marinate in the refrigerator for 1 hour or up to 1 day, stirring occasionally. Using a slotted spoon, remove from the marinade and set aside on a plate. Add the zucchini, onion, and bell pepper chunks to the marinade and stir until evenly coated.

Thread the chicken and vegetables onto 8 to 10 long skewers.

Lightly brush a grill grate, electric indoor grill, or stovetop grill pan with vegetable oil and heat to medium-high heat.

Grill the skewers, adjusting the heat up or down as needed to avoid scorching or flare-ups. Turn them occasionally and baste with the reserved marinade. Cook the chicken until it's firm to the touch, with clear juices, 10 to 15 minutes.

Let rest for 5 minutes. Serve on or off the skewers sprinkled with parsley and with lemon wedges on the side.

POMEGRANATE MOLASSES AND TAHINI KEBABS

1½ pounds boneless, skinless chicken thighs
1 tablespoon minced garlic
2 teaspoons minced fresh ginger
1½ cups chopped onion
1 teaspoon sugar
½ teaspoon dried mint
¼ teaspoon crushed red pepper, optional

2 tablespoons vegetable oil, plus more for the grill and basting
3 tablespoons Pomegranate Molasses (page 212) or purchased, divided
2 tablespoons fresh lime or lemon juice
1 tablespoon unseasoned rice vinegar
1 tablespoon soy sauce
Tahini Sauce (page 210)

Cut the chicken into 1½-inch chunks and set aside.

In a food processor or blender, combine the garlic, ginger, onion, sugar, mint, crushed red pepper (if using), oil, 1 tablespoon of pomegranate molasses, the lime juice, vinegar, and soy sauce and process until fairly smooth. Transfer to a large bowl. Add the chicken and mix until coated. Marinate, covered with plastic wrap, for 1 hour in the refrigerator, turning every 20 minutes.

Thread the chicken onto 8 to 10 long skewers. Lightly brush a grill grate, electric indoor grill, or stovetop grill pan with oil and heat to medium-high heat.

Grill the skewers, adjusting the heat up or down as needed to avoid scorching or flare-ups. Turn them occasionally and baste with oil. Cook until the chicken is firm to the touch but not hard, with clear juices, 10 to 15 minutes.

Let rest for 5 minutes. Swirl the remaining 2 tablespoons of pomegranate molasses through the tahini sauce and pass at the table.

MAKE IT IN ADVANCE: *The kebabs can be grilled 1 day in advance, stored in an airtight container, and refrigerated.*

MAKE IT SHABBAT:

STARTER/APPETIZER: *Almost Homemade Hummus (page 96) with vegetable sticks*

MAIN COURSE: *Za'atar Kebabs or Pomegranate Molasses and Tahini Kebabs*

SIDE DISH: *California Hakol Salad (page 130)*

ACCOMPANIMENT: *Yellow Rice (page 160)*

BREAD: *Flatbreads*

DESSERT: *Bundt Cake with Black and White Glazes (page 180)*

LEMONGRASS AND GINGER BARBECUED FLANKEN

Serves 4

After I had lemongrass and ginger beef skewers at a street café in Cambodia, I kept thinking how good the flavor combination would taste on grilled flanken (cross-cut or sliced beef short ribs), so when I got home I adapted the flavors and created a very flavorful but messy finger food.

Lemongrass is available in Asian and specialty and produce markets and some supermarkets. Choose stalks that are fragrant, feel firm, and are mostly green. Store wrapped in plastic wrap for up to 2 weeks in refrigerator (Freeze for longer storage). If fresh lemongrass is not available, use lemon zest.

I like to serve the short ribs with a cucumber-herb salad (page 150), which is how a similar dish was served in Cambodia.

4 tablespoons roasted unsalted peanuts (see Note)

2 fresh lemongrass stalks or 1 tablespoon minced lemon zest

2 teaspoons chopped fresh ginger

3 tablespoons chopped garlic

½ teaspoon ground turmeric

1 teaspoon minced lime zest

3 tablespoons peanut or vegetable oil, plus more for the grill

3 tablespoons soy sauce

1 tablespoon apple cider vinegar

1 tablespoon sugar

1 teaspoon chicken or vegetarian bullion powder

3 pounds flanken (cross-cut) short ribs (¼- to ½-inch-thick slices)

MAKE IT SHABBAT:

STARTER/APPETIZER: *Fruit and Vegetable Rice Paper Salad Rolls (page 136)*

MAIN COURSE: *Lemongrass and Ginger Flanken*

SIDE DISH: *Cucumber-Herb Salad (page 150)*

ACCOMPANIMENT: *Rice*

BREAD: *Flatbreads*

DESSERT: *Fruit Juice Sorbet (page 191) or Turkish Coconut Pudding (page 190)*

Roughly chop the peanuts and place in a food processor. Cut off the roots and the top 2 inches of the lemongrass. Strip off and discard any hard outer leaves off the remaining lemongrass. Crush the inner sections of each stalk, and then finely chop. (You should have about 3 tablespoons of minced lemongrass.) Add the lemongrass, ginger, garlic, turmeric, lime, peanut oil, soy sauce, vinegar, sugar, and bullion to the food processor and process, scraping down the sides of the bowl as needed, until a thick paste forms.

Spread a thin layer of the paste on the bottom of an 8-by-12-inch baking pan. Cover the paste with a layer of flanken. Spread the paste on the ribs and add another layer of meat. Repeat with the rest of the meat and paste. Cover and refrigerate for at least 4 hours or up to 1 day.

Lightly brush a grill grate, electric indoor grill, or stovetop grill pan lightly with oil and heat to medium-high heat. Add the flanken slices and grill, adjusting the heat as needed and turning once, until firm and cooked through, 7 to 10 minutes (the meat is very thin, so start checking early.) Transfer to a plate, cover with foil, and let rest for 5 minutes before serving. The ribs can also be cooked under a broiler or in a closed, panini-style grill, but the timing will vary.

NOTE: *The peanuts should not have skins. If roasted unsalted peanuts are not available, use raw peanuts and toast them before using.*

Chabad Shabbat

Some of my most memorable travel experiences have been at the Shabbat dinners I have shared with others around the world. Some of those have been under the auspices of the Chabad-Lubavitch movement. The organization has a network of Chabad Houses, or community centers, in 100 countries.

The dinners usually start with a fish course and vegetable salads, then chicken soup, a meat or chicken main course, and a simple dessert. Some dinners offered a taste of local flavors. One in Cambodia served a fresh green peppercorn and beef stir-fry. A Vietnamese one offered a ginger-chicken soup with rice.

Guests vary from locals to Israeli and other Jewish ex-pats and their families to college students and business people in the area to travelers passing through.

To find the Shabbat dinners in the United States, go to www.chabad.org and use the Chabad locator function. For centers outside the United States, click on the locator function, go to advance search and use the global locator.

GRILLED RIB EYE STEAKS WITH PRESERVED LEMON AND GREEN ONION SAUCE

Serves 4

The green onions and the salty, sour, and pickled taste of preserved lemons offset the richness of the steak. If desired, the steaks can be pan-fried in 2 tablespoons of oil in a heavy skillet over medium-high heat instead of grilled.

If preserved lemons (see page 147) are not available, substitute 1 tablespoon minced lemon zest, 2 tablespoons minced lemon without the peel, and ¼ teaspoon salt. For this recipe, seed the preserved lemon and then chop both the flesh and the skin.

MAKE IT SHABBAT:

STARTER/APPETIZER: *Gefilte Fish with Smashed Tomato Topping (page 118)*

MAIN COURSE: *Grilled Rib Eye Steaks with Preserved Lemon and Green Onion Sauce*

SIDE DISH: *Charred Greens (page 163)*

ACCOMPANIMENT: *Oven-Baked Garlic Fries (page 157)*

BREAD: *Friday Night Challah (page 204)*

DESSERT: *Challah Fritters with Sweet Tahini Sauce (page 188)*

FOR THE RUB

4 boneless rib eye steaks, (2 to 2½ pounds total)
1 garlic clove, cut in half lengthwise
¼ teaspoon salt
¼ teaspoon paprika
¼ teaspoon ground black pepper

FOR THE SAUCE

½ cup olive oil
¼ cup minced chopped garlic
2 cups chopped green onions, divided
2 tablespoons minced preserved lemon
2 tablespoons fresh lemon juice
2 cups chopped fresh flat-leaf parsley, divided
2 teaspoons Harissa (page 214) Z'hug (page 213) or spicy salsa
Salt

FOR GRILLING

Vegetable oil for the grill

TO MAKE THE RUB

Place the steaks on a large plate and rub them all over with the cut sides of the garlic clove. In a small bowl, mix together the salt, paprika, and black pepper and rub it all over the steaks. Let rest for at least 20 minutes or for up to 1 hour.

TO MAKE THE SAUCE

In a medium skillet or sauté pan, heat the oil over medium heat. Add the garlic and 1½ cups of green onions and sauté, stirring often, until the garlic begins to color and the green onions begin to soften, 3 to 4 minutes.

Lower the heat to medium-low. Add the preserved lemon, lemon juice, and 1 cup of parsley and cook, stirring often, until the parsley begins to wilt, about 4 minutes. Stir in the harissa and cook for 1 minute. Remove from the heat. Stir in the remaining ½ cup of green onions and 1 cup of parsley, taste, and add salt, if desired. Set aside.

TO GRILL THE STEAKS

Lightly brush a grill grate, indoor electric grill, or stovetop grill pan with oil and heat to medium-high. Place the steaks on the grill and cook, turning occasionally, until cooked to your desired doneness. A 1-inch-thick steak takes about 12 minutes total for medium-rare. A rare steak should register 125°F on an instant-read thermometer and feel firm but have a lot of give when touched. A medium-rare steak should register 130°F and feel firm but spring back when touched. A medium steak should register 135°F and feel firm but not hard. Medium-well should register 145°F and feel firm with very little give. Well-done steak should register 155°F and feel firm with no give.

TO SERVE

Let rest, covered with foil, for 7 to 10 minutes before cutting into slices. The sauce can be served warm or at room temperature on top of grilled steaks or on the side.

Buying and using preserved lemons

Preserved lemon is an ingredient in many Jewish North African dishes. The lemons are packed in brine in bottles and are available in some grocery stores, specialty shops, and Middle Eastern stores, and online. This recipe uses about half of a small preserved lemon. You can also mix a few tablespoons of rinsed and chopped preserved lemon into the Chicken and Vegetable Tagine (page 106), the Almost Homemade Hummus (page 96), or the Paella with Chicken and Sausage (page 139). Chopped preserved lemons can also add a zing to salad dressings and are an ingredient in the Tuna Freekah Salad (page 153). Once the jar is open, store the lemons in the refrigerator for up to 6 months.

Preserved lemons are sold in slices, halves, or whole. To use, remove them from the jar and rinse off the salt. Halve if necessary. Remove the seeds and chop as instructed in your recipe. Chop the peel and flesh together unless your recipe specifies otherwise.

LAMB HUMMUS BOWLS

Serves 4

The lamb topping makes a bowl of hummus a meal. Earthy, creamy hummus really is the perfect base for the aromatic lamb and onion topping. It's inspired by the toppings I ate in Israel and that I find in my favorite Middle Eastern and Israeli restaurants at home. In addition to the garnishes suggested below, add a drizzle of Z'hug (page 213) or Harissa (page 214) hot sauce if desired.

MAKE IT SHABBAT:

STARTER/APPETIZER: *Middle Easten Grilled Corn (page 134)*

MAIN COURSE: *Lamb or Mushroom-Eggplant Hummus Bowls*

SIDE DISH: *California Hakol Salat (page 130)*

BREAD: *Friday Night Challah (page 204) or pita*

DESSERT: *Turkish Coconut Pudding (page 190)*

FOR THE LAMB TOPPING

2 tablespoons olive oil
½ cup chopped onion
1 tablespoon minced garlic
½ teaspoon salt
½ teaspoon ground cinnamon
½ teaspoon ground cumin
½ teaspoon dried oregano
¼ teaspoon ground black pepper
⅛ teaspoon cayenne pepper
1 pound ground lamb
2 tablespoons finely chopped fresh mint
2 tablespoons finely chopped fresh flat-leaf parsley

FOR SERVING

6 cups Almost Homemade Hummus (page 96) or purchased plain hummus

FOR THE GARNISHES

Pickled Red Onions (page 165)
Paprika or ground sumac
Chopped fresh cilantro, mint, dill, or flat-leaf parsley
Tahini Sauce (page 210)

TO MAKE THE LAMB TOPPING

In a large skillet, heat the olive oil over medium heat. Add the onions and sauté until golden, 10 to 12 minutes. Add the garlic and sauté until golden, 1 to 2 minutes. Stir in the salt, cinnamon, cumin, oregano, black pepper, and cayenne and sauté for 1 minute. Add the lamb and sauté, breaking up any clumps with a spoon, until well browned, cooked through, and no longer pink, 10 to 12 minutes. Stir in the mint and parsley. The topping can be served hot, warm, or at room temperature.

TO SERVE

For each serving, swirl 1½ cups of the hummus in an 8- to 10-inch bowl and top with a fourth of the lamb topping. Add the pickled onions, sprinkle with paprika and cilantro, and drizzle with tahini sauce.

VARIATION: *Mushroom-Eggplant Hummus Bowls—Replace the lamb with 2 cups chopped eggplant and 2 cups chopped cremini or white button mushrooms. Once the onions and garlic are golden, add the seasonings. Stir in the eggplant and sauté until it starts to soften, 7 to 10 minutes. Add oil if necessary. Add the mushrooms and sauté until the mushrooms and eggplant are tender and the flavors have melded, about 7 minutes. Stir in ¼ cup chopped fresh parsley or cilantro. Serve the topping hot, warm, or at room temperature.*

MAKE IT IN ADVANCE: *This can be made up to 3 days in advance. Refrigerate the topping and hummus in separate airtight containers.*

ADANA BURGERS WITH POMEGRANATE MOLASSES BARBECUE SAUCE

Serves 6 to 8

Usually the mixture for these spicy beef and lamb burgers is wrapped around sword-like metal skewers and grilled as kebabs. I've taken the meat off the stick and formed it into juicy patties, which is much easier to prepare, and serve with a pilaf, on buns, or stuffed into pitas. The recipe is based on the Adana kebabs I've eaten in the United States, Israel, and Turkey. I like mine a bit on the spicy side, but you can cut back on the hot pepper for a tamer version.

The key to authentic flavor is Turkish pepper paste, available online and in many Middle Eastern markets in both hot and mild varieties. A few tablespoons stirred into soups, stews, and Mostly Make-It-Ahead Shakshouka (page 100) makes a great addition.

MAKE IT SHABBAT:

STARTER/APPETIZER: *Almost Homemade Hummus (page 96) with vegetable sticks*

MAIN COURSE: *Adana Burgers with Pomegranate Molasses Barbecue Sauce*

SIDE DISH: *Cucumber-Herb Salad*

ACCOMPANIMENT: *Bulgur Pilaf (see page 152) or Oven-Baked Garlic Fries (page 157)*

BREAD: *Flatbreads or pita*

DESSERT: *Raisin and Almond Twirls (page 187)*

FOR THE BARBECUE SAUCE

½ cup Pomegranate Molasses (page 212) or purchased
2 tablespoons tomato paste
1 teaspoon sugar
⅛ teaspoon salt

FOR THE CUCUMBER-HERB SALAD

½ cup rice vinegar or apple cider vinegar
¼ cup chopped red onion
¼ teaspoon salt, plus more if desired
½ teaspoon freshly ground black pepper or ¼ teaspoon crushed red pepper
2 large cucumbers, peeled and thinly sliced
¼ teaspoon sugar, optional
¼ cup mixture of finely chopped fresh mint, cilantro, dill and/or flat-leaf parsley

FOR THE ADANA BURGERS

1 small onion, finely minced
½ teaspoon salt
½ teaspoon ground black pepper
½ to 1 teaspoon cayenne pepper
⅛ teaspoon dried mint
1 teaspoon paprika
2 teaspoons mild Turkish red pepper paste or 2 teaspoons tomato paste mixed with an additional 1 teaspoon paprika
1 pound ground beef
1 pound ground lamb
Vegetable oil for the grill

TO MAKE THE BARBECUE SAUCE

In a small saucepan over low heat, mix together the molasses, tomato paste, sugar, and salt. Cook, stirring occasionally, for 20 minutes. Do not allow to boil. Transfer the mixture to a bowl and set aside to cool and thicken. Leftovers can be stored in an airtight container and refrigerated for up to 5 days.

TO MAKE THE CUCUMBER-HERB SALAD

In a large bowl, mix together the vinegar, onion, salt, and pepper. Add the cucumber slices and toss until evenly coated. Taste and add sugar, if desired. Just before serving, add the fresh herbs and toss again.

TO MAKE THE BURGERS

In a large bowl, mix together the onion, salt, black pepper, cayenne, mint, paprika, and pepper paste. Add the beef and lamb and knead with your hands until well mixed. Cover and refrigerate for 1 hour.

Shape the meat mixture into 8 to 10 patties.

Oil a grill grate or grill plate of a charcoal or gas grill, electric grill, or stovetop grill pan. Preheat to medium-high. Grill the burgers, turning occasionally and adjusting the heat as necessary, until cooked to your desired doneness, 8 to 10 minutes for medium-rare.

Serve the patties topped with the sauce and alongside the cucumber salad.

Turkish Jews

The first Jew in Turkey may have been Noah, whose ark landed atop Mount Arafat in what is now eastern Turkey. Historians place the first Jewish migration to Turkey about 2,400 years ago when Romaniote Jews from the Eastern Mediterranean settled there, but it was the rise of the Ottoman Empire and its welcoming of exiled Iberian Jews more than a thousand years later that created many of the Sephardic food ways we know today.

Even before their expulsion in 1492, the Sephardic Jews of Spain, Portugal, Naples, and Sicily with their extensive business, trade, and family networks were already sharing foods that were brought to Spain by the Moors, who had introduced eggplants, rice, almonds, sugar cane, citrus, lettuce, artichokes, carrots, spinach, and hard wheat to the Iberian peninsula.

Once the Jews settled in Turkey and elsewhere in the Ottoman Empire, Spanish and Moorish ingredients combined with Jewish and local food ways. Turkey was also a nexus of the overland spice trade, which impacted its cuisine.

As a result of this merger of traditions, techniques, and ingredients, the Jews who settled in Turkey (and throughout the Ottoman Empire) developed the stuffed vegetables, cheese, vegetable, and grain fillings wrapped in dough or vegetable leaves, kebabs, rice, sauces, and other dishes we associate with Sephardic cuisine.

Today more than half of the estimated 450,000 Jews with Turkish heritage live in Israel, with up to 22,500 living in Turkey (mostly in Istanbul) with large populations in the United States and Canada.

FREEKAH PILAF AND TUNA FREEKAH SALAD

Serves 4 to 6

Pilaf is my favorite way to cook freekah and bulgur, resulting in flavorful grains that are tender with just a hint of chewiness. Nomenclature, ingredients, and techniques vary but pilaf is a mainstay throughout the Jewish world. (For Rice Pilaf, see page 161).

Freekah (or frikah) is made from sun-dried, roasted young wheat and has a delicately smoky flavor. It comes whole or cracked. It takes longer to cook than bulgur, which is whole-grain kernels of wheat that are parboiled, dried, and cracked in various sizes. For bulgur pilaf, choose coarse or medium. The pilaf can be made up to 1 day in advance.

FREEKAH PILAF

1½ cups whole or cracked freekah or coarse- or medium-grind bulgur
2 tablespoons extra-virgin olive oil
2 cups chopped red onion
1 tablespoon minced garlic
¼ teaspoon salt, plus more if desired
1 teaspoon dried mint
½ teaspoon crushed red pepper
½ teaspoon ground sumac or 1 teaspoon grated lemon zest

About 4 cups of Vegetable Broth (page 197) or purchased, divided
2 cups halved cherry or grape tomatoes, optional
1 cup thinly sliced green onions
¼ cup chopped fresh flat-leaf parsley
½ cup chopped fresh mint
¼ cup chopped fresh dill
2 tablespoons grated lemon zest

If using whole freekeh, combine it in a bowl with cold water to cover and soak for 10 minutes. Remove any floating debris and drain well. (Skip this step if using cracked freekah or bulgur.)

In a large, deep sauté pan or a pot, heat the oil over medium-high heat. Add the red onion and sauté until softened, 5 to 7 minutes. Add the garlic and sauté until golden, 1 to 2 minutes. Add the salt, mint, crushed red pepper, and sumac and sauté for 1 minute. Add the freekah and stir until coated in oil. Sauté for 2 minutes. Add 1 cup of broth, bring to a simmer, and cook, stirring occasionally, until the broth is absorbed. Repeat twice more, cooking each time until the liquid is absorbed before adding more. The freekah should be cooked through but still firm in the center. If necessary, repeat with 1 more cup of broth. If you are making the Tuna Freekah Salad, stop here.

Toss with the tomatoes (if using), green onions, parsley, fresh mint, dill, and lemon zest. Serve hot or warm.

TUNA FREEKAH SALAD

Freekah Pilaf, made up to adding the
  tomatoes, at room temperature
2 (5-ounce) cans solid white albacore tuna,
  drained and flaked
2 cups halved cherry or grape tomatoes
1 cup thinly sliced green onions
½ cup chopped fresh flat-leaf parsley,
  divided
½ cup chopped fresh mint
¼ cup chopped fresh dill
2 tablespoons minced preserved lemon peel
  (see page 147) or grated lemon zest

¼ teaspoon salt, plus more if desired
⅛ teaspoon cayenne pepper
¼ teaspoon ground sumac or 1 teaspoon
  minced lemon zest
½ teaspoon dried mint
½ cup fresh lemon juice
½ cup extra-virgin olive oil
About 4 cups arugula or other greens
½ teaspoon paprika
2 tablespoons grated lemon zest, for garnish

In a large bowl, mix together the pilaf, tuna, tomatoes, green onions, ¼ cup parsley, mint, dill, and preserved lemon.

In a separate bowl, mix together the salt, cayenne, sumac, mint, lemon juice, and olive oil.

Just before serving, pour the dressing over the freekeh mixture and toss until well combined. Taste and add salt, cayenne, oil, and/or lemon juice, if desired. Arrange the arugula on a platter or individual plates and top with the freekeh salad. Garnish with paprika and the remaining ¼ cup of parsley and grated lemon zest and serve.

MAKE IT SHABBAT:

STARTER/APPETIZER: Leek-and-Mint Fritters
(page 62) with Garlic Sauce (page 210)

MAIN COURSE: Grilled Lamb Chops (page 116)

SIDE DISH: Tamarind Okra or Zucchini
(page 168)

ACCOMPANIMENT: Freekah Pilaf

BREAD: Friday Night Challah (page 204)

DESSERT: Twice-Baked Lemon Cookies (page 185)
and/or Chocolate and Cookie Truffles (page 186)

side dishes & accompaniments

TAHINI MASHED POTATOES

Serves 8 to 10

This recipe results in a textured mashed potato that includes bits of the peel. For a smoother or peel-free alternative, peel before cooking or put the cooked potatoes through a food mill or potato ricer instead of using a potato masher.

3 pounds Yukon, red, or new potatoes, cut into large chunks

1½ cups Tahini Sauce (page 210) made with garlic, divided

¼ cup extra-virgin olive oil

1 tablespoon minced garlic

½ teaspoon salt

¼ teaspoon ground black pepper

1 teaspoon paprika, for garnish

3 tablespoons chopped fresh flat-leaf parsley, for garnish

In a large pot, combine the potatoes with enough water to cover. Bring to a boil over high heat. Lower the heat to medium and cook until the potatoes are soft and can easily be pierced through by a fork. (Timing will vary depending on potato size.)

Reserve 1 cup of the cooking liquid. Drain the potatoes, discarding the rest of the water. While the potatoes are still hot, mash with potato masher until somewhat smooth.

Add 1 cup of tahini sauce to the potatoes along with the minced garlic, ½ cup of the reserved potato cooking liquid, olive oil, salt, and pepper and mash until combined. Stir in 6 tablespoons of tahini sauce. If not smooth enough, add more cooking liquid and continue mashing, but be careful not to make the potatoes watery. Taste and add more salt and/or pepper if desired. Keep warm or reheat when ready to serve. Drizzle with the remaining 2 tablespoons of tahini sauce, sprinkle with paprika, and scatter parsley on top. Serve hot.

MAKE IT IN ADVANCE: *Make it up to 2 days in advance and store in an airtight container in the refrigerator.*

OVEN-BAKED GARLIC FRIES

Serves 4

These fries are double cooked, which gives them a crunchy crust and rustic appeal. Not a garlic fan? Skip it (and the parsley too if you want), the fries will still be very satisfying. For extra crunch, I leave the peels on the potatoes.

4 to 5 medium-large russet, Idaho, or large Yukon gold potatoes
½ cup olive oil, plus additional for the baking sheets
1¼ teaspoon salt, divided
½ teaspoon crushed red pepper, optional
3 tablespoons minced garlic
¼ cup chopped fresh flat-leaf parsley

Scrub or peel the potatoes. Cut each potato in half lengthwise. Cut each of those sections into 4 long pieces.

Preheat the oven to 475°F. Oil 2 baking sheets.

Bring a large pot of water and ¼ teaspoon of salt to a boil over high heat. Add the potatoes. Return to simmer and cook until almost tender (a fork should be able to easily pierce potato but meet resistance at the center), 6 to 8 minutes. Timing varies depending on type and thickness of potato. Drain well. (Don't worry if the potatoes have lost a bit of their shape or the skins have begun to separate.)

In a large bowl, combine the potatoes, olive oil, ½ teaspoon of salt, and crushed the red pepper (if using) and gently toss until evenly coated. Wipe out the bowl to use later.

Spread out the coated potatoes in a single layer on the baking sheets. Bake for 25 to 30 minutes, until the bottoms are brown and crispy. Turn the potatoes over with a spatula. Bake for another 12 to 15 minutes, until the fries are brown and crisp on both sides without being burnt.

Place fries in bowl. Toss with the remaining ½ teaspoon of salt or more, if desired, garlic, and parsley and serve hot.

POTATO LATKES

Makes about 24; serves 6 to 8

The word "latke" means "little oily thing" in Yiddish, which is just one aspect of this delicious and crisp potato pancake. Fried foods symbolize the Hanukkah miracle of the oil for the menorah lasting eight days. Latkes evolved from Italian savory pancakes and ricotta cheese pancakes cooked in oil olive. Ashkenazi Jews originally ate latkes (levivot in modern Hebrew) made from vegetables or rye or buckwheat flour cooked in goose or chicken fat. With the arrival of the New World potato, an enduring tradition was begun. For a taste of the past, fry the latkes in chicken fat (schmaltz) or duck fat.

Serve the latkes by themselves with applesauce and/or sour cream sprinkled with green onions or herbs, or serve plain as an accompaniment to saucy dishes such as Pulled Turkey with Pomegranate Molasses (page 65) or one of the brisket or pot roast recipes (see pages 38, 73, or 114). Try them topped with salsa, Z'hug (page 213), or even amba (see page 135) or Yellow Curry Sauce (page 211) or purchased mango chutney.

Some families have a tradition of sprinkling plain latkes with sugar. I think they would also be good drizzled with Pomegranate Molasses (page 212) or silan (see page 25), topped with hummus, or crowned with fried eggs.

2½ pounds Idaho, russet, or Yukon gold potatoes
1 large onion, cut into large chunks
1 teaspoon minced garlic
3 large eggs, beaten
1 teaspoon salt
¼ teaspoon ground black pepper
3 tablespoons flour or ¼ cup matzo meal
Vegetable oil for frying

Hannukah foods

Two types of foods dominate Hanukkah tables, those fried in oil and those made with dairy products. The dairy connection dates back to a fourteenth-century interpretation of the story of Judith and involves her feeding an enemy general salty cheese until he was thirsty then plying him with wine. Once he passed out, Judith cut off his head. The story is no longer associated with Hanukkah but dairy foods are.

Set a wire rack over a pan or line two plates with paper towels.

Scrub the potatoes well or peel them. Using a food processor fitted with the grating attachment, grate the potatoes, alternating with chunks of onions, emptying the work bowl as necessary into a large bowl. (The onions will help keep the potatoes from browning, but if the potatoes do end up turning brown, they will taste just as good.) If grating with a hand grater, combine the batches in a large bowl.

Working over a sink or second bowl, take handfuls of the potatoes and onions and squeeze out as much liquid as you can. Place the wrung-out potatoes and onions in a large dry bowl. Repeat with the remaining shreds.

Change to the food processor's steel blade. Put ⅓ of the potato back in the work bowl and pulse until finely chopped. (If making by hand, chop with a knife.)

Add the chopped potato and onions to the bowl with the shreds. Add the garlic, eggs, salt, and pepper. Sprinkle the flour on top and mix well. Let rest for 10 minutes. Sprinkle in more flour if the batter seems wet and doesn't stick together when compressed. Stir well.

Heat a 10- to 12-inch skillet over medium-high heat. Add ¼-inch oil. Take 3 to 4 tablespoons of batter and, working over a bowl (not the latke batter bowl) to catch drips, squeeze the batter with your hands to form a compact patty 2½ to 3 inches in diameter.

When the oil is hot but not smoking (a shred of potato tossed into the hot oil should sizzle on contact, about 350°F on a deep fry thermometer), use a spatula to gently slide the first 3 to 5 latkes into the pan. Do not crowd them. Adjust the heat as necessary. Press down to flatten with a spatula.

Fry for about 4 minutes until the center of the latke has become firmer, the edges have browned, a spatula can easily be inserted underneath without tearing the latkes, and the bottom is golden brown. Flip it over and cooked until the other side is browned, 3 to 4 minutes. (If a latke falls apart during the flip, use the spatula to pat it back in shape.)

Drain on the prepared rack. Bring the oil back to sizzling and repeat until all the latkes are cooked. If you need to add oil between batches, make sure the oil is sizzling again before cooking.

VARIATION: *Make It Vegan—Omit the eggs and increase the flour or matzo meal by 1 tablespoon or use an egg replacer.*

VARIATION: *Make It Gluten-Free—Replace the flour or matzo meal with potato starch (not potato flour) or one-for-one all-purpose gluten-free flour baking mix.*

MAKE IT IN ADVANCE: *The latkes can be cooled, wrapped, and refrigerated overnight or wrapped individually and frozen for up to 3 months.*

YELLOW RICE

Serves 6 to 8

This simple, spiced rice dish is a great accompaniment to Spice Trade Fish Stew (page 78) or any roast or grilled chicken, fish, or meat dish.

2 cups white basmati rice
2 tablespoons olive oil
1 cup chopped onion
1 tablespoon hawaij for soup or Instant Almost Hawaij (page 216)
3 cups water

Place the rice in a bowl and rinse it in several changes of water until the water runs clear. Cover with warm tap water and let sit for 20 minutes. Drain the rice and set aside.

In a large saucepan, heat the oil over medium-high heat. Add the onion and sauté until golden, 5 to 7 minutes. Add the hawaij and rice and stir until evenly coated. Add the water, stir well, raise the heat to high, and bring to a boil. Cover, lower the heat to low, and simmer for 15 minutes. Remove from the heat and let rest, covered, for 10 minutes. Fluff the rice with a fork before serving warm.

MAKE IT IN ADVANCE: *Place in an airtight container and refrigerate up to 1 day in advance or freeze for up to 3 months.*

RICE PILAF

Serves 6 to 8

This comforting side dish is packed full of vegetables. Because it is not spicy, it makes a great side dish for highly seasoned dishes such as Shawarma Roast Chicken (page 110), or Adana Burgers (page 150). Switch out the bell peppers and eggplant for other favorite vegetables. I like to serve it topped with a Chopped Tomato Salad (page 162), which adds color and a bit of zing.

3 tablespoons olive oil, divided, plus more as needed
1 cup chopped onion
2 teaspoons minced garlic
1 cup chopped red and yellow bell pepper
2 cups chopped eggplant
2 cups long-grain white rice, rinsed
3 to 4½ cups warmed Vegetable Broth (page 197) or purchased
¼ teaspoon salt
¼ teaspoon ground black pepper
Chopped Tomato Salad (page 162), optional

In a large, skillet, heat 2 tablespoons of the olive oil over medium-high heat. Add the onions and sauté until softened and golden, 8 to 10 minutes.

Add the garlic and sauté until golden, 1 to 2 minutes. Add the bell peppers and sauté until they begin to soften, 3 to 5 minutes. Add the remaining 1 tablespoon olive oil and heat for 30 seconds. When the oil is sizzling, add the eggplant and sauté until it begins to soften and lightly brown, 3 to 5 minutes. Add more oil if needed to prevent sticking. Add the rice, stir well to coat in the oil, and sauté for 1 minute. Add 2 cups of the broth, lower the heat to medium-low, and simmer, stirring occasionally, until the broth is absorbed, 10 to 15 minutes. Repeat with another 1 cup of broth.

Once the broth has been absorbed (5 to 10 minutes), bite into a grain of rice to see if it is tender with a little resistance in the center. If the rice is not ready, add 1 cup of broth, and simmer until absorbed. Test again for doneness and, if needed, add broth ¼ cup at a time, letting it absorb before adding more. Taste, and add salt and pepper.

Serve topped with Chopped Tomato Salad (if using).

MAKE IT IN ADVANCE: *The rice can be stored in an airtight container and refrigerated for up to 1 day.*

CHOPPED TOMATO SALAD

Serves 2 to 3 as a salad, or 6 to 8 as a topping

This makes a great side salad, or serve it on top of Rice Pilaf (page 161), Freekah Pilaf (page 152) or any cooked rice or grain.

2 cups chopped red onion
2 cups chopped tomatoes
2 tablespoons chopped fresh flat-leaf parsley
½ teaspoon salt
¼ teaspoon ground sumac or 1 teaspoon minced lemon zest
⅛ teaspoon ground pepper
2 tablespoons extra-virgin olive oil
1 tablespoon fresh lemon juice

In a medium bowl, mix together the onion, tomato, parsley, salt, sumac, black pepper, olive oil, and lemon juice. Taste and adjust seasonings, if desired.

CHARRED GREENS

Serves 4 to 6

Be sure to scrape up any browned bits and stir them into the vegetables as they cook, as that's where a lot of the flavor comes from. To prepare the greens for cooking, wash and shake off moisture, but do not dry. The greens should still be wet when added to the skillet. Hardier greens such as kale or cabbage will take longer to cook than more tender ones such as chard or arugula. If your kale, chard, or other hardier greens have stems, trim off the leaves and chop the stems into ½-inch pieces. Sauté the stems with the onions and proceed with the recipe instructions.

2 tablespoons olive oil
1 cup chopped onions
1 tablespoon minced garlic
1 teaspoon salt
½ teaspoon ground black pepper
½ teaspoon crushed red pepper
10 to 12 cups roughly chopped kale, chard, arugula, dandelion greens, cabbage, or other greens
1 cup water, divided, plus more if needed
¼ teaspoon sugar, optional
1 tablespoon grated lemon zest, optional

In a heavy 12-inch skillet (do not use nonstick), heat the olive oil over medium-high heat. Add the onions and sauté until soft, 7 to 10 minutes.

Add the garlic and sauté until golden, 1 to 2 minutes. Stir in the salt, black pepper, and crushed red pepper. Increase the heat to high. Add one-fourth of the chopped greens and cook, stirring occasionally, until they begin to char or brown. Add another one-fourth of the greens to the pan (leaving the first batch in the pan) and repeat. Repeat with the remaining 2 batches.

Add ½ cup of the water, stir, and cover the pan. Let the greens steam until the pan dries out and the greens are totally wilted and tender, 1 to 2 minutes. If not quite cooked, stir and add the remaining ½ cup water and steam again for 1 to 2 minutes. Check for doneness; repeat, adding a little more water at a time, if needed.

Lower the heat to low and stir the greens. Taste, and if the greens are bitter, add the sugar and stir until combined. Add salt, if desired. Remove from the heat, sprinkle with the lemon zest (if using), and serve.

NORTH AFRICAN CARROT SALAD

Serves 4 to 6

Cooked carrot side dishes, referred to as salads, are common in Morocco and North Africa. They are traditionally served warm or at room temperature, though this take on the classic is also good chilled or hot. Serve on a bed of arugula or other greens for a more substantial side.

1 pound medium carrots, peeled and cut into ⅛-inch rounds
1 teaspoon salt, divided
2 tablespoons extra-virgin olive oil
1 cup chopped onion
2 teaspoons minced garlic
½ teaspoon caraway seeds, optional
½ teaspoon ground cardamom
½ teaspoon dried mint
½ teaspoon paprika
½ teaspoon ground cumin
¼ cup fresh lemon juice
¼ teaspoon sugar, plus more if desired
1 teaspoon grated lemon zest
¼ cup chopped fresh mint, cilantro, or flat-leaf parsley
Harissa (page 214) or other hot sauce

Place the carrots and ½ teaspoon of salt in a saucepan, add enough water to cover, and bring to a simmer over medium heat. Lower the heat to medium-low, stir, cover, and simmer until the carrots are tender but still very crisp in the middle, about 5 minutes. Do not overcook. Drain and set aside.

In a large skillet, heat the oil over medium-high heat. Add the onions and sauté until softened, 5 to 7 minutes.

Add the garlic and sauté until golden, 1 to 2 minutes. Add the caraway seeds (if using) and sauté for 1 minute. Add the cardamom, mint, paprika, cumin, and the remaining ½ teaspoon of salt and sauté for 1 minute. Add the carrots and stir until coated in the oil. Add the lemon juice and sauté until the carrots are heated through, 3 to 5 minutes.

Taste, and add salt or sugar, if desired. Stir in the lemon zest and mint and serve with the harissa. If serving cold, refrigerate in an airtight container until cold. Taste, and adjust the salt and sugar, if desired. Just before serving, stir in the lemon zest and mint, and serve with Harissa at the table.

MAKE IT IN ADVANCE: *Can be made up to 3 days in advance, stored in an airtight container, and refrigerated. Stir in the lemon zest and mint before serving.*

PICKLED RED ONIONS

Makes 1 quart

These versatile quick pickles add a piquant taste to meat, chicken, and vegetable mains. They go great with kebabs and burgers and bring a bit of zing to cheese-based dishes. For a sweeter taste, double the sugar. For less of a vinegar bite, reduce the vinegar to 1½ cups and add ½ cup of water. As the red onions marinate in the vinegar brine, they will become a light pink and the liquid will turn red.

1 pound small or medium red onions, thinly sliced

1 large bay leaf, optional

2 cups apple cider vinegar

1½ teaspoon salt

3 teaspoons whole black peppercorns, lightly crushed

2 tablespoons sugar

Fill a clean 32-ounce glass jar with boiling water and pour the boiling water over the inside of the jar lid. Let sit for 10 minutes.

Empty the water from the jar. Pack the onions tightly into the jar along with the bay leaf (if using).

In a saucepan, mix together the vinegar, salt, peppercorns, and sugar and cook over medium heat, stirring often, until the salt and sugar have dissolved and the liquid is simmering.

Carefully pour the liquid into the jar, covering the onions completely. (If there is not enough liquid, top it off with more vinegar.) Secure the lid and let cool to room temperature. Refrigerate until cold. The onions are ready to eat after 1 hour but the flavor will mature and color deepen when chilled for a few days. The pickled onions can be refrigerated for up to 1 month.

IRAQI-ISRAELI VEGETABLE PICKLES

Makes 1 quart

This is my adaptation of the popular ruby-hued Middle Eastern and Near Eastern vegetable pickles. Its jolt of color and sharp flavor brighten up any meal. For a milder pickle, use 1 cup cooking liquid and 1½ cups of vinegar. You'll need 2 or 3 medium beets, 1 medium large turnip, and about ½ small head of cauliflower for this recipe.

½ pound beets (weight without stems and leaves), scrubbed, trimmed, and peeled
¼ pound turnips (weight without greens), scrubbed, trimmed, and peeled
1 cup (1-inch) cauliflower florets
2 cups of distilled white vinegar
1 teaspoon mustard seeds, lightly crushed
½ teaspoon Sichuan peppercorns (see page 46), lightly crushed, optional
½ teaspoon black peppercorns, lightly crushed
¼ teaspoon coriander seeds, lightly crushed
2 tablespoons salt
2 tablespoons sugar
¼ teaspoon crushed red pepper

Fill a clean 32-ounce glass jar with boiling water and pour additional boiling water over the inside of the jar lid. Set aside.

Cut the beets into 1-by-½-inch sticks. Place the beets in a large saucepan, cover with water, and simmer, covered, over medium heat until the beets are just beginning to soften but are still fairly hard, 5 to 10 minutes.

While the beets are simmering, cut the turnips into 1-by-½-inch sticks. When the beets have begun to soften, add the turnips to the pan. Simmer, covered, until the outsides of the turnips and beets are tender while the interiors still offer resistance when pierced with a fork, 5 to 10 minutes. Remove from the heat.

Strain the vegetables in a colander set over a bowl and set them aside. Reserve the cooking liquid. Carefully pour out the hot water from the glass jar. Put half the cooked vegetables into the jar, pushing down with a spoon to pack them in. Top with half the cauliflower, pressing down with the spoon to pack them in. Repeat, leaving about 1 inch of headroom at the top of the jar.

Add ½ cup of the reserved cooking liquid and the vinegar to the saucepan. Add the mustard seeds, Sichuan peppercorns (if using), black peppercorns, coriander seeds, salt, sugar, and crushed red pepper, and stir well. Bring to a simmer over medium heat and cook, stirring occasionally, until the salt and sugar are dissolved.

Pour the hot liquid into a heat-proof measuring cup with a spout and then pour the hot liquid over the vegetables, filling the jar until the vegetables are covered. If there is not enough liquid, mix 1 part of the remaining cooking liquid with 3 parts vinegar and top off the jar. Let cool, uncovered. Secure the lid and refrigerate until cold.

The pickles are ready to eat once cold, but the taste will mature over a few days. The pickles can be refrigerated for up to 1 month.

TAMARIND OKRA OR ZUCCHINI

Serves 4

Sweet and tangy tamarind paste or concentrate can be found in Middle Eastern, Asian, Latin American, and Indian grocery stores. It is nicely balanced by the salty savoriness of soy sauce in this dish, which complements a wide range of main courses. Use a jarred, seedless tamarind paste or concentrate. The paste is thicker than the concentrate.

Okra is found in Southern, African, Middle Eastern, Near Eastern, and Indian cooking. Choose fresh, green, firm (but not hard or woody) okra from supermarkets, international markets, and produce stores. Okra pods should be 2 to 3 inches long and have tips that can be cleanly snapped off when fresh. When cooked, it should be tender but not mushy. Zucchini is a good substitute.

1 tablespoon plus 1 teaspoon tamarind paste or 1 tablespoon plus 2 teaspoons tamarind concentrate
1 cup warm water, plus more as needed
2 teaspoons sugar or as needed
1 teaspoon soy sauce
2 tablespoons olive oil
2 cups chopped onion
1 tablespoon minced garlic
1 to 2 teaspoons finely chopped fresh bird's eye, jalapeño, or serrano chiles (seeded if desired)
6 cups (½-inch-thick slices) okra or zucchini

In a bowl, mix together the tamarind paste, warm water, sugar, and soy sauce until smooth. Set aside.

In a large skillet, heat the oil over medium-high heat. Add the onion and sauté until golden, 10 to 12 minutes.

Add the garlic and 1 teaspoon of chiles (add more if you like more heat) and sauté until the garlic is golden, 1 to 2 minutes. Add the okra and sauté until the okra is beginning to soften, 3 to 4 minutes.

Stir the tamarind mixture, pour it into the pan, and stir until the okra is covered, adding more water as needed. Continue to cook, stirring occasionally, until the okra is just tender, 4 to 5 minutes. The sauce should be very thick. Serve immediately.

GEFILTE FISH WITH SMASHED TOMATO TOPPING pg. 118

SPINACH AND DILL PHYLLO PIES pg. 126

MIDDLE EASTERN GRILLED CORN pg. 134

ZA'ATAR KEBABS WITH VEGETABLES pg. 142

LAMB HUMMUS BOWL pg. 148 **TAHINI SAUCE** pg. 210

BUNDT CAKE WITH BLACK AND WHITE GLAZES pg. 180

CHALLAH FRITTERS WITH SWEET TAHINI SAUCE pg. 188

FRIDAY NIGHT CHALLAH pg. 204

desserts

FLOURLESS CHOCOLATE BERRY CAKE

Serves 4 as a main course, or 8 as a side dish

This not-too-sweet cake is fudgy and dark with an almost pudding-like interior. It is a dense and gluten-free chocolate cake with a subtle floral note of rose water and the sweet tang of raspberry jam. Rose water can get strong fast, so be sure to taste as you go. It's available in specialty, Middle Eastern, and Indian markets. The cake is worthy of your best-quality chocolate but semi-sweet chocolate chips will work fine. It is very rich when topped with whipped cream. It is suitable for Passover if made with kosher-for-Passover–certified ingredients.

½ cup unsalted butter or vegan stick margarine, plus more for the pan

10 ounces bittersweet or semi-sweet chocolate, chopped

6 large eggs, divided

1¼ cup sugar

1 teaspoon vanilla extract

½ cup unsweetened cocoa

1 cup almond flour

1 cup seedless raspberry jam

½ to 1 teaspoon rose water

3 tablespoons confectioners' sugar or additional unsweetened cocoa, optional

Whipped cream topping, optional (see Note)

Raspberries or sliced strawberries for garnish, optional

Preheat the oven to 400°F. Grease a 9-inch spring form pan with butter. Line the bottom with parchment paper and grease the paper.

Cut the butter into cubes. In a 7- to 8-inch heatproof mixing bowl, combine the butter and chocolate. Put a few inches of water in the bottom of a 5- to 6-inch saucepan and place the bowl over it. Water should not touch the bottom of the bowl. (Or use a double boiler.) Bring the pan of water to a simmer over medium heat. Lower the heat to low and stir occasionally until the mixture is melted and smooth. Turn off the heat, but leave the pan and bowl in place.

Separate 4 eggs. In a medium bowl, whip the whites with an electric hand or stand mixer until stiff peaks form. In a separate bowl, beat the yolks, remaining 2 eggs, the sugar, vanilla, cocoa, and almond flour until smooth. Working in batches, fold the chocolate mixture into the almond flour mixture. Working in batches, gently fold the egg whites into the chocolate mixture. Pour into the prepared pan.

Bake for 35 to 40 minutes, or until the top is somewhat firm and springs back to the touch. (The cake will still be wet and fudgy inside.) Let cool in the pan. Remove the sides, invert onto a plate, and remove the bottom of pan and the parchment. Using a long, serrated knife, gently cut the cake in half horizontally, creating two layers.

In a small bowl, mix together the jam with ½ teaspoon of rose water. Taste, and add additional rose water, if desired. Place one cake layer cut side up on a platter. Spread it with jam, place the second layer on top cut side down. Sprinkle with confectioners' sugar or spread with whipped cream (if using). Decorate with raspberries (if using).

NOTE: *To make whipped cream topping, in a large bowl, whip ½ pint heavy cream with 2 tablespoons sugar and ½ teaspoon rose water with an electric hand or stand mixer until soft peaks form. Taste, and add more rose water, if desired.*

BUNDT CAKE WITH BLACK AND WHITE GLAZES

Makes 1 standard Bundt cake, 18 mini-Bundt cakes, or 24 cupcakes

This slightly lemony cake reminds me of the black-and-white cookies my grandmother used to buy. Use regular confectioners' sugar here—using organic will turn the white glaze gray.

Besides the alternating chocolate and white glazes described in the directions, I sometimes make mini-Bundt cakes and glaze half of them with one glaze and half with the other. Then I drizzle them with the contrasting glaze. I also like the classic black-and-white cookie look where the top of each one is half black and half white. You can also skip the glazes altogether and serve slices of the cake with Sweet Tahini Sauce (page 188).

FOR THE CAKE

¾ cup plus 1 tablespoon vegetable oil, plus more for the pan
3 cups flour, plus more for the pan
1½ teaspoons baking powder
¾ teaspoon salt
2 cups sugar
4 large eggs, beaten
1 cup unsweetened non-dairy milk
2 teaspoons vanilla extract
2 teaspoons lemon extract
1 tablespoon minced lemon zest, optional

FOR THE GLAZES

4 cups confectioners' sugar, divided
¼ to ½ cup boiling water, divided
¼ teaspoon lemon extract
¼ teaspoon vanilla extract
2 ounces semi-sweet or bittersweet chocolate, chopped
1 tablespoon vegetable oil

TO MAKE THE CAKE

Preheat the oven to 350°F. Brush oil all over the inside of a 12-cup Bundt pan, making sure to cover any indentations and the center tube. Sprinkle flour inside the pan and shake it to distribute the flour throughout the interior. Shake out any excess. Do the same if using mini-Bundt pans or cupcake tins without liners.

In a medium bowl, mix together the flour, baking powder, salt, and sugar. Set aside.

In a large bowl, combine the eggs, non-dairy milk, vanilla extract, lemon extract, lemon zest (if using), and oil. Beat with an electric hand or stand mixer on high speed until light, about 2 minutes. Reduce the speed to medium and, with the motor running, add the flour mixture in batches until combined and continue to beat until smooth, 2 to 3 minutes.

Pour the batter into the prepared pan. It should be about two-thirds full. Place the pan on a baking sheet and bake for 50 to 55 minutes, or until the top is set and golden and the sides are pulling away from the Bundt pan. A toothpick inserted into the cake should come out clean.

Let cool in the pan on a wire rack for 5 minutes pan side down. Turn the pan upside down and let cool for another 5 minutes cake side down. Immediately turn the pan over again and, using a spatula or a flexible knife, loosen the cake from the edges of the pan and from around the center tube. Turn the pan over and gently jiggle the pan until the cake is released. If it doesn't release, tap across bottom of the pan and jiggle again. If cake hasn't released from the pan, return it to the warm oven (do not turn it on) and let it sit for 10 minutes. Then repeat the process to remove the cake from the pan.

Let cool completely flat side down on the wire rack. At this point you can glaze the cake or wrap it in plastic wrap and store it at room temperature for up to 2 days.

Brush any crumbs off the top of the cooled cake. Place the cake on a wire rack over a baking sheet to catch drips.

TO MAKE THE WHITE GLAZE

Place 2 cups of confectioners' sugar in a bowl. Slowly stir in 2 tablespoons of the boiling water and stir until smooth. Add the lemon extract, and stir to combine. If the glaze is too thick, gradually add hot water 1 tablespoon at a time and stir constantly until the mixture is thick but still spreadable. If the glaze is too thin, stir in more confectioners' sugar, 1 tablespoon at a time. Immediately spoon or brush the glaze over the top of the cake, making sure the glaze runs down the sides and leaving space to alternate with the chocolate glaze. (If the glaze is not opaque enough on the cake, add a second layer.)

(recipe continues)

TO MAKE THE BLACK GLAZE

Put several inches of water in a 5- to 6-inch saucepan and place 2 cups of confectioners' sugar in a heatproof 5- to 7-inch bowl set over the top, making sure the water does not touch the bowl. (Or use a double boiler.) Stir in 2 tablespoons of the boiling water into the sugar and stir until smooth, When the glaze is thick and spreadable, stir in the vanilla extract. Bring the water in the pan to a simmer over medium heat. Turn the heat to low. Add the chocolate and oil and stir until the chocolate is melted and smooth. Add confectioners' sugar or hot water as needed to make sure the glaze can be spooned or brushed over the cake. Immediately spoon the glaze over the cake, alternating with the white glaze already in place, making sure glaze runs down the sides of the cake.

Cut the cake into slices and serve.

NOTE: *If your Bundt cake tin holds less than 12 cups, bake any excess batter in a cupcake tin.*

VARIATION: *Mini-Bundts—Pour the batter into greased and floured mini-Bundt pans and bake for 30 to 35 minutes. If necessary, bake in batches, letting the pan cool completely and greasing and flouring between batches. Makes about 18. Yield and baking time may vary depending on the capacity of mini-Bundt pans.*

VARIATION: *Cupcakes—Grease and flour or line 2 (12-cup) cupcake pans. Pour in the batter and bake for 18 to 20 minutes. Cool on rack. Remove the liners, if desired.*

MAKE IT IN ADVANCE: *Wrapped airtight, the unglazed cake(s) can be kept at room temperature for up to 2 days and frozen for up to 2 months.*

ONE-PAN BANANA BREAD

Makes 12 slices

This recipe is adapted from one by Dawn Margolin, who makes this recipe regularly for Shabbat dinner (see page 28). She prefers hers without nuts. My husband prefers his without chocolate. I like both, so I split the difference. Pick the variation that works for you. (For all chocolate, omit the walnuts and use 1 cup chocolate chips. For all nuts, leave out the chocolate and use 1 cup walnuts).

The special feature to this cake is that it all mixes in the pan it bakes in. Be sure your bananas are ripe and your pan is well greased. Choose vegan margarine and chocolate for a dairy-free dessert.

½ cup unsalted butter or vegan margarine, melted
1 cup brown sugar
1 cup flour
1 teaspoon baking powder
¼ teaspoon salt (omit if using margarine)
1 large egg, beaten
½ cup chopped walnuts
½ cup semi-sweet chocolate chips
2 large, ripe bananas cut into ¼-inch slices

Preheat the oven to 350°F. Pour the butter into a 5-by-9-inch loaf pan and, using a pastry brush or crumbled paper towel, lightly and completely coat the pan with some of the butter.

Sprinkle the brown sugar on top of the melted butter and mix well. Add the flour, baking powder, and salt. Lightly stir the dry ingredients and then mix in with the butter and sugar. Add the egg and mix well. Add the nuts and chocolate and mix well. Gently stir in the banana slices.

Bake for 40 to 50 minutes, or until browned and the edges are pulling away from pan. The top should spring back when touched. Let cool in the pan. Using a knife, loosen the edges if necessary, cut into slices, and serve directly from the pan or turn out onto a platter.

MANGO AND CARDAMOM MINI CHEESECAKES

Makes 24 individual cheesecakes

These lush mini cheesecakes are popular, easy to make ahead, and are my go-to to-go dessert. The recipe was given to me by my friend Marcia's mom and has evolved over time. She made the original recipe with vanilla wafers and without the cardamom, ginger, or mango purée and topped the cheesecakes with seasonal fresh fruit. Use Philadelphia-style "brick" cream cheese. Make sure it is at room temperature before using.

24 ginger snaps, lemon snaps or wafers, or vanilla wafers

1½ cup fresh or defrosted frozen mango chunks, divided

3 (8-ounce) packages regular or light cream cheese, at room temperature

3 large eggs, beaten

1 cup sugar

½ teaspoon ground cardamom

¼ teaspoon salt

¼ teaspoon ground ginger

1½ teaspoon vanilla extract

1 teaspoon fresh lemon juice

Preheat the oven to 375°F. Line two 12-cup cupcake pans with paper or foil liners. (If you don't have enough tins, use foil cupcake liners on a baking sheet.)

Put a cookie in the bottom of each liner. (Break the cookies to fit and cover the bottom of the liner if necessary.)

In a blender, purée ¾ cup of mango chunks until smooth. Set aside.

Cut the cream cheese into 1-inch chunks. In a large bowl, combine the eggs, sugar, cardamom, salt, ginger, vanilla extract, and lemon juice and beat with an electric hand or stand mixer until light and lemony in color, 1 to 2 minutes. Add the cream cheese chunks in 3 batches, incorporating each batch before adding the next. Beat on medium-high speed until totally smooth, 3 to 4 minutes.

Fill each cupcake liner two-thirds full. Place 1 teaspoon of the mango purée in the center of each cake. Using a knife, swirl the purée through the batter to create a marbleized look.

Bake for 20 minutes, or until the centers of the cheesecakes are a bit loose and jiggly, puffed up, and pale in color. Turn off the oven, open the oven door, and leave the cheesecakes there for 30 minutes. Transfer the cheesecakes to a wire rack and let cool. (The tops of the cakes will collapse.) Place the cheesecakes in the refrigerator until chilled.

To serve, remove the cheesecakes from the liners, if desired. Chop the remaining ¾ cup of mango and spoon it onto the cheesecakes. Serve cold or cool.

MAKE IT IN ADVANCE: *Wrap the cooled cheesecakes well and refrigerate without the topping for up to 3 days or freeze for up to 3 months. If freezing, use foil iners. Defrost them in their wrappings in the refrigerator before serving.*

TWICE-BAKED LEMON COOKIES

Makes 2 dozen cookies

Call them biscotti, mandelbrot, biscochadas dulces, or almond rusks, these cookies have roots in twice-baked cookie traditions from around the world. The cookies are crunchy, not too sweet, and they have a citrus twist. They are good by themselves, alongside ice cream, Fruit Juice Sorbet (page 191), or dunked in tea, coffee, milk, or even a sweet wine. They crisp as they cool and taste even better the next day.

Vegetable oil for the baking sheets
2 large eggs
⅔ cup sugar
1½ teaspoons lemon extract
½ teaspoon almond extract
2 tablespoons grated lemon zest
¼ cup extra-virgin olive oil
1⅔ cups flour, plus more as needed
1 teaspoon baking powder
¼ teaspoon salt
1 cup sliced or chopped almonds

Preheat the oven to 325°F. Grease 2 baking sheets with vegetable oil.

Put the eggs and sugar in a mixing bowl and beat with an electric hand or stand mixer on high speed until pale yellow and thickened, 1 to 2 minutes. Add the lemon extract, almond extract, lemon zest, and olive oil and beat until combined.

In a separate bowl, mix together the flour, baking powder, and salt. Slowly add the flour mixture to the eggs in 3 batches and beat on medium speed, making sure each batch is combined before adding the next, until smooth, about 2 minutes. Using a spoon, stir in the almonds. The mixture will be very stiff (if not, add more flour 1 tablespoon at a time, until the dough is stiff enough to maintain shape and not spread).

Sprinkle 1 to 2 tablespoons of flour on a clean, dry work surface. The dough will be sticky, so wet or oil your hands. Shape the dough into 2 loaves, each about 10 inches long, 1½ inches wide and 1 inch tall. Transfer each loaf to the center of one of the prepared baking sheets. (If the loaf cracks or becomes misshapen, pat it back into shape. Using two spatulas to transfer helps.)

Bake for 25 minutes, or until golden and the top has small cracks. Leave the oven on. Transfer the pans to a wire rack and let cool for a few minutes, until just cool enough to handle. Transfer the loaves to a cutting board and cut them into ¾-inch slices. Arrange the slices flat side down on the same baking sheets.

Bake for 15 minutes. Transfer the pans to the wire rack and let cookies cool in the pan. The slices will become crunchier as they cool.

MAKE IT IN ADVANCE: *The cookies can be stored in an airtight container at room temperature for up to 5 days or wrapped tightly in plastic wrap and frozen for up to 3 months.*

CHOCOLATE AND COOKIE TRUFFLES

Makes twelve 1-inch truffles

I first had a version of these at a falafel restaurant in California and they called these no-bake treats "chocolate falafel," referring more to their round shape than the ingredients or technique since no chickpeas or deep frying were involved. I later learned they are popular in Israel as kadorei shokolad.

My take uses a chocolate-nut spread and graham crackers. It's a great project for young children. Choose from the toppings listed or find your own favorites. The amount shown for each is enough to generously coat 12 truffles. Adjust quantities if using multiple toppings.

For vegans, use a non-dairy chocolate spread. Roll the truffles in your choice of toppings. Sub out any plain or vanilla flavored sturdy cookie for the graham crackers.

3½ ounces (6 whole sheets) of graham crackers
¾ cup purchased chocolate-hazelnut or chocolate-almond spread
¼ teaspoon almond extract
⅛ teaspoon ground cinnamon
Vegetable oil for your hands

TOPPINGS (CHOOSE 1)

1 cup finely chopped nuts
¾ cup finely shredded dried unsweetened coconut
¼ cup confectioners' sugar
¼ cup unsweetened cocoa powder
¼ cup ground cinnamon
¼ cup pumpkin pie or chai masala spice

In a food processor, process the graham crackers into fine crumbs. Alternatively, you can place the crackers in a heavy-duty zip-top plastic bag, lay it flat on a sturdy cutting board, and bash with a meat mallet, hammer, or rolling pin.

In a bowl, mix together the chocolate spread, almond extract, and cinnamon. Add 1 cup of the graham cracker crumbs and mix until well combined. Try forming a 1-inch ball. If the mixture does not hold its shape, add more crumbs as needed.

Oil your hands and roll the mixture into twelve 1-inch balls. Roll the balls in your choice of topping(s). Serve immediately, or place them in an airtight container, separating the layers with waxed paper, and refrigerate until ready to use. Serve chilled or let sit at room temperature for about 20 minutes before serving.

MAKE IT IN ADVANCE: *The truffles can be made up to 4 days in advance. Store in an airtight container in the refrigerator.*

RAISIN AND ALMOND TWIRLS

Makes 12 twirls

In Judaism, almonds are a symbol of hope, prosperity, happiness, and fertility, while raisins are a symbol of the sweetness of life. With lots of flaky phyllo layers and a shape and filling a bit like a strudel, this dessert complements a variety of menus. For more on using phyllo dough, see the Mushroom and Cheese Strudels on page 98. The cooled roll can be stored at room temperature for up to 2 days. Cut into slices before serving.

1 cup Pomegranate Molasses (page 212) or purchased
½ cup water
1 teaspoon grated lemon zest
1 tablespoon fresh lemon juice
4 tablespoons sugar, divided
¼ teaspoon salt
2 cups raw whole almonds, toasted and roughly chopped
2 cups raisins
4 tablespoons almond flour, divided
½ cup oil, divided
5 (13-by-17-inch) sheets phyllo dough, at room temperature
½ cup semi-sweet or white chocolate chips

In a large saucepan, combine the pomegranate molasses, water, lemon zest, lemon juice, 3 tablespoons of sugar, and salt and bring to a simmer over medium-low heat. Cook, stirring occasionally, for 5 minutes. Stir in the almonds, raisins, and 2 tablespoons almond flour and simmer, stirring occasionally, for 5 minutes. Set aside.

Preheat the oven to 350°F. Line a baking sheet with parchment and brush with oil.

Place 1 phyllo sheet on a work surface with a long side closest to you. Brush it lightly with oil. Place a second sheet on top and brush it lightly with oil. Repeat with the third and fourth sheets. Top with the fifth sheet but do not oil. Sprinkle the top sheet with 2 tablespoons of almond flour.

About 2 inches from the long end nearest you, spread a 3-inch-wide ribbon of the filling, leaving a 1-inch border along the short ends. Scatter with the chocolate chips.

The rolling resembles making a burrito. Fold in the phyllo sheet's short sides 1 inch at either end toward the filling. (Folded up ends will overlap the edges of filling.) Roll the strudel starting from the long end, at the 2-inch margin closest to the filling. Compress and turn as you roll up, creating a compact roll. Place it seam side down on the prepared baking sheet. Brush the top and sides of the roll with oil and sprinkle with 1 tablespoon of sugar. Score the roll into 12 even pieces, cutting about one-third of the way through the roll and making sure not to cut all the way through.

Bake for 30 to 35 minutes, or until golden. Let cool completely. Cut the roll into sections at the score lines and serve.

CHALLAH FRITTERS WITH SWEET TAHINI SAUCE

Makes about 40 fritters

The fritters are about the size of dough-nut holes and are perfect for Hanukkah. It's also a great use for day-old or stale challah. The recipe halves well.

FOR THE FRITTERS

1 (1-pound) loaf plain challah
4 large eggs, beaten
1 cup milk or unsweetened non-dairy milk
1½ cups mashed ripe bananas
½ cup sugar
1 teaspoon ground cinnamon
½ teaspoon ground nutmeg
¼ teaspoon salt
½ teaspoon vanilla extract
Vegetable oil for frying
Confectioners' sugar or cinnamon sugar, optional
Homemade or purchased chocolate sauce, warmed, optional

FOR THE SWEET TAHINI SAUCE

½ cup tahini (stir in the jar before measuring)
¼ cup cold water, plus more as needed
2 tablespoons fresh lemon juice
⅛ teaspoon salt
3 to 4 tablespoons agave syrup
2 teaspoons silan (see page 25), optional

TO MAKE THE FRITTERS

Shred the challah into ¼-inch pieces and place them in a large bowl.

In a separate large bowl, mix together the eggs, milk, bananas, sugar, cinnamon, nutmeg, salt, and vanilla. Add the shredded challah and stir until well combined. Cover with plastic wrap and refrigerate for 20 minutes. Stir well.

Wet your hands. Using your hands, roll about 1 tablespoon of batter into a ball. Press it together firmly and roll it again, squeezing to compact it into a firm ball about 1 inch in diameter. Place it on a plate. Repeat with the remaining batter.

In a 12-inch wide, heavy pot, heat ½ inch of oil over high heat to 350°F (for best results, use a deep-fry or candy thermometer, but the oil is ready when a bit of fritter batter bubbles as soon as it is added to the pan). Line a large plate with paper towels.

Roll the fritters between your hands to make sure they are compact, then gently roll them off your hand and into the hot oil until you have 8 to 10 in the pot, being careful not to crowd the pan. Adjust the heat as needed to maintain the proper temperature and prevent burning, and cook until the bottoms of the fritters are dark golden brown, 2 to 3 minutes. Flip the fritters with a slotted metal spoon or tongs and cook until the other side is browned, 1 to 2 minutes. Transfer the fritters to the prepared plate using tongs or slotted spoon. Add oil as needed and be sure to return the oil to the proper temperature between batches. (If desired, keep the fritters warm in a 250°F oven on an ungreased baking sheet.)

TO MAKE THE SWEET TAHINI SAUCE

In a medium bowl, mix together the tahini, cold water, lemon juice, salt, and 3 tablespoons of the agave syrup until very smooth (the mixture will seize up but loosen as you continue to stir). Add water 1 tablespoon at a time until the sauce is still thick but can be poured. Taste, and add more agave syrup, if desired. Transfer to a serving dish, drizzle with silan, if using.

Sprinkle the fritters with confectioners' sugar (if using) and serve with the sweet tahini sauce and warmed chocolate sauce (if using), on the side for dipping.

VARIATION: *Jam Challah "Doughnut Holes"—Omit the bananas, cinnamon, nutmeg, salt, and vanilla. Stir in 1 cup seedless fruit preserves or jam and proceed with the recipe instructions. Serve sprinkled with confectioners' sugar and with warmed chocolate sauce.*

MAKE IT IN ADVANCE: *The fritters can be made 1 day in advance, stored in an airtight container, and refrigerated. The Sweet Tahini Sauce can be made 2 days in advance without the silan and stored in an airtight container in the refrigerator.*

TURKISH COCONUT PUDDING

Serves 6

Sutlach or sütlaç (sutlag in Ladino, the traditional language used by many Sephardic Jews) is such a part of Turkish Jewish culture and celebrations it even appears in a Jewish fairy tale about a maiden in disguise. She reveals her true identity by hiding a ring in a bowl of sutlach she makes for a prince. My version is vegan and gluten-free. I suggest some garnishes but others you can try include rose or fruit-flavored syrups or jams, ground cinnamon, slivered almonds, honey, chopped dried dates or apricots, and fresh berries.

3 (13½-ounce) cans full-fat coconut milk

⅔ cup white rice flour or unflavored cream of rice cereal (not instant)

¼ cup plus 3 tablespoons sugar

⅛ teaspoon salt

¼ teaspoon ground cardamom

2 tablespoons orange blossom water, optional

¼ cup plus 2 tablespoons toasted coconut chips or large, unsweetened shreds

¼ cup plus 2 tablespoons shelled pistachios

¼ cup plus 2 tablespoons pomegranate seeds

Shake the coconut milk cans very thoroughly, remove the lids, and pour them into a large pitcher or jar. Use a spoon to scrape out any liquid or solids that remain in the cans. Stir or whisk well until the mixture is somewhat smooth (if necessary, place the pitcher in a bowl of hot tap water to speed the process). Break up any large chunks and mash them into the mixture. It is okay if the milk is still a bit lumpy.

In a large saucepan, combine the rice flour, sugar, and salt. Slowly add 1 cup of coconut milk while stirring until a relatively smooth paste forms. Slowly stir in the remaining coconut milk. Place the pan over medium heat and cook, stirring constantly, until the mixture is bubbling and has begun to thicken, 9 to 10 minutes.

Lower the heat to low, add the cardamom, and cook, stirring often, until bubbling, thickened, and there is no raw taste, 4 to 5 minutes. Stir in the orange blossom water (if using) and pour the mixture into serving dishes.

Garnish with coconut chips, pistachios, and pomegranate seeds and serve immediately. You can also press plastic wrap against the top of the pudding before garnishing and refrigerate until cold. Garnish and serve chilled or at room temperature.

MAKE IT IN ADVANCE: *The plastic-wrapped pudding dishes can be refrigerated for up to 3 days.*

FRUIT JUICE SORBET

Serve 6 to 8

This sorbet can be made with or without an ice cream maker. Allow time for the sugar syrup to chill before making. Sorbet made in an ice cream maker may need a half hour or so to harden in the freezer before using. If you are making this without an ice cream maker, plan for 4 to 6 hours for the sorbet to freeze.

I've made this with orange, tangerine, lemon, mango, and many other juices. Use fresh squeezed or juiced fruit or purchased fresh, refrigerated juice. Try adding 1 tablespoon of chopped fresh herbs, such as basil or rosemary, or grated fresh ginger to the simmering water and sugar for an added level of flavor. Strain the mixture after chilling and before adding the syrup. If you are not using an ice cream maker, chill a 2- to 3-inch-deep, 8-inch-square metal baking pan in advance for faster freezing.

1¼ cups water
1¼ cups sugar
1½ cups cold orange, lemon, or other fruit juice
2 tablespoons fresh lime juice or as needed

(recipe continues)

In a saucepan, combine the water and sugar and bring to a simmer over medium heat, stirring occasionally, until the sugar is dissolved. Refrigerate the mixture until chilled, 2 to 3 hours. (Can be made and refrigerated up to 5 days in advance.)

In a bowl, combine 1½ cups of the sugar syrup and fruit juice, and lime juice. Stir well and taste. Add up to ½ cup more of sugar syrup if needed. (Coldness dulls the sweet flavor, so the sorbet base should taste a bit sweeter than you would normally prefer.) Add more lime juice for a tarter flavor. (If you have syrup leftover, keep in the refrigerator for up to 1 month. It can be used as a base for cocktails or as a sweetener for cold drinks.)

If using an ice cream maker, freeze according to the manufacturer's instructions. After churning, the sorbet will be soft. Serve immediately or pack it into an airtight container and freeze for 30 to 60 minutes to harden. Once the sorbet freezes completely, make sure to remove it from the freezer 10 to 20 minutes before you want to serve it for easiest scooping. The sorbet can be made and frozen up to 3 days in advance.

If not using an ice cream maker, pour the mixture into a 2-to-3-inch-deep, 8-inch-square chilled metal baking pan. Cover with plastic wrap and place it in a flat spot in the freezer for 1 hour. Using a fork, break up any ice clumps and stir the sorbet. Return to the freezer for 2 hours. Stir again. Freeze for 2 more hours and stir. Remove from freezer a few minutes before serving. Break up any ice clumps with a wooden spoon (or scrape a fork across the top of the sorbet to turn the sorbet into crystals), scoop, and serve.

fundamentals

CHICKEN BROTH

Makes about 3 quarts

Broth is truly a building block for Jewish cooking. You'll find it as a base ingredient in everything from rice dishes to stews to soups, including the iconic Ashkenazi Chicken Soup with Matzo Balls (page 196). Use this broth for any recipe that calls for chicken broth. I use a whole raw chicken and lots of root vegetables to give the broth a deep flavor. I like the peppery sharpness the turnip gives the broth. Leave it out or substitute celeriac, parsley root, or kohlrabi. The onion peels and saffron help give the soup its golden hue.

For the best color and taste, don't let the broth come to a full boil. To reduce fat, make the broth the day before and refrigerate. When chilled, skim off the fat. (Discard or save it and use for frying or sautéing.)

1 (4½-to-5-pound) whole chicken

12 cups water, plus additional water as needed

3 medium carrots, cut into 1-inch chunks

1 large unpeeled parsnip, cut into 1-inch chunks

1 medium-large unpeeled onion, rinsed and cut in quarters

1 large unpeeled turnip, cut into 1-inch chunks

3 large celery stalks with leaves, cut into 1-inch chunks

4 large garlic cloves, peeled and smashed

1-inch piece fresh ginger, unpeeled and cut in half

1 large leek

Bunch of fresh flat-leaf parsley

1 large bay leaf

1 tablespoon grated lemon zest

½ teaspoon whole black peppercorns

½ teaspoon salt, plus more if desired

⅛ teaspoon saffron threads

Remove the internal organs and any excess fat from inside the chicken and discard. (Save the neck if available.) Be sure all bits of deep red tissue are removed from inside the chicken (they can turn a broth bitter). Rinse the chicken inside and out, being careful not to splatter work surfaces.

Place the chicken (with neck if available) in a large, deep pot, add the water, adding more if needed to cover, and bring to a simmer over medium heat. Add the carrots, parsnip, onion, turnip, celery, garlic, and ginger and stir.

Trim the roots and deep green tips off the leek. Cut it in half lengthwise and rinse well to remove any sand or soil. Cut the halves into 1-inch pieces and add to the pot. Add the parsley, bay leaf, lemon zest, peppercorns, and salt and bring back to a simmer. Crumble the saffron into the pot, cover, and keep it at a simmer, lowering the heat if necessary, to prevent it from coming to a rapid boil.

Simmer for 3 to 4 hours, stirring occasionally and skimming off any foam that might form, until the chicken is falling off the bone, the vegetables are soft, and the broth tastes rich and full of flavor. Add more salt if desired. Let cool.

Strain the broth into a large container. Taste the chicken meat. If it still has good texture and flavor, shred it and use it to make Chicken Soup with Matzo Balls (page 196). If it is tasteless or dry, discard it along with the other solids.

TO PRESSURE-COOK (STOVETOP OR ELECTRIC PRESSURE COOKER OR MULTI-COOKER)

For pots 8 quarts or larger, use a 4½- to 5-pound chicken and 12 cups water. For 6-quart pots, use a 3½- to 4-pound chicken and 8 to 9 cups of water. Reduce the other ingredients by about one-third. Do not overfill.

Combine the chicken, water, vegetables, and seasonings (except the salt and lemon zest) to the pot. Add 1/4 teaspoon of salt. Seal the pressure cooker. For stovetop cookers, put on high heat. Once it reaches high pressure, cook for 35 minutes (adjust the heat up or down to maintain pressure). For electric pressure cookers or the pressure function of multi-cookers, cook for 40 minutes on high pressure (or follow manufacturer's directions). Let the pressure release naturally and let the broth cool. Strain. Taste, and stir in lemon zest and additional salt, if desired. The yield may vary.

SLOW COOKER OR MULTI-COOKER

Make adaptations for the chicken size and ingredients (including reducing salt and eliminating the zest) as described in the Pressure Cooker variation. Add the ingredients to the slow cooker, cover, and cook on low for 8 to 10 hours in a slow cooker or 9 to 11 hours in a multi-cooker, until golden, rich tasting, and full flavored. Strain. Taste, and stir in additional salt, if desired. Proceed with the recipe.

MAKE IT IN ADVANCE: *The broth can be made up to 3 days in advance, stored in an airtight container and refrigerated. Freeze for up to 6 months.*

Troubleshooting

• If the broth is too salty, cut a large, scrubbed, unpeeled potato in half and simmer in the strained broth until soft. Discard the potato. It should absorb some of the excess salt. Repeat if necessary.

• If the broth is slightly watery tasting, simmer the strained broth for 20 minutes over low heat until it reduces to concentrate the flavors. You can also poach 1 pound of boneless chicken (or 1½ to 2 pounds skin-on bone-in chicken) in the strained simmering broth until

it's cooked through, 15 to 35 minutes. Remove the chicken and save it to make soup or for another use. Taste and adjust the seasonings. Strain the broth again before proceeding.

• To brighten the flavor without adding more salt, stir in 1 tablespoon of fresh lemon juice. Taste and add more, if desired.

• If the broth is not "golden" enough, add ¼ teaspoon of turmeric to the simmering, strained broth.

CHICKEN SOUP WITH MATZO BALLS

Serves 8 as a starter

Chicken soup is more than physical sustenance. It is the essence of Jewish soul, probably the ultimate food for meal-based celebrations. From Shabbat dinner to the High Holiday table and from Brooklyn to India, a bowl of rich, fragrant chicken soup has become a defining part of the global Jewish kitchen.

Chicken Broth (page 194)
1 leek
1 medium parsnip, peeled and chopped
3 medium carrots, peeled and chopped
1 large turnip, peeled and chopped
2 large celery stalks, chopped
16 cooked Matzo Balls (page 199), at room temperature, or 3 cups cooked rice, pasta, or noodles

2 to 3 cups cooked shredded chicken
½ teaspoon salt, optional
½ teaspoon ground black pepper, optional
1 tablespoon fresh lemon juice, optional
½ cup finely chopped fresh dill or flat-leaf parsley or a combination of the two

If the chicken broth is chilled, skim off fat, if desired. (Leaving some fat makes a richer soup.) Put the broth in a large pot and bring to a simmer over medium heat (do not let it come to a rapid boil).

While the broth comes to a simmer, trim the roots and deep green tips off the leek. Cut it in half lengthwise and rinse well to remove any sand or soil and chop. Add the parsnips, carrots, turnip, leek, and celery to the simmering broth, and cook until the vegetables are just starting to soften, 6 to 8 minutes.

Add the matzo balls (or cooked rice or noodles) and shredded chicken, stir to combine, and simmer until heated through, the vegetables are cooked, and the soup is hot, 15 to 20 minutes. Taste, and add salt, pepper, and lemon juice (if using). Serve in bowls topped with dill.

VEGETABLE BROTH

Makes about 3 quarts

A rich, full-tasting vegan alternative to chicken broth. Use this in the Vegetable Soup with Matzo Balls (page 198) as well as in the Hawaij Vegetable Soup (page 104). You'll also see vegetable broth called for in many stews, pilafs, and other dishes.

2 medium onions, unpeeled, rinsed, and cut in quarters

8 large garlic cloves, peeled and smashed

1 large leek, trimmed and cut into 1-inch pieces

3 medium carrots, cut in 1-inch chunks

1 large unpeeled parsnip, cut in 1-inch chunks

1 large unpeeled potato, cut in 1-inch chunks

1 large unpeeled turnip, cut in 1-inch chunks

12 small white or brown mushrooms, trimmed and cut in half

3 large stalks celery, with leaves, cut in 1-inch pieces

3 medium tomatoes, halved

1 large bay leaf

½-inch piece fresh ginger root, unpeeled and cut in half, optional

1 tablespoon grated lemon zest

1 bunch fresh flat-leaf parsley

About 12 cups water

1 teaspoon salt, divided, plus more if desired

½ teaspoon whole black peppercorns

½ teaspoon ground black pepper, divided, plus more if desired

¼ teaspoon ground turmeric

In a large pot, combine the onion, garlic, leek, carrots, parsnip, potato, turnip, mushrooms, celery, tomatoes, bay leaf, ginger root, lemon zest, and parsley. Add the water or enough to cover, about 12 cups, and stir. Add ½ teaspoon salt, the peppercorns, ¼ teaspoon of black pepper, and the turmeric, stir, and bring to a boil over medium-high heat. Cover, lower the heat to medium-low and simmer until the vegetables are soft and the broth is full tasting, 30 to 45 minutes. If the broth is too strong, add some water. If the broth is too weak, remove the cover, return to a boil, and cook until the liquid is reduced and the broth has the desired strength. Taste and add remaining ½ teaspoon salt and ¼ teaspoon black pepper, plus more, if desired. Strain the broth into a large bowl, pressing down on the vegetables to extract the liquid. Discard the solids. Return the broth to the pot and return to a simmer.

MAKE IT IN ADVANCE: *The broth can be made up to 5 days in advance, stored in airtight containers, and refrigerated or frozen for up to 6 months.*

VEGETABLE SOUP WITH MATZO BALLS

Serves 8 as a starter

Vegetable soup is not just an alternative to chicken soup, it is delicious and filling in its own right. For a main-course vegetable soup, add 3 to 4 cups of cooked white beans or chickpeas with the matzo balls. For a vegan soup, use the cooked rice or pasta instead of the matzo balls.

Vegetable Broth (page 197)
1 leek
1 medium parsnip, peeled and chopped
3 medium carrots, peeled and chopped
1 large turnip, peeled and chopped
2 large celery stalks, chopped
2 cups thinly sliced brown or white
  mushrooms

16 cooked Matzo Balls (page 199), at room
  temperature or 2 to 3 cups cooked rice,
  pasta, or noodles
½ teaspoon salt, optional
½ teaspoon ground black pepper, optional
1 tablespoon fresh lemon juice, optional
½ cup finely chopped fresh dill and/or flat-
  leaf parsley

Bring the broth to a simmer in a large soup pot over medium heat. While the broth is coming to a simmer, trim the roots and deep green tips off the leek. Cut it in half lengthwise and rinse well to remove any sand or soil. Cut the halves into 1-inch pieces. Once the broth is simmering, add the leeks, parsnips, carrots, turnip, celery, and mushrooms to the broth and return to a simmer. Stir and cover until the vegetables are just tender, 6 to 8 minutes.

Add the matzo balls (or cooked pasta, noodles or rice) and return to a simmer, adjusting the heat if needed, and cook until the soup is hot and the vegetables and matzo balls are heated through, about 15 minutes. Taste, and add salt, pepper, and lemon juice (if using). Ladle the soup into bowls and sprinkle with dill and/or parsley.

MATZO BALLS

Makes 20 to 22 dumplings

Everyone who has ever eaten a matzo ball seems to have an opinion on the appropriate ingredients and technique, and as to whether the matzo balls (also known as knaidlach) should be light and fluffy (floaters) or dense and chewy (sinkers). Positions are taken young and kept for life. This basic matzo ball recipe is adapted from my husband's late Aunt Betty, and falls into the floaters category.

4 large eggs, separated
⅓ cup vegetable oil, plus more if needed
½ cup plain seltzer or water

½ teaspoon salt, divided
¼ teaspoon ground black pepper
1 cup matzo meal

All about matzo balls

• Taste your matzo meal before using. If it tastes stale or rancid, your matzo balls will, too.

• Leave time for the batter to chill for easier matzo ball shaping.

• Handle the dough as little as possible if you want fluffy matzo balls. Allow room in the pot for them to expand. The balls will be a little rough looking but very tender inside.

• Compact the batter into smooth, round balls if you want picture-perfect, pleasantly chewy matzo balls. Put more in the pot to allow less room to expand.

• Choose your fat. Using neutral-tasting oil probably gives the fluffiest results. Slightly cooled, melted chicken schmaltz (commercially available or homemade rendered chicken fat) or the fat left over from skimming the chilled chicken broth adds a lot of taste, but be careful not to over handle the dough if you want floaters.

• Select the right liquid to mix in. Water is fine, but legions of Jewish cooks (including me) swear that plain, unflavored seltzer water (not sparkling mineral water or club soda) makes for lighter and fluffier knaidlach. Strained chicken or vegetable broth adds flavor.

• Cook matzo balls in simmering—not boiling—water. Intense boiling can break apart the dumplings. If doubling the recipe, be sure to use multiple pots or simmer in batches.

• Bring matzo balls to room temperature before reheating in simmering soups or water.

(recipe continues)

Lightly grease a large plate with oil and put in the refrigerator to chill. Place 2 wire racks over 2 baking sheets.

In a small bowl, whisk together the egg whites until foamy, about 1 minute. In a large bowl, beat the egg yolks until combined. Add the oil, seltzer, ½ teaspoon of salt, and the pepper to the yolks and mix well. Slowly stir in the matzo meal with a fork until well combined. Fold in one-third of the egg whites and stir until incorporated. Fold in another one-third of the egg whites and stir. Add the remaining third and gently stir to make sure everything is combined. Cover with plastic wrap and refrigerate for at least 2 hours or overnight. The batter will thicken as it chills.

Fill 1 or 2 large pots with water and ½ teaspoon salt and bring to a boil over medium-high heat. (Because you are making floaters, cook in 2 pots or in batches to avoid overcrowding. You should be able to cook 10 or 11 matzo balls at a time in a 12-inch diameter pot.)

Wet or oil your hands and gently shape the mixture into 1-inch rough balls, being careful not to over handle or compress the dough. Place them on the chilled plate. To cook, gently drop the balls into the simmering water. Once the water has returned to a simmer and the matzo balls are floating on top, cover and keep at a simmer for 30 to 45 minutes. After 30 minutes of simmering, check for doneness by cutting 1 matzo ball in half. There should be no raw spots. A fluffy dumpling should be a uniformly creamy white inside. A denser matzo ball will be more compact and darker, but still uniform. Both types should taste cooked through. Remove the balls with a slotted spoon and place them on the wire racks to drain.

NOTE: *The floaters expand to double or triple the size you make them, so be careful to adjust the size of the shaped balls as needed. Cooking times will also vary.*

VARIATION: *Sinkers (chewy and denser matzo balls)—Do not separate the eggs. In a large bowl, beat the eggs until combined. Reduce the oil to ¼ cup. Instead of seltzer, use water or chicken broth and reduce the amount to 3 tablespoons. Mix all the ingredients with the beaten eggs. Form them into firm balls and cook them in one pot of simmering salted water. Cooking time may vary. Matzo balls will not expand as much as floaters but they will still increase in size.*

VARIATION: *Herbed Matzo Balls—Follow the main floater recipe or the sinker variation and add ¼ cup finely chopped parsley, 2 tablespoons finely chopped dill, and 2 tablespoons finely chopped chives or green onions to the batter with the matzo meal.*

VARIATION: *Jalapeño and Cilantro Matzo Balls—Follow the Herbed Matzo Balls directions, using ¼ cup minced cilantro or parsley, 1 teaspoon minced jalapeño (seeded for milder taste), and 2 tablespoons minced green onions.*

MAKE IT IN ADVANCE: *The matzo balls can be made up to 3 days in advance, stored in airtight containers, separated with layers of oiled wax paper, and refrigerated. They can also be frozen in a single layer on a baking sheet and then stored in an airtight container or plastic bag in the freezer for up to 3 months.*

PEPPERS, EGGPLANT, AND ONIONS
IN TOMATO SAUCE

Serves 4 to 6

My Grandma Clara was Italian-Hungarian Jewish and this recipe is influenced by her Italian-style tomato sauce and lecsó, a Hungarian paprika–laden stew of peppers and onions. Despite 2 tablespoons of paprika, the dish is not very spicy, so add the crushed red pepper for more heat. Use it on its own or with the Make-Ahead Meatballs (page 112) over pasta or polenta, or wherever a flavorful tomato sauce would be an asset.

2 tablespoons vegetable oil, plus more as needed
4 cups chopped onion
1 tablespoon minced garlic
2 teaspoon salt
2 tablespoons paprika
¼ to ½ teaspoon crushed red pepper, optional

1 teaspoon dried oregano
4 cups (½-inch pieces) chopped eggplant
4 cups (½-inch pieces) chopped red or yellow bell peppers
1 (28-ounce) can crushed tomatoes
1 teaspoon sugar
¼ cup water, plus more as needed
1 tablespoon olive oil

In a Dutch oven or large pot, heat the oil over medium-high heat. Add the onion and sauté until softened and translucent, 5 to 7 minutes.

Add the garlic and sauté until golden, 1 to 2 minutes. Add the salt, paprika, crushed red pepper (if using), and oregano and sauté for 1 minute. Add the eggplant and sauté until it is lightly browned and softened, adding more oil if needed, 7 to 10 minutes. Add the peppers and sauté until they begin to soften, about 5 minutes. Stir in the tomatoes with their juices, sugar, and water and bring to a simmer, stirring occasionally. Cover, lower the heat to medium-low and keep at a simmer, stirring occasionally, until the vegetables are tender (but not mushy) and the flavors are blended, about 20 minutes. Stir in the olive oil and simmer, uncovered, for a few minutes, until the sauce is the consistency of a very thick pasta sauce, but not at all dry (add water as needed).

MAKE IT IN ADVANCE: *The sauce can be refrigerated in an airtight container for 3 days or frozen for up to 3 months.*

REAL DEAL CHOPPED CHICKEN LIVER

Serves 8 to 10

This is the type of chopped liver I grew up with, coarsely chopped where in every luscious mouthful the punch of liver is brightened by salt and smoothed by chicken fat, caramelized onion, and hard-boiled egg. I do play with tradition by adding a pinch of cayenne pepper, garlic, and a splash of sweetened Concord grape wine (the stuff that's traditional for Friday night blessings for many American Jews). Substitute Concord grape juice or 1 tablespoon Pomegranate Molasses (page 212) mixed with 1 tablespoon of water.

Broiling the livers replicates the taste of old-fashioned chopped liver but may not qualify as properly kashering the livers. (See But Is It Kosher? page 12) Adjust the recipe if that is a concern.

¼ cup chicken schmaltz, vegetable oil, or vegetable shortening, plus more if desired

2 pounds onions, thinly sliced

2 teaspoons minced garlic

1 teaspoon salt, divided

2 pounds chicken livers

1 teaspoon Diamond Crystal kosher salt (see Kosher Salt, page 17)

4 large hard-boiled eggs, peeled and roughly mashed

2 tablespoons sweetened kosher Concord grape wine, plus more if desired

½ teaspoon ground black pepper, plus more if desired

¼ teaspoon cayenne pepper

In a large skillet, heat the schmaltz over medium-high heat until it's liquid. Add the onions and sauté, stirring occasionally, until they begin to color, 10 to 12 minutes. Add the garlic and ½ teaspoon salt and stir until combined. Lower the heat to medium-low and cook, stirring occasionally, until the onions are caramelized (add more schmaltz as needed) and they have a deep, rich bronze color, are very soft, and have a slightly sweet taste, 30 to 40 minutes. Remove one-third of the onions, chop them roughly, place in a container, and refrigerate. Place the remaining onions and all the schmaltz from the pan in a large bowl.

While the onions are cooking, preheat the broiler. Trim the livers of any connective tissue, green spots, and visible fat. Rinse and pat dry with paper towels. Place the chicken livers in a single layer on a perforated broiler pan or a rack with a drip pan beneath (work in batches if necessary). Sprinkle with half of the kosher salt. Broil for 5 minutes. Turn the livers and sprinkle with the remaining kosher salt. Broil for 5 to 7 minutes, or until the livers are brown inside with a pink center. Transfer the livers to the bowl with the onions.

Add the mashed eggs, wine, black pepper, and cayenne to the liver and onions and mix well.

Using a wooden chopping bowl and a mezzaluna (half-moon-shaped knife), chop the mixture in batches. Alternatively, you can pulse the mixture in batches in a food processor. Be careful not to over chop. The mixture should have a rough, slightly crumbly texture; it should not be finely chopped or puréed. Transfer the chopped mixture to a second large bowl.

Mix well and taste. Add the remaining ½ teaspoon of salt or more, if desired, and additional black pepper, if desired. If the mixture is too dry and not spreadable, stir in additional schmaltz or oil 1 tablespoon at a time. If it's too strong tasting, stir in additional wine 1 tablespoon at a time.

Cover with plastic wrap and refrigerate for several hours. Serve at room temperature, topped with the reserved caramelized onions.

MAKE IT IN ADVANCE: *The chopped liver can be stored in an airtight container in the refrigerator for up to 3 days or frozen for up to 2 months.*

FRIDAY NIGHT CHALLAH

Makes 2 medium loaves or 1 large loaf; serves 8 to 10

Bread is the heart of the Friday night dinner. Ritually, bread makes the meal and it is doubly blessed (see About Challah, page 207). The best-known Shabbat bread is the braided loaf known as challah. Like many recipes that have become family traditions, there are innumerable variations. The recipe below represents mine, which is based on a recipe made by the children at my synagogue's preschool.

When the house's temperature dips below 70 degrees, I proof my challah in the oven on the upper rack with the heat off and the light on. When it gets even colder, I'll add a pan of boiling water to the bottom rack to encourage the rise. Don't go by time; go by how much the dough has risen. The only special equipment I use is my instant-read thermometer for the warm water and for checking the progress of the baking challah.

FOR PROOFING THE YEAST

½ cup warm water (100 to 110°F)
1 teaspoon sugar
2¼ teaspoons active dry yeast (not instant or quick-rise)

FOR MAKING AND SHAPING THE DOUGH

3 large eggs, divided
1 tablespoon plus ¼ cup room-temperature water, divided, plus more as needed
2 tablespoons vegetable oil, plus more for the bowl and baking sheets
2 tablespoons sugar
1½ teaspoons salt
3 to 4 cups white bread flour

OPTIONAL TOPPING

¼ to ½ cup topping of your choice, such as sesame seeds, poppy seeds, za'atar, kosher or coarse sea salt, cinnamon or cinnamon sugar, or purchased "everything" topping (a mixture of black sesame seeds, white sesame seeds, kosher or flaked salt, dried onion flakes, dried minced garlic, and poppy seeds), optional

TO PROOF THE YEAST

Place the warm water in a 2-cup measuring cup or bowl. Stir in the sugar and sprinkle the yeast on top. Let sit until the mixture is foaming and bubbly, 5 to 10 minutes. If the yeast doesn't proof (bubble and foam), the water was either too warm or too cold, or the yeast was no longer active due to age or exposure to heat. If the yeast does not proof, the bread will not rise.

TO MAKE AND SHAPE THE DOUGH

Separate 1 egg and place the yolk in a small bowl and the white in a large bowl. Add 1 tablespoon of room-temperature water to the yolk, stir until blended, cover, and refrigerate.

Add the remaining eggs to the large bowl with the egg white and beat with a wooden spoon. Add the oil, sugar, salt, and ¼ cup water and stir well until combined. Pour in the yeast mixture, making sure to scrape out the container to get all the liquid and foam, and stir well.

Add 1 cup of flour and stir until it is fairly well incorporated. Repeat with the second and third cups. (If the dough gets hard to stir, mix with your hands). Keep mixing and adding flour, 1 tablespoon at a time if necessary, until the dough forms a rough, shaggy, sticky ball. Knead the mixture in the bowl with your hands for 2 to 3 minutes. If more flour is needed, flour your hands and work it in as you knead, until the dough is cohesive but still sticky. Let rest for 5 minutes.

Lightly dust a clean, dry work surface with flour. Turn out the dough onto the work surface and knead for about 8 minutes, until it's slightly tacky, smooth looking, elastic, and springy (a pinch of dough feels as resilient as a pinching the bottom of your ear lobe). If more flour is needed as you knead, flour hands and work in, but be careful of adding too much flour and creating a dense, stodgy loaf. Sprinkle with a few drops of water at a time and knead it in if the dough becomes dry. It is better for the dough to be slightly under kneaded than over kneaded and to be tackier rather than drier.

Place the dough in a bowl lightly greased with oil large enough for the dough to double in size. Turn the dough in the bowl so all sides are coated with oil. Cover the bowl with plastic wrap or a clean dish towel, place in a warm, draft-free place, and let rise until doubled in size, 45 minutes to 3 hours.

Press your fist down into the dough to let some of the air out (this is known as punching down the dough). Return the dough to the work surface and knead for a few minutes. Cut the dough into 3 equal pieces for one loaf or 6 equal pieces for 2 loaves. Roll each section into a ball and then roll it on a work surface or between your hands to form ropes about 18 inches long for large loaves and 12 inches long for medium. (If the dough is too springy to shape, let rest for 10 minutes, then try again.)

Take 3 of the ropes and place them flat on the work surface. Pinch them together at one end. Pick up the rope on your right and pass it over the center rope. The rope that started on the right is the new center rope. Take the rope on the left. Pass it over the center one. (The original center rope is on the right, the original right rope is on the left, and the original left rope is now the center.) Continue braiding. It should not be too tight nor too loose, but it should keep its shape and have room to rise. Pinch the ropes together at the end. Tuck both pinched ends underneath the loaf for a neat finish. Repeat with second loaf if making two.

Line 1 or 2 large baking sheets with parchment paper. Lightly grease with oil.

(recipe continues)

Place the challah(s) in the center of the pan(s), cover with clean kitchen towel(s), and put in a warm, draft-free place to rise until doubled in size, 30 minutes to 2 hours. The dough should look pillowy and soft. The dough is ready when a knuckle pushed into it leaves an indent that fills in slowly and not all the way. If it fills in rapidly it is not yet ready. Be careful of the bread rising too much (over proofing) at this stage, so if in doubt, go ahead and bake even if it is not quite doubled in size.

About 20 minutes before it looks like the second rise will be done, preheat the oven to 350°F.

TO FINISH

After the second rise, remove the egg yolk mixture from the refrigerator. Use a pastry brush or basting brush to lightly coat the top and sides of dough with the egg wash. Be careful not to get the glaze on the parchment or foil to avoid burning.

Leave the dough plain or sprinkle the top and sides with your choice of topping.

Bake for 10 minutes. Remove the pan from the oven (shut the oven door to keep the heat in) and lightly brush any newly exposed dough with some of the remaining egg wash. If using a topping, sprinkle a bit more over the freshly egg-washed sections.

Bake for another 15 to 25 minutes, rotating the pans in the oven if necessary, until the bread is evenly golden brown, the bottom sounds hollow when tapped, and an instant-read thermometer reads 190°F. Let cool on a wire rack.

VARIATION: *Vegan Challah–Omit the eggs. Use 3 tablespoons sugar, ¼ cup of oil, and ¼ cup plus 2 tablespoons of water. Brush the challah(s) with maple syrup or non-dairy milk before baking instead of using the egg wash.*

VARIATION: *Challah Pull-Apart Rolls–Grease a 9- or 10-inch round cake pan. After the first rise, divide the dough into 10 equal pieces and roll or shape them into balls. Place one ball in the center of the pan and the remainder along the inside rim. After the second rise, brush with the egg wash and sprinkle generously with any desired toppings. Bake in a 350°F oven as instructed for 20 to 25 minutes, or until golden and an instant-read thermometer reads 190°F.*

MAKE IT IN ADVANCE: *The bowl with dough can be covered with plastic wrap and held overnight in the refrigerator. Punch down the dough and return it to room temperature. Let rise until doubled, then finish as instructed. Baked and cooled challah can be tightly wrapped and stored at room temperature for up to 2 days or frozen for 3 months. Defrost in the wrappings at room temperature.*

About challah

This braided, enriched bread is named after challah (or more exactly, the taking of challah), a religious ritual that burns a small piece of the raw dough as an offering and a thank you to God.

The tradition of having ritual bread for Shabbat stretches back to showbread, which was twelve loaves displayed in two rows of six, each on a special marble table in the Temple. The breads were replaced every Shabbat.

After the destruction of the Temple, the showbreads were replaced by blessing two loaves of bread on Shabbat, representing the double portion of manna that was provided before Shabbat during the Exodus.

What was considered a special Shabbat bread varied based on geography, economics, and local traditions, but in most European communities it became a custom to use refined wheat flour. The bread we know today as challah got its start as a braided bread in Germany that was adapted by local Jews in the fifteenth century, with the first reference to this bread being called challah in 1488. These early challahs were not sweetened and contained no eggs except for the glaze.

There are many Shabbat customs around bread including what constitutes what is ritually acceptable. The bread should be made of at least 20 percent of at least one of five grains (wheat, rye, spelt, oats, and barley) for it to be used for the blessing for bread (see page 15).

Once the Hamotzi is recited, the meal formally begins, but first everyone eats a bit of the Shabbat bread. There are many traditions around this. My favorite is a Sephardic one, where to celebrate the joy of Shabbat, pieces of bread are tossed to guests.

MATZO CRACKERS

Makes 6 rounds

Homemade matzos are not just for Passover. My take produces a thin, blistered round that crisps up as it cools and when broken into pieces makes crackers to use year-round for Almost Homemade Hummus (page 96) or Charred Eggplant Dip (page 131). Traditionally, once water and flour are mixed for matzos, the crackers must be made and baked within 18 minutes to ensure that the dough doesn't ferment and rise (hence unleavened bread). I've kept the yield low so the time frame is attainable. With practice or helpers, the recipe can be multiplied and production time still kept to 18 minutes. (Of course, when using the matzos outside of Passover, there are no time restrictions, which makes multiplying the recipe much easier.)

1 cup flour, plus more for the work surface
¼ cup plus 2 tablespoons warm water, plus more as needed
½ teaspoon salt
Kosher salt or coarse ground sea salt, optional (see page 17), for topping

Matzo for Passover

Making unleavened bread is a bit like time travel, since the concept goes back to the age of Moses and beyond. Jews have been making matzos for millennia. It is the most famous and universal Jewish food and is a staple for Passover rituals and meals.

Today, most Americans know matzo only as uniform, machine-made boxed crackers, but until the 19th century, matzo was hand-produced in rounds, either in the home or by community bakers. Over the years, Ashkenazi tradition resulted in a dry, cracker type of matzo, but it was originally a round and thicker soft flatbread, a type of matzo that is still favored by many non–Eastern European Jews.

For many, homemade matzo is an alternative to the commercially made versions. Please note that this matzo, even if made in under 18 minutes and only with flour, water, and salt, won't meet the ritual requirements for Passover unless the flour has been guaranteed to have not come in contact with any fermentation agents. All utensils, work surfaces, and the oven must be specially cleaned for Passover.

Chabad centers, Sephardic and Mizrahi congregations, and other organizations often sell specialty matzos before Passover.

Preheat the oven to 475°F with 2 baking sheets inside. Lightly dust a clean, dry work surface with flour.

In a medium bowl, mix together the flour, ¼ cup plus 2 tablespoons of water, and salt with a wooden spoon until a dry, shaggy dough forms. If the dough seems dry, add water 1 teaspoon at a time, mixing between additions. If wet, add flour 1 tablespoon at a time. The dough should not be sticky or tacky. Knead a few times in the bowl with your hands until the dough smooths out and forms a ball.

(If not using for Passover, cover the dough with a kitchen towel and let rest 10 to 15 minutes. This will make the dough easier to handle. If using for Passover, go right to the next step.)

Turn the dough out onto the floured work surface and knead for 3 minutes. Divide the dough into 6 pieces and keep them covered with a kitchen towel.

Take out 1 piece of dough, roll into a ball, and flatten it into a round with your hand. Using a rolling pin, roll it out into a free-form, rough round or oval about 6 inches in diameter and ⅛-inch thick or even thinner. (Too thick and the matzos will not crisp up.) Prick the surface all over with a fork. Repeat with the other dough pieces.

Brush off any excess flour from the rounds. If topping with the kosher salt, lightly brush the top of the dough with water and sprinkle it over the top.

Place the dough on the heated baking sheets, making sure they don't touch each other, and bake for 2 to 3 minutes, or until golden and blistered in spots. Using long metal tongs, quickly reach into the oven and flip the matzos over, closing the oven door as quickly as possible to retain the heat. Bake another 2 to 3 minutes, until golden and blistered. (Crackers with toppings may need more time.) Let cool on a wire rack. The matzos will crisp as they cool. Break it into pieces once cool if using as crackers.

VARIATION: *Matzo with Toppings—Before baking, replace some or all of the kosher salt in the topping with za'atar, Za'atar in a Pinch (page 217), or sesame seeds.*

MAKE IT IN ADVANCE: *The matzo can be made up to 2 days in advance, cooled, wrapped in plastic wrap, and stored at room temperature.*

TAHINI SAUCE

Makes about 1 cup

This is a basic tahini sauce and I use it throughout the book. For a less pungent sauce, leave out or reduce the garlic. Make sure you stir the tahini before measuring. See The World of Tahini (page 37) for more about tahini.

1 teaspoon minced garlic
1½ tablespoons fresh lemon juice, plus more if desired
¼ cup plus 2 tablespoons very cold water, plus more if desired
¾ cup tahini
¼ teaspoon salt, optional

In a medium bowl, stir together the garlic, lemon juice, and water. Stir in the tahini paste with a fork. The mixture may thicken and seize, but keep stirring, until smooth and thick but still pourable. Add cold water 1 teaspoon at a time to reach the desired consistency. Taste and add salt and/or lemon juice, if desired. Store in an airtight container in the refrigerator for up to 3 days.

GARLIC SAUCE

Makes about 1 cup

This lemony garlic sauce is inspired by toum, a creamy Lebanese staple. It's definitely for garlic lovers. It makes a nice non-dairy alternative for a creamy garnish or even an aioli-style dip for crudites. It complements Falafel Pizza with Feta and Herbs (page 102), Peppers Stuffed with White Beans, Chard, and Tomatoes (page 54), or Whole Roasted Cauliflower (page 58) as well as cooked vegetables and grilled meats.

¼ cup peeled garlic cloves
⅓ cup fresh lemon juice
½ cup extra-virgin olive oil
¼ teaspoon salt

In a blender, combine the garlic, lemon juice, olive oil, and salt and purée on high speed until smooth. The sauce can be stored in an airtight container in the refrigerator for up to 5 days. Bring to room temperature before using.

YELLOW CURRY SAUCE

Makes about ¾ cup

This slightly spicy and tart yogurt-based sauce punches up the flavor of grilled or roasted vegetables or fish. It's also a great garnish for Mostly Make-It-Ahead Shakshouka (page 100), Falafel Pizza with Feta and Herbs (page 102), and Almost-Homemade Hummus (page 96).

I developed this sauce as a stand in for amba (see page 135), an Iraqi-Israeli fermented sour mango sauce available in some kosher, Middle Eastern, and Indian groceries. Amba is bright yellow and has a slightly tart and spicy finish. It is a favorite drizzled on falafel and sabich (fried eggplant) sandwiches in Israel, but it can be hard to find elsewhere.

½ cup plain Greek yogurt
1 teaspoon minced lemon zest
1 tablespoon fresh lemon juice
1 teaspoon curry powder
½ teaspoon ground turmeric
⅛ teaspoon sugar
2 tablespoons milk plus more if needed

In a bowl, mix together the yogurt, lemon zest, lemon juice, curry powder, turmeric, and sugar until smooth. Slowly stir in the milk, adding more, if needed, until the sauce can be drizzled. Store in an airtight container in the refrigerator for up to 3 days.

POMEGRANATE MOLASSES

Makes 2 cups

If pomegranate molasses is not available in your area, make it yourself with this recipe. I like to splash it over everything from yogurt to vegetables, stews to roasts, and even desserts for a tangy punch of flavor. Fresh pomegranate juice is available at most supermarkets in the refrigerated section.

2 cups homemade or purchased fresh
  pomegranate juice
1 tablespoon fresh lemon juice
¼ cup sugar

In a saucepan, combine the pomegranate juice, lemon juice, and sugar and bring to a boil over medium heat. Lower the heat to low and simmer until the liquid is reduced to ½ cup, 50 to 60 minutes. Store in a sealed jar at room temperature for up to 2 weeks. For longer storage, refrigerate for up to 3 months. Bring to room temperature for easier pouring.

The versatility of pomegranate molasses

Pomegranate molasses is not molasses (a sugar byproduct) but a very thick sweet-and-sour syrup made by cooking down pomegranate juice. The best brands are made from pomegranate juice, sugar, and lemon juice and don't use additives or high-fructose corn syrup.

It is a staple in my kitchen and an important ingredient in Sephardic and Mizrahi cooking, as well as in foods all across the Middle East, Central Asia, the Near East, the Caucuses, and Turkey. It adds a fruity, tangy sweet-tart flavor associated with many Jewish cuisines and depending on the country, it may be used in savory or sweet dishes. I like to

make my own, but the syrup is widely available. The balance of sweet to sour varies from brand to brand, so while cooking, taste and adjust as needed.

Pomegranate syrup, which is thick and viscous, or pomegranate concentrate can be used in place of pomegranate molasses. (Thinner syrups meant for beverages and cocktails are not suitable substitutes.) Taste before using, since they can be sweeter or more sour than pomegranate molasses, and you'll need to adjust the recipe accordingly.

Once open, pomegranate molasses can be stored at room temperature away from heat or light.

Z'HUG

Makes about 2 cups

This spicy hot sauce originated in Yemen. It is best if made at least a few hours before using. Seed the peppers if you prefer a milder flavor. Thin some of the hot sauce with olive oil for a pourable garnish for all sorts of grilled or roasted meats, vegetables, fish or chicken. It also perks up beans and rice.

9 ounces jalapeños, stemmed and roughly chopped
3 tablespoons extra-virgin olive oil
1 cup roughly chopped fresh cilantro, or ½ cup fresh cilantro and ½ cup flat-leaf parsley
4 large garlic cloves, crushed and minced
2 teaspoons hawaij for soup or Instant Almost Hawaij (page 216)
1 teaspoon salt
⅛ teaspoon ground caraway seeds, optional

In a food processor, combine the chiles and olive oil and process until finely chopped but not puréed. Transfer the mixture to a bowl. Add the cilantro to the food processor and process until finely chopped. Transfer the cilantro to the bowl with the chiles. Add the garlic, hawaij, salt, and caraway (if using), to the bowl and stir until combined.

Alternatively, make the sauce in a blender: Combine the chiles, oil, and cilantro together in batches and blend until finely chopped. Add each batch to the bowl. Stir in the garlic and spices.

Store in an airtight container in the refrigerator for up to 2 weeks.

HARISSA

Makes about 1¼ cups

Harissa is a hot sauce originally from Tunisia that has become popular throughout North Africa and in Israel. It is an important condiment with soups, stews, tagines, and other dishes. I use it frequently in recipes like Whole Roasted Cauliflower (page 58) and the Middle Eastern Grilled Corn (page 134). Harissa is available in jars, cans, and tubes in specialty and Middle Eastern markets, but I prefer to make my own.

This recipe uses a mix of dried Mexican chiles, which are easier for me to find than the traditional North African ones. Choose a combination of mellower New Mexican, ancho, and/or pasilla chilies for a base and add in some arbol, guajillo, pequin, and/or other hot dried chiles for more heat. Most chiles are available online or in Latin American markets. If the resulting sauce is too hot, stir in 1 to 2 tablespoons of tomato paste.

5 ounces dried hot red chiles or 4 ounces crushed red pepper
Boiling water
2 tablespoons chopped garlic
½ teaspoon salt
2 tablespoons lemon zest
1 tablespoon fresh lemon juice
½ teaspoon ground cumin
½ teaspoon ground coriander
⅛ teaspoon ground or finely crushed caraway seeds, optional
½ cup plus 2 tablespoons extra-virgin olive oil

Stem and seed the dried chiles and place them in a bowl. Cover with boiling water and let sit until soft, about 30 minutes. (If using the crushed red pepper, cover with boiling water and let soak until softened, about 5 minutes.) Drain.

In a food processor, combine the softened chiles, garlic, salt, lemon zest, lemon juice, cumin, coriander, and caraway (if using) and purée until smooth and thick. Add ½ cup of olive oil and process until combined. Transfer the harissa to a glass jar with a lid. Top the sauce with the remaining 2 tablespoons of olive oil and secure the lid. Store in the refrigerator for up to 2 months.

BASICALLY BERBERE

Makes about ⅓ cup

Nothing can replace an authentic berbere made from freshly roasted and ground whole spices, but this combination is a good compromise if the real thing is not available. You can find prepared berbere in well-stocked gourmet, Ethiopian, and African markets, spice shops, specialty stores, and online. Use it in Bebere Lentils and Cauliflower (page 26) and in Ethiopian Spiced Pot Roast (page 73). It also makes a spicy rub for barbecued chicken or meats. For more about Ethiopian Jews, see page 75.

2 to 3 teaspoons cayenne pepper
3 tablespoons paprika
1 teaspoon ground black pepper
1 teaspoon ground ginger
½ teaspoon ground cinnamon
½ teaspoon ground cardamom
½ teaspoon ground cumin
½ teaspoon ground fenugreek
¼ teaspoon salt
⅛ teaspoon ground cloves
⅛ teaspoon ground turmeric

In a glass jar with a lid, combine 2 teaspoons of cayenne (use 3 teaspoons if you like more heat), paprika, black pepper, ginger, cinnamon, cardamom, cumin, fenugreek, salt, cloves, and turmeric. Seal the lid and shake until combined. The mixture can be stored in an airtight container at room temperature away from direct sunlight for up to 1 year.

INSTANT ALMOST HAWAIJ

Makes about ½ cup

This spice mix is an important component of many Yemeni Jewish dishes, especially soups and stews but can be hard to find in the United States. Hawaij adds a sweet and spicy, almost curry-like note and bright yellow color to Yemeni Grilled Chicken (page 141) and Hawaij Vegetable Soup (page 104). Check Middle Eastern, kosher, and specialty stores, spice shops and online. If you can't find it, try this hawaij replacement mix.

3 tablespoons ground turmeric
3 tablespoons ground cumin
1 tablespoon ground black pepper
2 teaspoons ground cardamom
2 teaspoons ground coriander
1 teaspoon ground ginger
¼ teaspoon ground cloves

In a small jar with a lid, combine the turmeric, cumin, black pepper, cardamom, coriander, ginger, and cloves, secure the lid, and shake until combined. Store it in an airtight container away from direct sunlight for 1 year.

ZA'ATAR IN A PINCH

Makes ½ cup

Za'atar is an earthy and tangy mix of dried herbs and spices that flavors many Middle Eastern dishes. Although it can be found in many grocery stores and Middle Eastern markets, I prefer to make my own. Traditionally used with olive oil as a topping for pita and other flatbreads, I like to use it in marinades for recipes such as Za'atar Roast Turkey (page 108) and Za'atar Kebabs with Vegetables (page 142), to flavor salads such as in the Lemon, Za'atar, and Garlic Dressing (page 219), and as a topping for breads such as the Friday Night Challah (page 204).

1 tablespoon sesame seeds
¼ cup dried oregano leaves
2 tablespoons dried thyme leaves
2 teaspoons ground sumac
1 teaspoon coarse sea salt or Diamond Crystal Kosher Salt (see page 17)

Heat a small skillet over medium heat. Add the sesame seeds and stir constantly until golden, about 1 minute. (Be careful not to burn or over brown.) Pour the seeds into a bowl and let cool.

Pick through the oregano and thyme leaves, discarding any stems or twigs. Add the oregano, thyme, sumac, and salt to the toasted seeds and stir until combined.

To make in a spice grinder: Place the mixture in a spice grinder and process in batches until just finely ground but not powdery.

To make in a blender: Put the mixture in a blender and process on high, stopping and shaking or scraping down the sides as necessary, until finely ground, but not powdery.

To make by hand: Crumble the oregano and thyme as finely as possible into a small bowl. Replace the coarse sea salt with ¾ teaspoon finely ground salt and add it to the bowl with the sesame seeds and sumac.

Store in an airtight container at room temperature, away from direct sunlight, for up to 3 months or in the refrigerator for up to 1 year.

VARIATION: *Whole Seed—Toast the sesame seeds and let cool but do not add to the mix. After the za'atar is finely ground, stir in the whole seeds. This is particularly nice when using za'atar as a topping for challah or flatbreads.*

WHOLE ROASTED GARLIC

Serves 4

Roasting whole garlic transforms its raw pungency into a savory sweetness. To eat, squeeze out a roasted clove from its peel and spread the garlic directly on baguettes or crackers. It adds a mellow kick as an accompaniment to stews, roast chicken, and as a garnish in the Spice-Rubbed Chicken on Root Vegetables (page 28)

4 small heads or 2 large heads of garlic
1 tablespoon extra-virgin olive oil or as needed

Preheat the oven to 350°F.

Peel off just the outer, most papery layers of the head. Cut off the top of each head, just exposing the cloves. Drizzle olive oil on top and rub the outside of the heads with the oil. Wrap each head individually in aluminum foil, place on a baking sheet, and roast for 40 minutes, or until soft. The roasted garlic can be wrapped tightly and refrigerated for up to 1 day. Bring to room temperature before using.

WHOLE LEMON DRESSING

Makes about 1¼ cups

---

2 small lemons, scrubbed
1 teaspoon minced garlic
1 teaspoon salt
¼ teaspoon ground black pepper
⅛ teaspoon cayenne pepper
½ cup extra-virgin olive oil
½ cup fresh lemon juice
2 tablespoons water

Grate the zest from the lemons and place the zest in a jar with a lid. Cut away the white pith from the lemons and discard. Chop the lemon flesh into ¼-inch pieces and add to the jar. Add the garlic, salt, black pepper, cayenne, olive oil, lemon juice, and water. Seal the lid and shake until combined. Taste and adjust the seasoning, if desired. The dressing can be made up to 3 days in advance and kept airtight in the refrigerator. Stir or shake well before using.

LEMON, ZA'ATAR, AND GARLIC DRESSING

Makes about 1¼ cups

½ cup extra-virgin olive oil
¼ cup vegetable oil
¼ cup fresh lemon juice
¼ cup water
½ teaspoon za'atar or Za'atar in a Pinch
  (page 217)
⅛ teaspoon sugar
⅛ teaspoon salt
⅛ teaspoon ground black pepper
1 to 2 tablespoons minced garlic

In a jar with a lid, combine the olive oil, vegetable oil, lemon juice, water, za'atar, sugar, salt, black pepper, and garlic. Seal the lid and shake until combined. Taste and adjust the seasoning, if desired. The dressing can be made up to 3 days in advance and kept airtight in the refrigerator. Stir or shake well before using.

NORTH AFRICAN DRESSING

Makes about 1¼ cups

½ cup extra-virgin olive oil
¼ cup vegetable oil
¼ cup fresh lemon juice
¼ cup water
¼ teaspoon ground cumin
¼ teaspoon dried oregano
⅛ teaspoon paprika
⅛ teaspoon sugar
⅛ teaspoon salt
⅛ teaspoon ground black pepper

In a jar with a lid, combine the olive oil, vegetable oil, lemon juice, water, cumin, oregano, paprika, sugar, salt, and black pepper. Seal the lid and shake until combined. Taste and adjust the seasoning, if desired. The dressing can be made up to 3 days in advance and kept in an airtight container in the refrigerator. Stir or shake well before using.

TAHINI DRESSING

Makes 1½ cups

½ cup extra-virgin olive oil
¼ cup apple cider vinegar
2 tablespoons fresh lemon juice
½ cup tahini
¼ cup cold water, plus more if needed
2 teaspoons minced garlic.
½ teaspoon salt
¼ teaspoon ground black pepper
¼ teaspoon paprika
¼ teaspoon dried mint

In a jar with a lid, combine the olive oil, vinegar, lemon juice, tahini, and water. Secure the lid, and shake until smooth, adding water 1 tablespoon at a time if needed until the dressing is the consistency of a thin cream. Add the garlic, salt, black pepper, paprika, mint, and cumin, secure the lid, and shake until combined. Taste and adjust the seasonings, if desired. The dressing can be made up to 3 days in advance and kept airtight in the refrigerator. Stir or shake well before using.

resources

These books are a good starting point to explore the global Jewish kitchen and have been resources for me:

Abadi, Jennifer Felicia. *A Fistful of Lentils: Syrian-Jewish Recipes from Grandma Fritzie's Kitchen*. Boston: The Harvard Common Press, 2002.

Cohen, Jayne. *Jewish Holiday Cooking: A Food Lover's Treasury of Classics and Improvisations*. New York: John Wiley and Sons, Inc., 2008.

Larkey, Sue Spertus. *Bone Soup and Flipped Bread: The Yemenite Jewish Kitchen*. Jerusalem: Gefen Publishing House, 2017.

Marks, Gil. *Encyclopedia of Jewish Food*. New York: John Wiley and Sons, Inc., 2010.

Nathan, Joan. *King Solomon's Table: A Culinary Exploration of Jewish Cooking from Around the World*. New York: Alfred A. Knopf, 2017.

Roden, Claudia. *The Book of Jewish Food: An Odyssey from Samarkand to New York: A Cookbook*. New York: Knopf Illustrated, 1996.

Spieler, Marlena. *The Complete Guide to Traditional Jewish Cooking*. Dayton: Lorenz Press, 2014.

Stavroulakis, Nicholas. *Cookbook of the Jews of Greece*. Istanbul: Bosphorus Books, 1986.

These websites offer personal stories, interviews, information and recipes on the international Jewish food experience

Jews Indigenous of the Middle East and North Africa (JIMENA). www.jimena.org

The Jewish Food Society. www.jewishfoodsociety.org

From traditional to interfaith, from highly personal to more standard observances, here are a sample of websites that offer information, prayers, and resources for shabbat, holidays, and other jewish rituals

My Jewish Learning. www.myjewishlearning.com

Reform Judaism movement. www.reformjudaism.org

Ritualwell: Traditions and Innovation. www.ritualwell.org

One Table. www.onetable.org

The Shabbat Project. www.theshabbosproject.org

18 Doors. www.18doors.org

Be'chol Lashon. www.globaljews.org

measurement conversions

All recipes in this cookbook use standard U.S. measurements. There are many measurement conversion websites that give precise equivalents, which may be especially helpful for baked goods. The conversions below have been rounded up or down for convenience. For most recipes the slight difference will be undetectable.

U.S. VOLUME TO METRIC

General rule – each fluid (liquid) ounce equals about 30 milliliters

U.S. VOLUME	METRIC
⅛ teaspoon	0.5 ml (milliliter)
¼ teaspoon	1 ml
½ teaspoon	2 ml
¾ teaspoon	4 ml
1 teaspoon	5 ml
1 tablespoon (3 tsp)	15 ml
¼ cup (2 oz., 4 tbsp)	60 ml
⅓ cup (3 oz.)	75 ml
½ cup (4 oz.)	120 ml
¾ cup (6 oz.)	180 ml
1 cup (8 oz.)	240 ml
2 cups (16 oz., 1 U.S. pint)	480 ml
1 quart (32 oz., 4 cups)	1 L (liter)

U.S. WEIGHT TO METRIC

General rule – each ounce equals about 28 grams

U.S. WEIGHT	METRIC
½ ounce	15 g (grams)
1 ounce	30 g
¼ pound (4 ounces)	115 g
½ pound (8 ounces)	225 g
1 pound (16 ounces)	450 g
2 ¼ pounds	1 kg (kilogram)

U.S. LENGTH TO METRIC

U.S. LENGTH	METRIC
⅛ inch	3 mm (millimeters)
¼ inch	5 mm
½ inch	1.25cm (centimeters)
¾ inch	2 cm
1 inch	2.5 cm
12 inches (1 foot)	30 cm

FAHRENHEIT TO CELSIUS OR GAS MARK

F	250°	300°	350°	375°	400°	425°	450°	475°	500°
C	120°	150°	180°	190°	200°	220°	230°	240°	260°
GAS MARK	½	2	4	5	6	7	8	9	10

If using a fan-assist (convection) oven, reduce temperatures by 25°F or 20°C or as directed by the manufacturer instructions. Timing may vary.

index

acknowledgments

52 Shabbats would not exist without the inspiration and assistance of so many.

Most of all, my thanks go to my husband, Gary, who makes everything possible; my sons and daughter-in-law—Noah, Seth, and Sinead—my favorite taste testers and biggest supporters; and my granddaughter, Reese, whom I hope will grow up loving to explore, cook, and write as much as I do.

Special thanks go to a friend who will never see this book but somehow knew I would one day write it. Thank you, Lita. Your memory has been a blessing.

My mother was a fearless cook and encouraged me to experiment in the kitchen when I was growing up, even when the result was inedible. My sisters, Laura Rock-Smith and the late Beth de la Torre, and I always connected through food, and both helped me develop recipes. I miss being with them in the kitchen.

I am also thankful for the support of the editors and staff of the *j, The Jewish News of Northern California*. Writing my cooking column and getting feedback from readers shaped my concept of Jewish food. The *j.* is where earlier versions of some of the recipes in this book first appeared.

Thank you to Angela Engel and the team at the Collective Book Studio for turning my recipes and stories into this book. Editor Amy Treadwell was always available for advice and help. Designer Andrea Kelly gave the book its good looks aided by photographer Clara Rice and food stylist Bebe Black Carminito.

A big thank you goes to Karen and Rabbi Mark Bloom and Dianne Jacob for reading and commenting on sections of the manuscript. Mala Johnson, Maureen Gomberg, and Jody Hoffman all cooked up recipes for the photo shoots. Special thanks to Dawn Kepler, of Building Jewish Bridges, Dawn Margolin, and the family of the late Pola Silver for sharing their stories, Shabbat traditions, and recipes.

There are so many people who helped me on this journey that it is impossible to single them all out. My thanks go to the many friends and family members who encouraged me, tested and tasted my recipes, and celebrated Shabbat and holidays with me, as well as the people I met on my travels or at restaurants, farm stands, markets, produce stores, butcher shops, and elsewhere who shared anecdotes, cooking tips, and treasured recipes.

Faith Kramer is a food writer and recipe developer concentrating on the food ways, history, and customs of the Jewish diaspora. She writes about Jewish customs and food, travel, and global ingredients with accompanying recipes at faithkramer.com. As a columnist for *j., the Jewish News of Northern California,* she writes articles on food and cooking along with original recipes. Faith has taught cooking classes around the world, presented programs on Jewish customs, celebrations, and holidays, and led food-related walking tours that explore the economic, geographic, and political underpinnings of the food as well as how to use international ingredients in other contexts. She lives with her family in the San Francisco Bay Area.